Between Exits

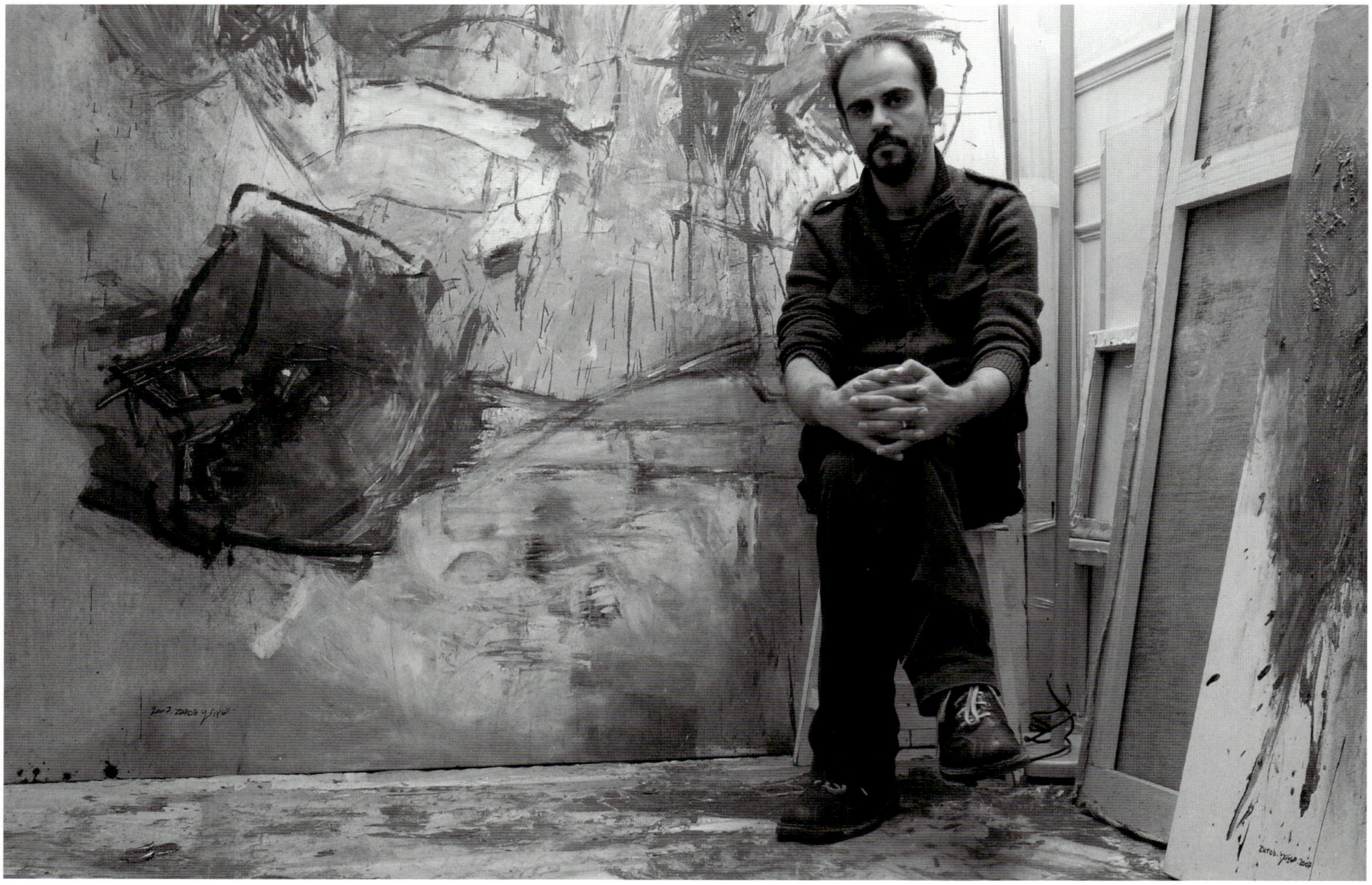

Hani Zurob at his home studio,
Paris, 2007.

Between Exits

Paintings by Hani Zurob

Kamal Boullata

Introduction by Jean Fisher

black dog publishing
london uk

For Muhammad, Yasmine and Ziad.

Contents

Preface and Acknowledgements

In a homeland enduring over 40 years of military occupation, where art is saturated with nationalist clichés and tired iconographic images, how does a young and ambitious talent like Hani Zurob break away from the binds of the local mainstream to explore his own originality in painting? Having been born and raised in a cultural ghetto where he had been cut off from the world history of art as well as from the art history of his own culture, where could he go with the minimal studio training he received? Deeply rooted in Arab culture which is predominated by oral and verbal expression, in what way does such a tradition allow us to read his visual expression? These are some of the key questions that this book attempts to elucidate.

Since Vasari, artists' lives have been considered a cornerstone in the understanding and interpretation of their art. This book, in focusing on a selection of paintings by a contemporary artist, attempts to trace the evolution of his work in concordance with his lived experiences at home and in exile. Foremost among these experiences is that of space. In studying Zurob's painting, the reader senses how the artist's lived experiences are manifested in his pictorial space. Thus, I hope this book widens the scope of my findings in previous writings on Palestinian art.

I have noted in previous writings that right after the fall of Palestine in 1948 and before the advent of globalisation, which granted instantaneous accessibility of images from everywhere at the tap of a finger, that paintings by Palestinian artists growing up in refugee camps, as well as those living in proximity of the homeland, have on the whole employed a figurative mode of expression. The further away their places of residence were from their country of birth, the more abstract elements entered into their art. The decade of art production that is discussed in the present book, covering the period the artist moved from his home studio in Ramallah to his exile in Paris, illustrates how his painting can be characterised by shuttling between figuration and abstraction.

Born and raised in a refugee camp in the Gaza Strip, Hani Zurob belongs to the first generation of Palestinian artists whose work evolved at the turn of the twenty-first century. His life has encompassed a range of trying experiences that were marked by the period stretching between the first popular uprising against the Israeli Occupation in 1987 when he was 11 years old and what has been known as 'the Oslo Years', which refer to the aftermath of the ill-fated Peace Accords reached between Israeli and Palestinian political leaders in 1993. Two decades of waiting followed the signing of the agreement and none of the Palestinians' rights cited in the Accords were granted. Despair plagued the people of Palestine as their political leadership failed to deliver any of its promises.

Keeping this political background in mind, the text of the present book was conceived on the basis of close observation of the evolution Hani Zurob's painting underwent between 2002 and 2012. Since his arrival in Paris in 2006, protracted conversations with the artist have additionally

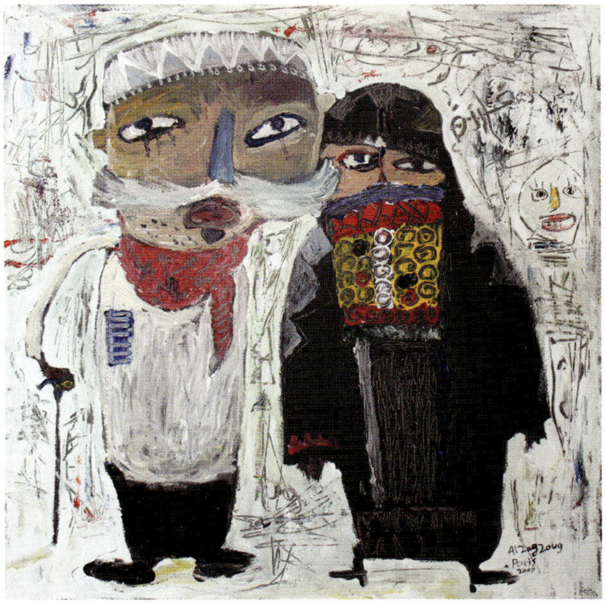

Shadi Alzaqzouq
Hani & Sabreen, Paris, 2007.
Acrylic and pastel on canvas,
50 x 50 cm.

allowed me to learn how his life experiences continued to unfold in the context of the political developments back home. Through the discussion of his art, the reader can see how the artist was, as it were, living simultaneously in two places; one of memory, where his friends and relatives continue to undergo the savageries of war; and the other a place of residence, where he is pursuing his art career in alienation from his environment. The sporadic gatherings of a small circle of male friends from Gaza who ended up living in Paris have occasionally provided him with an experience of home away from home.

One such evening I attended in 2007, Gaza artist Shadi Alzaqzouq invited a bunch of his friends to his studio at the Cité Internationale des Arts in Paris to view his most recent paintings. By the evening's end, I found myself surrounded by a number of compatriots all of whom were from the Gaza Strip. They were taking turns in recounting home news emanating from Israel's siege and the outcome of its bombing raids. Jokes punctuated the description of distressing anecdotes related to the deteriorating living conditions aggravated by the electricity blackouts, fuel shortages and the scarcity of drinking water in Gaza's boiling summers. Thinking of our collective exile, I mentioned some of Hani's ordeals and the tribulations of those Gaza men who obtained immigration rights to work in the farthest north of Norway where a freezing world extends for endless months of perpetual night. Wisam al-'Abed snapped, "that is all Gaza-lite!" Everyone roared with laughter.

Along with correlating Zurob's painting and his life experiences, the book discusses in what way his art corresponds with verbal expression and how it incorporates associations affiliated with an Arabic literary tradition particularly in relation to verbal metaphors and cultural references that may be read in his painting. But it is interpretation of space, the principal field of a visual artist, which charts the course of this study.

Writing on the experience of space at home, Palestinian poet Mourid Barghouti noted in a personal memoire, "[o]ne of the Occupation's cruellest crimes is the distortion of distance in the individual's life." He later added, "[t]he soldier of the Occupation stands on a piece of land he has confiscated and calls it 'here' and I, its owner, exiled in a distant country, have to call it 'there'."[1] In this study, I attempt to illustrate the different modalities in which the 'here' and the 'there' are manifested in Hani Zurob's art.

•

The idea of this book was first entertained during the spring of 2010 after Hani Zurob asked me to write an introduction to an exhibition catalogue featuring paintings he had just finished working on during an art residency in Essoyes. The Renoir Association, which had offered him the grant to work for nine months in the favourite village of the French master, was sponsoring the exhibition. After viewing the new paintings I was all set to begin writing the catalogue's introduction when Steve

Sabella, a colleague of the artist, urged me to turn it into a book. The suggestion caught me by surprise, especially because it was put forth by a visual artist who first met Hani as a contender in an art competition in which I happened to serve as a member of the jury. In an art world plagued by competitions and ruthless rivalries, the generosity of spirit expressed by an artist friend compelled me to consider his proposal. What tipped the scale was my realisation that the expression of such a rare solidarity amongst artists is a result of both artists belonging to the same generation which as children surprised the world as it watched them consolidating the frontline of the First Intifada, the popular uprising against the Israeli military occupation of the West Bank and the Gaza Strip in 1987. The book project has taken me close to two years of intermittent writing to complete. Thanks to Steve for urging me to write it and to the Renoir Association for readily supporting it.

As for the writing itself, it could not have been possible without the unmitigated collaboration of Hani Zurob. As soon as he knew of my project he made all his work accessible for me to view and was available to respond to my inquiries at all hours of the day and night. When we could not meet in Paris, protracted conversations on the phone became the order of the day. Occasionally, the same questions were posed more than once to verify earlier notes I had taken down in passing. At times I have further asked him to write down a certain chronology of events, to make sure I do not miss any important detail. It is impossible to thank him enough for his cooperation and for putting up with my incessant probing into his personal life, a matter which at times evoked some bitter memories. Though his answers often helped in contextualising my perception of his painting in relation to the period in which he had worked on a certain canvas I was studying, needless to say, I alone remain responsible for the interpretation of his work and for any shortcomings I may have overlooked. The artist's mother, Intisar Za'rur, was my main source of the family history before and after 1948. To her I owe special thanks.

This book could not have been realised if it were not for the generosity and support of friends, to whom I owe more thanks than anybody should owe a friend or a well-wisher. Despite her overloaded working schedule as the General Delegate of Palestine to the European Union, Leila Chahid had always made the time to enjoy art and foster cultural projects. Her enthusiasm for the book proved to be contagious. Words fail me were I to thank the valued friend she has always been. I am particularly grateful to Nader Abou Dagga, Tayseer Barakat, Hani Kalouti, Nabil Qaddumi and Rana Sadik for their enthusiasm and generosity. Amel and Gamal M. Abouali deserve thanks beyond measure for their generosity and unequivocal support throughout the period I was working on the book; it was thanks to their unfeigned faith in my work that this book finally came to light.

Living in a small town far from a reference library I was especially grateful to Steve Tamari and Tida Tippapart who assisted me in tracking down hard-to-find historical data that needed verification. I am no less grateful to Karma Nabulsi, Nur Masalha and Ilan Pappé whose exchange of emails over a question I raised enlightened my research. I also wish to thank Norwegian artist Henrik Placht who, during a visit to Menton, clarified to me his role in establishing the International Academy of Art in Ramallah with the grant provided by his government's Ministry of Foreign Affairs.

As for the book's illustrations, I would have liked to include all the beautiful images sent by artists whose work is discussed as well as those whose art is merely referred to in the text but, due to space restrictions, it was not possible to include all images received. Nevertheless, I wish to thank each and every one of the artists for their contribution. In particular, thanks to Tamam al-Ak-hal, Shadi Alzaqzouq, Samira Badran, Taysir Batniji, Ahmad Na'wash, Steve Sabella and Larissa Sansour. Besides the photographs taken by the artist of himself in his Paris home studio and the others he kindly furnished me with, including his grandfather's portrait photograph along with the rare snapshots taken of him as a boy with family members and childhood friends, I am thankful to his partner Sabreen Daoud, his cousin Ahmad Zurob and his colleagues Hazem Harb, Mo'een Hassouna, Ramzi al-Taweel each of whom was there at the right moment to capture one of the photographs illustrating the book. Our common friend Najwan

Darwish may have continued to travel in every direction away from his native Jerusalem, but ever since Hani and I met with him in Paris, Najwan remained present for me through his poetry, which made me see how the aesthetic sensibility of the artist's generation was taking a new turn. To Najwan I owe many thanks for being there as a friend and for his generosity, commitment and unflagging support of the book project.

Colin Pearson deserves my special thanks for his professional assistance in practical matters at a time when I wished to concentrate solely on my writing. At the same time, I am especially grateful to Duncan McCorquodale for his light hand in copyediting the manuscript. Thanks to him and to each member of the staff at Black Dog Publishing who brought this book into being.

No set of acknowledgements could be complete, however, without mention of Jean Fisher for making the time to read the manuscript and write the introduction. Her insightful contribution marks the crowning of a friendship that was kindled over two decades ago just before she became Editor of *Third Text*. At the time, as Associate Editor of the journal, Jean heralded the publication of the first essay I ever wrote in English on Palestinian art. Thanks to her and to Rasheed Araeen, the journal's foremost Editor, it was also the first essay that *Third Text* ever issued on the subject.[2] After having published pioneering studies on contemporary art by Native American, Irish, Mexican and Black British

Diaspora artists, her introduction to the works of a Palestinian artist does not only invite readers to dive into the book but it sets the ground for seeing Zurob's art in a broader critical perspective.

Now that the writing on Hani Zurob's painting for this book has come to a close, I would like to take this opportunity to thank the directors of the Cité Internationale des Arts who repeatedly extended his art residency over successive periods during which he produced many of the paintings selected for my study. On behalf of all viewers who are interested to see the evolution of his art, I wish to extend particular thanks to Madame Catherine Peyge, Mayor of Bobigny for offering him a spacious studio in which to work uninterruptedly over the coming two years.

Last but not least, thanks to my partner Lily Farhoud for being my first reader and unsparing critic while this work was being written. Her patient perusal and her ever-pressing concern for clarity compelled me to continually clarify my thoughts. No one knows better than her in how many ways I am indebted to her.

Kamal Boullata

Menton, 25 July 2012.

Introduction

As I was preparing to receive Kamal Boullata's manuscript, *Between Exits*, on the life and art of Hani Zurob, three new reports were published on the treatment of Palestinian children in Israeli military detention: *Bound, Blindfolded and Convicted: Children held in Military Detention*; *The Impact of Child Detention: Occupied Palestinian Territory*; and *Children in Military Custody*.[1] In addition to the shocking catalogue of systematic abuse of children as young as 12 years old, contravening the UN Convention against Torture, Israel was found to be in breach of articles 65 and 76 of the Fourth Geneva Convention (translation of military orders into the language of the prisoner and prohibiting the transfer of prisoners out of occupied territories) and several articles of UN Conventions on the Rights of the Child.[2] *The Impact of Child Detention* focuses on the traumatising effects of Israel's brutal detention of children and their subsequent struggle with mental health problems and social reintegration, finding that, of around 700 children detained every year, 90.6 per cent suffer symptoms of post-traumatic stress disorder.[3] This report is prefaced with a quote by an Israeli spokesperson: "The test of a democracy is how you treat people incarcerated, people in jail, and especially so with minors."[4]

The alleged 'crime' of the majority of incarcerated children is throwing stones.

With these reports preying on my mind, I became more aware than I might otherwise have been that childhood, with its implications of memory and inheritance, is a leitmotif that resonates throughout *Between Exits*, a book that provides a vivid insight into one artist's life written by another of an earlier exiled generation, Kamal Boullata, who is not only a distinguished painter in his own right but also the leading authority on Palestinian art history.[5] Indeed, his text is itself a collaboration between two generations that opens onto a third: it begins with Hani Zurob's early life in Gaza and the serial displacements that marked his formative years as a painter and concludes with his attentiveness to the emotional tenor of the exilic experience of his son Qudsi, as yet too young to understand why his father cannot travel with him to visit his maternal family in Jerusalem. Between these two beginnings, Kamal Boullata weaves a richly textured narrative of the sociopolitical and cultural forces that inform the Gaza artist's paintings, and in so doing reveals the immeasurable anguish of a people dispossessed of their ancestral homeland yet defiant in its refusal to 'disappear' and in its will to maintain a collective memory and identity, against international political indifference and a shameless Zionist memoricide. As Edward Said insisted, "if there is no country called Palestine it is not because there are no Palestinians."[6]

However, collective identity—despite the interventions of nationalism—is not a fixed object but a transformative process; and for Hani, raised in a period when the visual representation of Palestinian national identity was reduced to simplistic clichés, "identity was not an abstract thought and its representation could not be generic, impersonal and divorced from the painter's self... national identity could only be experienced when one looks into another's face and recognises one's own self." Any artwork succeeds *in the world* to the extent that it speaks from the self to a universally shared human experience; and it is in this achievement that Hani Zurob's poetic consciousness, whilst deliberately eschewing the overtly nationalist and political rhetoric of earlier generations of Palestinian artists, is profoundly 'political'.

Boullata's attention to Hani's childhood experiences and how these are later interlaced with those of Qudsi has immense resonance as it opens a perspective on the Israeli colonial occupation that deserves more public scrutiny than it is usually given. It focuses our minds on the extent to which Israel cynically targets children in its strategy to destroy Palestinian society, identity and development *from the inside*. At the same time we are made aware that one of the few tools of resistance remaining to the Palestinians, whether living as exiles or refugees, in their own or the lands of others, is their investment of cultural memory and the flickering shadow of hope in successive generations. It is the oral transmission of stories of home and absent relatives that sustain the personal threads of Palestinian identity; and for us, it is Kamal Boullata who testifies to Hani's struggle to overcome the crippling experiences of occupation and exile, and those emotional memories of youth internalised and fashioned into the worldview of the adult, later to be expressed in his artistic choices.

We first meet Hani as a young boy living in Rafah, one of eight refugee camps set up in the Gaza Strip by UNRWA to house the thousands of Palestinians fleeing Zionist violence, in 1948, in 1967 and in 1979 following the Camp David Accords when Rafah itself was divided by the border with Egypt, separating family members yet again. For this creative boy, childhood pleasures of playing marbles, visiting the beach, and practising Arabic calligraphy were relegated to memory by the Israeli murder of Gazan workers, which precipitated the First Uprising of 1987. As with the Soweto Uprising against apartheid and the proposed formation of Bantustans in 1976, the young—armed with little more than their acute sense of injustice—were at the vanguard of resistance, and Hani joined in demonstrations, designing posters and spraying graffiti. All these early memories are to find their way into the young artist's paintings as he travels, mostly 'illegally', from city to city in his own homeland, seeking a professional art education, but finding in his own body and sensations his only viable conceptual and aesthetic resource, until he wins a residency to Paris, where for the first time he encounters freedom—and international art. And yet the Gaza home remains a pivotal point of reference.

Now confined to what visitors describe as an open-air prison, Gaza children in recent years have expressed their unity and longing for freedom through their skill at collective kite-flying; but among the many enlightening passages in this book we learn that flying as a metaphor for loss and longing is embedded in Arabic and Islamic literature and continues to reverberate throughout much of recent Palestinian art and filmmaking, becoming a central motif in Hani's paintings incorporating Qudsi's image.

In his writings, Boullata has consistently paid attention to the literary legacy embedded in Arabic visual arts, pointing out that "the verbal and the pictorial forms of art have never been identified as two equally independent fields of creative expression. Instead, the word has consistently dominated the image throughout the culture's history."[7] As Elias Khoury has similarly noted, "poetry in classical Arab culture was not merely the supreme art; it also combined all the arts in one. The poet was seen as a musician, a painter and an image-maker."[8] The use of time and space in Hani's paintings are themselves indicative of this symbiotic relation between Arabic visual and verbal arts. Speaking of the *Siege* paintings from the artist's sojourn in Ramallah, Kamal informs us:

> Far from being symbolic as one familiar with the tradition of Western painting may tend to read them, each detail alludes to metaphoric associations whose visual formulation stems from verbal expression. In that way, each painting represents an attempt to embody a meaning whose articulation unfolds like the cadence of a phrase in everyday speech.

Self-portraits in profile, achieved through the distancing device of two mirrors, are likened to an Arabic tradition where autobiography is expressed in the third person, except when the first person pronoun 'I' suddenly intervenes, which is equated with Hani's introduction of a frontal gaze, referred to as a "doubling of the narrative voice". Perhaps, following this train of thought, we can speculate that Hani's subsequent paintings of Qudsi also reveal an analogous doubling: the youthful memories of the father woven with those of a son's, yet to be articulated? For the exile, however, the mirror as a metaphor of self-other relations invokes an anxiety of estrangement; as Mourid Barghouti writes:

> Who can describe me
> if my mirror fails to?...
> Did I break the mirrors which the tribe held up,
> or did the mirrors break me?[9]

But this introduces another dimension to Zurob's work discussed in the book, namely, how the conflicting emotions of estrangement and belonging are expressed through a tension between the paint mark that defines a form and one that records a bodily gesture. The Gaza artist performs what the late Irish-born painter and voluntary exile Francis Bacon referred to as "a kind of tightrope walk between what is called figurative painting and abstraction".[10] Bacon rejected mere illustration as demanding only mental deciphering; and he rejected 'pure' abstraction as being too focused on the aesthetics of patterns or shapes. Important to Bacon was immediate sensation as the ground for provoking intellectual insight. And yet, it is also 'sensation' that accounts for Hani's occasional turn to painterly abstraction: the more abstract *Barrage* and *Projection* series, coincide with periods of deepening violence against the Gazan population, as if any form of naturalistic depiction would be inadequate to convey the artist's feelings. Altogether, despite their cultural and temporal distance, there is much in the author's analysis of Hani's work that recalls Bacon's preference for poetry as a primary source of inspiration as well as his own artistic responses to an earlier violent (European) reality.[11] For both artists the photograph is a central tool towards restaging a disassembled human form, reassembled in delineated frames or in the minimal outline of rooms, which function as fragile, often restrictive armatures for the body in space, but always, as Bacon said, as a "recording of being in the world".

The act of recording "being in the world" is attributed to the Mediaeval troubadours, a tradition to which Palestinian artists, musicians and writers, forced into an itinerant existence, have become its reluctant reincarnation.[12] We too often forget that the Arabic tradition of poetry and song was brought from al-Andalus to the royal courts and public squares of Europe via the travelling troubadours, among whose intellectual roles was to chronicle and interpret the sociopolitical realities of the times and engender new spaces of creative action. In an earlier text, Boullata noted that the border-crossing contemporary artist has become the intellectual "nomad" of our time, variously a witness, provocateur or soothsayer; whilst for Said "the traveller discovers other selves and identities... and transforms contest into creative interaction."[13] For Michel Serres, the troubadour (*trouvère* in French) has an exemplary, visionary status as the creator who 'does not seek but finds': "The inventive breath alone gives life, because life invents."[14]

These, then, are the modalities of the troubadour function that concern us here: to witness, to record and to engender cultural renewal, all of which enact the ethics of memory and its commitment to truth. In the Palestinian context they are the means of 'working through' what Paul Ricoeur identifies as the "wounds and scars of history", and, I would emphasise, of reclaiming agency.[15] In fact, Ricoeur offers several insights into how we may understand *Between Exits* as more than a narrative about its named actors. On the one hand, it becomes clear that the pathology of Zionism's abuses of memory and history, its attempts to 'disappear' or vampirise the Palestinian other, lies in the lack of Israeli-Jewish identity, for there can be no self without an other—and elsewhere Ricoeur notes that "the duty of memory is the duty to do justice, through memories, to an other than the self".[16] On the other hand, Palestinian resistance to the erasure of its own identity connects with what Ricoeur calls "the duty to remember", "which consists not only in having a deep concern for the past, but in transmitting the meaning of past events to the next generations."[17] In essence, this is Kamal Boullata's own ethical commitment: to give life and agency to the creativity of successive generations of Palestinian visual artists as a *collective* inheritance, in which language and memory of land are inseparable. In *Between Exits*, the collective troubadour's voice is given over to Hani Zurob, who finds his own artistic maturity and agency in expressing the time and space between memory and hope, cultural belonging and exilic longing, his own beginnings and those of Qudsi—for those who went before and for those who come after.

Jean Fisher

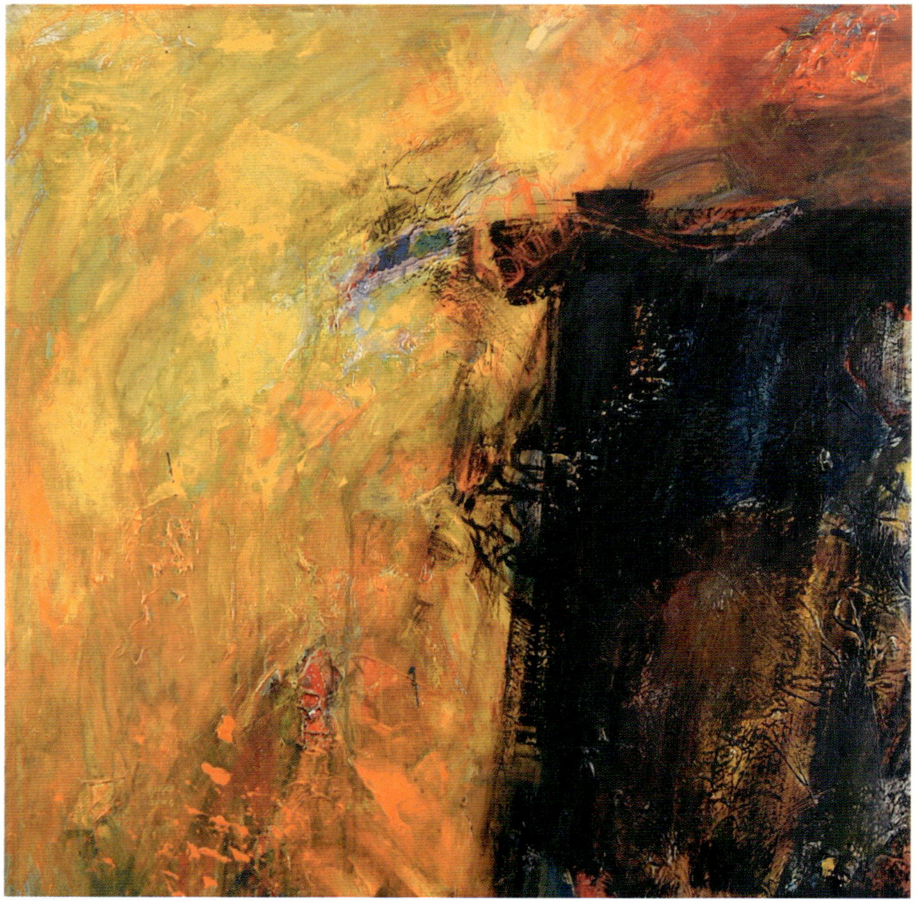

Siege no. 23, 2006.
Acrylic, pastel and charcoal
on canvas, 90 x 90 cm.
Private collection, Jerusalem

1.

Grounds

A nation's history becomes a family's history, becomes in turn a child's apparently idiosyncractic conscience.

Robert Cole

The Political Life of Children, New York: Atlantic Monthly Press, 2000, p. 310.

The past owns us.

Edward W Said

After the Last Sky, London: Faber & Faber Ltd, 1986, p. 14.

The sliver of fertile land bordering on sand dunes and ridges that flank the Sinai Desert in the south and stretching along the Mediterranean Sea in the west is known today as the Gaza Strip. Since antiquity, this corner of the world has been a region of crossroads between Egypt and the Levant as well as between Europe and Arabia. Old-world invaders including Pharaonic Egyptians, Babylonians, Assyrians, Israelites and Persians besieged it, colonised it and repeatedly destroyed its population centres but its people lived on to witness successive conquerors come and go from Alexander the Great to Napoleon Bonaparte. For four centuries under the Ottomans, the Gaza region was part of the province of Jerusalem. During the 26 years of the British Mandate, it was one of Palestine's six administrative districts with Gaza City as its capital.

With the creation of Israel along the Eastern coast of Palestine in 1948, the country's remaining portions came under the control of their neighbouring Arab states. Further east, the region which included the Old City of Jerusalem and its environs was annexed by the newly-formed Hashemite Kingdom of Jordan and it was called the West Bank in reference to being west of the River Jordan. Palestine's southern part fell under the military rule of Egypt. Since then it has been referred to as the Gaza Strip.

The war that was waged to make room for the establishment of a Jewish State in Palestine led to the dispersal of the country's Christian and Muslim Arab natives. Thousands of families who did not flee the firing lines were chased out of their towns and villages at gun point. In wave after wave, they poured into what was to become known as the West Bank and the Gaza Strip while other displaced families sought shelter further away in neighbouring Arab countries. Reaching the Strip by land and by sea, the masses of refugees were granted temporary asylums in mosques, churches and schools. Private houses also opened their doors to lodge relatives and their neighbours or fellow travellers of theirs who equally turned homeless overnight.

By December 1949, with the failure to repatriate the refugees, the UN General Assembly approved a resolution to establish the United Nations Relief and Works Agency (UNRWA). Thus, Palestine's refugees officially registered with UNRWA were eligible for shelter, food rations, education, health care, social services and some work opportunities. Families were first quartered in hurriedly built tent camps, which proved to be unsuitable once winter whipped across the region. Subsequently, blocks of concrete cubicles were constructed in rows everywhere within reach. UNRWA identified each block with a letter from the English alphabet. Harbouring the largest refugee population on what remained of historic Palestine, the Gaza Strip became the site of eight major refugee camps that were established in the sandy and flat lands and wherever refugees huddled together in great numbers.

Rafah

Hani Zurob was born in the summer of 1976 in a little house in the Rafah refugee camp which UNRWA divided into 17 blocks. The cubicle that it granted to his paternal grandfather was inherited by Hani's father who expanded it to accommodate his family of seven children. The house was lined up along what UNRWA named "Block-I". Locals, however, referred to its neighbourhood as the "Quarter of the Palm Tree" for in that sandy and barren area of the camp there was a stately palm tree up the road from the house.

Hani's family descended from an old peasant clan which had thrived for decades in the southern region of the Gaza Strip. The name of a hill in Rafah carrying the family name and known as "Tal Zu'rob" continues to be home for many distant relatives and a plot of land in it serves as the burial grounds of their ancestors and family members. Likewise, in the nearby town of Khan Yunis, there is a whole neighbourhood known as "Hay Zu'rob" where clan members continue to live.

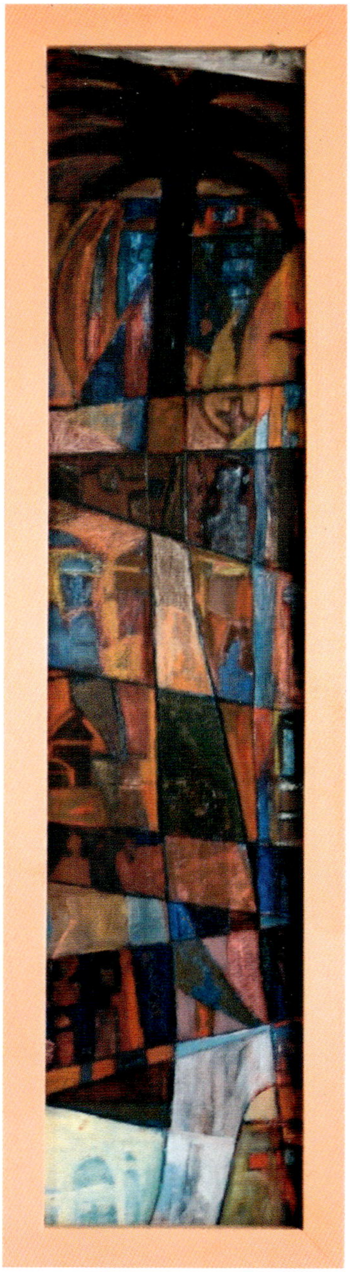

Palm tree, 2002.
Oil on canvas, 90 x 15 cm.
Private collection, Beirut.

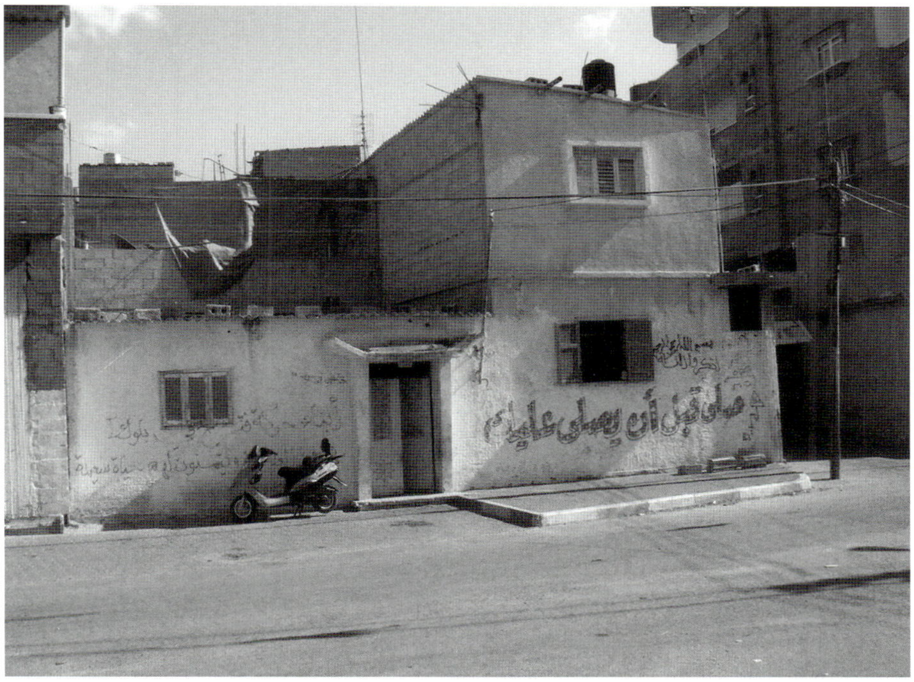

The Zu'rob's Rafah home, 2008.

Notwithstanding the legendary origins of the Zu'rob clan in the region, UNRWA counted Hani's family among the refugee population for being descendants of refugees, however, Hajj Thabet Zu'rob, Hani's paternal grandfather was in his youth a renegade from his clan. As soon as the Ottomans lost control of Palestine and new work opportunities loomed up north with the advent of the British Mandate, young Thabet bought a camel and left home to seize his chance of work away from the well-worn family tradition of tilling the soil. He settled in the shady village of Wadi Hunayn which lay on the outskirts of the old city of Ramleh. Over a few years his commercial success in running the business of transporting the village's fruit produce on his camel to the neighbouring town markets allowed him to buy an old truck and employ a driver to expand his business venture, which eventually was to include several trucks. To the villager's contentment, Hajj Thabet Zu'rob, who had built a stone house in the village following his marriage to a Rafah girl, was soon nominated to serve as *mukhtar*, the village's chief manager. But the prosperity he and the villagers attained was not destined to last. The peace for long enjoyed with their next door Jewish neighbours at Ness Ziona colony were, in the blink of an eye, to come to an end.

Within days of hearing about the horrors of the massacre perpetrated by Jewish armed militias in the village of Deir Yaseen on Friday 9 April

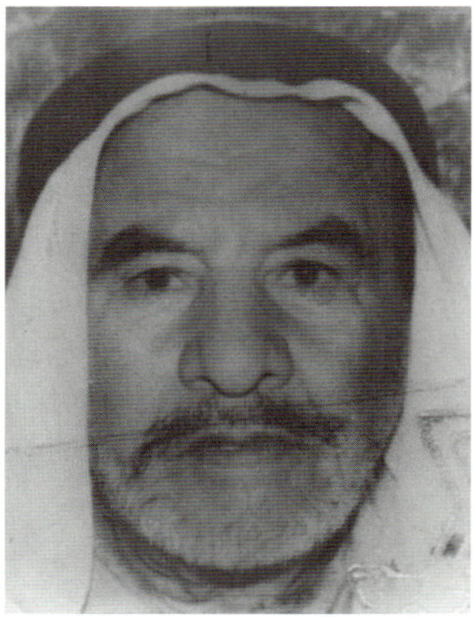

Grandfather Thabet Zurob (1900–1986), Rafat, 1980.

1948, even after the village elders had concluded a non-aggression pact with representatives of the neighbouring Jewish colony of Givat Sha'ul, all natives of Wadi Hunayn sought refuge elsewhere. Hajj Thabet and his family, together with the families of his neighbours, locked their houses and carrying only scanty belongings with them hopped on two of his trucks and headed south to Rafah where they thought they could wait in safety for the Jewish violence to subside. All members of the convoy were accommodated in family residences in Tal Zu'rob.

As Hani was growing up, he could not fully comprehend why all adults around him would speak of "waiting to return home". For him, 'home' was right there in Rafah where he enjoyed playing marbles in the camp's alleyways and the daily three kilometre walk to and from his UNRWA school was as much fun as walking to the beach in summer. 'Home' was where a whole hill in town has been named after his family's name and the abode imbued with the scent of his mother, the taste of her dishes and the aroma of coffee in the morning. 'Home' was most of all where he was proud to have a father who owned 'Hawaii Boutique' in the middle of town, a potpourri of a clothes' store whose income helped the family meet its growing needs over and above the food rations UNRWA provided.

The state of 'waiting to return home' became more palpable to the child every time he saw his grandfather bring out the seal of the village chief to stamp some official document that a Wadi Hunayn villager needed. The seal was fastened to the same waist-band engirdling the key of the house Hajj Thabet owned in Wadi Hunayn. Hani's father, Subhi, who was the youngest of his three boys was the chosen son to whom Hajj Thabet, bequeathed the key to the house in which his children were born.

That same state of 'waiting to return home' was further reinforced by Ahmad Za'rur, the stone builder of Hajj Thabet's house who eventually became Hani's maternal grandfather. Likewise, he never parted from the keys of his old house in his native Ramleh. The account of how he and his family were driven out of their homes at gunpoint when Hani's mother was only one year old was often retold. The seven members of the Za'rur family took turns in carrying the baby girl as they, together with some neighbours of theirs, had to walk under the threat of arms all the way from Ramleh to Jaffa where they joined tumultuous throngs that were hastily embarking on boats scurrying to safety. That day, Ahmad Za'rur decided to hire two fishermen's boats to secure that at least half the family could survive in case one of the boats was shot down. He asked both fishermen to head to Rafah, hometown of his closest friend from Wadi Hunayn.

At that time no survivors of the 1948 Palestinian exodus could imagine that in less than two decades their places of refuge were to be invaded. In the summer of 1967, the state of Israel launched a six-day blitzkrieg during which all the remaining parts of Palestine fell under its control. In addition, it took over Egypt's Sinai Desert and Syria's Golan Heights. With the fall of the Gaza Strip and the West Bank under Israeli military occupation, thousands of Palestinian families were to become refugees; some for the second time in their lives as the family of Hani's maternal grandfather did when they fled from Rafah to Amman, Jordan.

Hani's parents, who had got married that ominous year, remember well how within days following the Israeli military takeover, all men in Rafah between the ages of 18 and 40 were rounded up in school yards. At the end of a long summer day spent waiting in the sun, they were trucked to the borders and banished to Egypt. That year Hani's mother was expecting her firstborn. Her ageing father was obliged to return from his refuge in Jordan to stay with her up until the following year when her husband was among the men permitted to return to Rafah.

Growing up with such family memories, it was incomprehensible for the child to understand how his grandparents used to live in peace and harmony with their Jewish neighbours 'back home'. The first time he lived through the consequence of what was called 'peace' induced his earliest experience of anguish. It came after the signing of the peace agreement between Egypt and Israel. The agreement, which called for the return of the Sinai Desert to Egypt, stipulated that the international borders between the two states had to go through Rafah. This meant the division of the town into two halves and separating the families and their relatives from each other. A visit to Hani's aunts Aziza, Zakiyya and Huda who were living at a stone's throw away from their own block in the camp became a life-threatening venture. Every time he and other family members went for a visit, each had to slip through the barbed wires when no border patrols were in sight.

Unlike his grandparents, the only Jews the boy ever saw in Rafah were armed Israeli soldiers who ravaged the place and exacted death and destruction. From Tal Zu'rob where an Israeli military base had been installed, Rafah houses were shelled at will, killing family acquaintances and demolishing their homes. One of the earliest and closest encounters

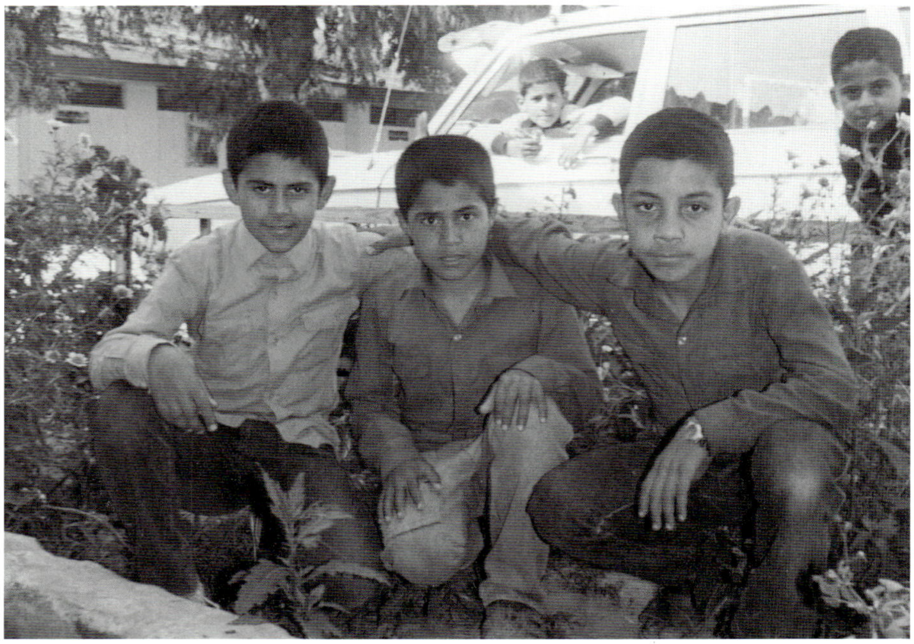

Hani (left) with schoolmates from Alif Elementary School, Rafah, 1986.

Hani had with an Israeli soldier took place in the middle of the night, right in his and his brothers' bedroom when he was about six years old. He abruptly woke to see an armed Israeli soldier flouncing his bedcovers. As he cringed on his floor mattress, he became aware that other soldiers were walking all over the house and wreaking havoc with the family's belongings and personal effects.

For two decades of living under Israeli military occupation, the grief, anger and humiliation that Palestinians went through dissipated their daily lives. The night raids, the sporadic blowing up of homes, the continuous confiscation of land and water sources, the imprisonment and deportation of emerging community leaders, and the random killings in the open fields and on the streets while the rest of the world was looking the other way was reaching a level beyond the limits of tolerance. Parents were thus not surprised to see their children defying their orders as Hani did and going out on the streets to call for an end to Israel's occupation. The new generation who felt their national cause was betrayed and abandoned by Arab leaders braced themselves to take things into their own hands.

The popular uprising that was to be internationally known by its Arabic name as the Intifada had been brewing for sometime before it swept all the Palestinian territories Israel occupied since 1967. The one incident that led up to the full scale protest occurred outside the Jabalya refugee camp north of the Gaza Strip. On 8 December 1987 an Israeli tank crashed into a line of cars and vans filled with workers returning from their day's work in Israel. Four men were killed and seven were seriously injured. That night the funeral turned into a massive demonstration. The following day spontaneous demonstrations broke out throughout the Gaza Strip. In no time, they spread to the West Bank. Children, teenagers and young adults were seen at the forefront of the protest.

Figuring that unruly youth were using school and university facilities to organise the protests, all educational institutions in the Gaza Strip and the West Bank were ordered to close. Curfews were imposed. Challenging the curfews, the young went out to dare Israeli soldiers on the streets and alleyways of their homes. Armed with slingshots and stones they confronted the army units who in turn responded with teargas canisters, rubber bullets and live ammunition. With what Israel called an "Iron Fist" policy, its soldiers were authorised to suppress all forms of nationalist expression. The Palestinian flag, which has been forbidden to be displayed anywhere, became a common feature of the protests and a number of children raising it were shot dead. Over the first two years of the uprising more than 800 civilians were killed on the streets of the Gaza Strip and the West Bank, among them over 200 children. Many of the survivors were maimed for life.

Lasting for about five years, the Intifada was first ignited as a spontaneous protest. In time, it was to become more organised by an underground coalition of local leaders who disseminated weekly leaflets with directives that were signed by what became known as the National Leadership of the Uprising (UNLU). Their directives which were all of a non-violent nature included the call for civil disobedience, demonstrations, general strikes, boycotts of Israeli products, refusal to pay taxes, constructing makeshift roadblocks with rocks and the burning of tires to obstruct the circulation of Israeli tanks and armoured vehicles. The young of all ages volunteered to devise these barricades.

Having participated in demonstrations and having been known at school for his distinguished Arabic calligraphy and his talent for drawing, Hani, who by then was in his mid-teens, was approached by an older schoolmate associated with the UNLU to join a team who were provided with slogans and equipment to spray graffiti on their neighbourhood's street walls and to create posters to be plastered throughout Rafah. Hani, who used to spend long hours at home during the curfew days copying illustrations from his father's collection of Arabic books and Egyptian periodicals including *Rose el-Yousef* and *Sabah al-Kheir*, jumped at the opportunity. He went immediately to work.

Spraying graffiti as well as designing the posters all had to be done after sunset and in hiding from his parents as well as from the Israeli patrols. The risk never ceased to be entailed with a secret joy of knowing that his creations were now being appreciated by people beyond his schoolteachers and classmates who were particularly fond of the pencil drawings he used to do of their favourite Egyptian singers and movie stars. Hearing a compliment by a member of the camp's community who did not know that he was the street artist behind some of the graffiti and posters diffused in town was most gratifying to Hani even though he knew most of his works did not last long; upon seeing them, Israeli patrols would usually order some passerby to peel off the poster and whitewash the slogans.

For about three consecutive years the posters he designed and the graffiti he enjoyed spraying on freshly painted walls furnished him with a thrill that transcended the simple delight he enjoyed in pencilling drawings at home. It even exceeded the excitement that surged every time the teacher handed him a bunch of colour felt-pens to create a new issue of the school's wall-newspaper. The larger the space to be covered on the wall the greater the thrill he experienced, especially when he was provided with colours other than the usual red and black spray-cans. By the time he graduated from al-Samaw-al Secondary School, Hani Zurob's mind was set. He wanted to learn how to become a professional artist. For him, however, there was nowhere around that could teach him anything new even though the Gaza Strip has been the bedrock of post-1948 Palestinian nationalist art inspired by the exodus and by life in the refugee camps.

Thanks to the UNRWA schools and its vocational training centres which offered art classes and to Nasser's Egypt for providing Palestinian students with a higher education free of charge, leading talents from the Gaza Strip would go to Egypt to study art education and some received training classes in painting and other studio arts. In the meantime, the yearly art exhibitions of students' work mounted in UNRWA schools had become a festive community event. By the mid 1950s, Gaza City had not only become the site of the first exhibition of young talents returning from their art studies in Egypt but it also was the birthplace of the first Union of Palestinian Artists.[1]

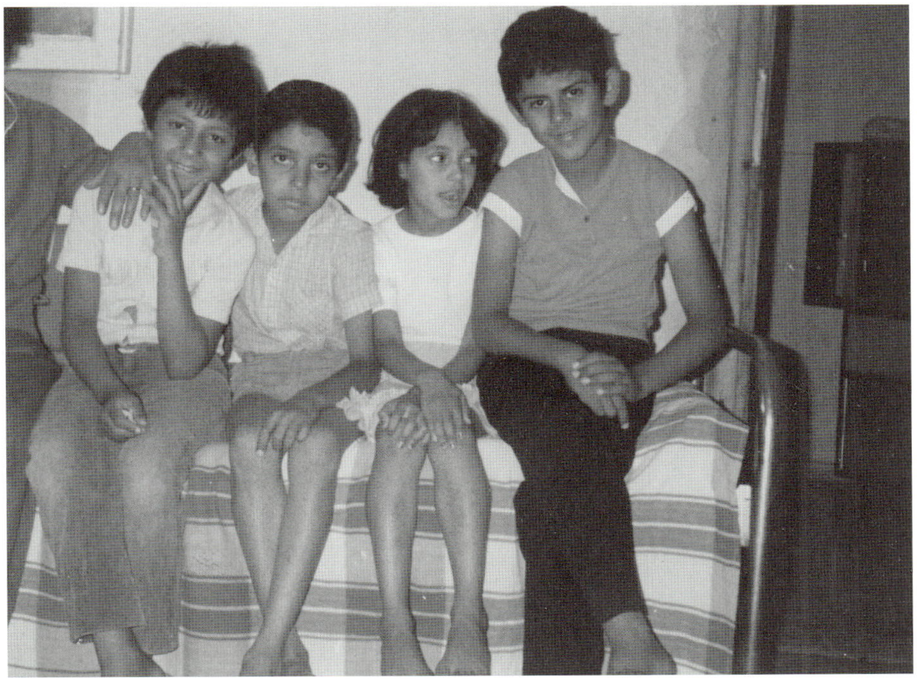

Hani (right) at home with relatives, Rafah, 1986.

Since the fall of the Gaza Strip under the Israeli military occupation, however, studying in Egypt was no longer an option for Hani. He was obliged to look elsewhere to further his studies and the only viable place he could think of was al-Najah National University in Nablus, the West Bank, which had expanded its art department into an independent college in 1992. Despite the rigid restrictions Israel had imposed on people from the Gaza Strip applying for permissions to travel to the West Bank, Hani continued hoping that the seeming changes in the region's political mood could possibly ease off the travel restrictions.

By the summer of 1994, Hani joined the masses of people coming from all over the Gaza Strip to his hometown to welcome the triumphant entry of Yasser Arafat, Chairman of the Palestine Liberation Organisation (PLO). Surrounded by green-bereted Palestinian guards and raising a victory sign, Arafat's crossing the Rafah border with Egypt announced the first step in the enactment of the Declaration of Principles agreed in the Oslo Peace Accords and signed in Washington the previous year. Following Arafat's celebrated visit, however, none of Israel's travel restrictions were lifted. In fact, they were tightened as the Palestinian National Authority was itself being restricted and its nominal territorial control was initially assumed to be nowhere beyond what became the newly autonomous areas of Gaza and Jericho.

Ironically, it had been the Israeli Prime Minister Yitzhak Rabin who shook Arafat's hand on the South Lawn of the White House who had presided over devising the atrocious system that ultimately led to caging Palestinians into cantons. At the time, the Palestinians may not have known that when Rabin in his White House address underlined the need for "a separation between us and them", the consequences of his message were to result in the kind of 'separateness' that literally translates to the word '*apartheid*' in Africaans. Notwithstanding, all Palestinians did recall was how it was Rabin in his position as Minister of Defence who had encouraged his soldiers to break the legs and arms of Palestinian kids who were caught throwing stones during the Intifada. Hani knew quite a few of them in his neighbourhood whose wrists and elbows ended up in casts, others who hopped on crutches and a few who moved around in wheel chairs. Most of all, like many Palestinians, Hani could not forget that it was the same Israeli Prime Minister who signed the peace agreement with Arafat in Washington who as commander of the Harel Brigade signed on Monday 12 July 1948 the order to expel the Palestinians from their homes in Lydda and Ramleh, which included the family of his maternal grandparents.

Nablus

Hani was determined to find a way to reach the city of Nablus which remained under Israeli military occupation. His application to travel there, however, was repeatedly rejected by the Israeli authorities. Finally, after the school year had started, as a last resort he decided to carry out the recommendation of a shrewd operator who suggested circumventing the Israeli intransigence by applying for travel to Amman. Thus he would manage to exit from the Eretz Crossing which at the time was the only Israeli checkpoint between the Gaza Strip and the Israeli border. Once his exit was secured he was told he could make it to Nablus if he could privately agree with the driver of the collective taxi he would ride to take him to Jerusalem instead of Amman, and from there it would be easy to go anywhere in the Occupied Territories of the West Bank. Hani had no choice but to take the risk. The taxi driver agreed to take him to Jerusalem as he had other passengers with permissions to go there.

Once in Nablus Hani was aware that according to the definitions of the Israeli occupation authorities he was considered an "illegal sojourner" in the West Bank and subject to imprisonment or deportation back to Gaza if he were caught. His thirst to learn all about art, however, exceeded his fears of retribution. Hence, he made sure to steer clear from all hot areas where Israeli army patrols could ask him for his papers. In the meantime, he managed to join a number of students from the Gaza Strip with whom he shared an apartment. To support himself, pay the university fees and cover the costs of his art supplies, he worked all his nights and throughout the holidays as waiter in a local cafeteria.

It was at art school that the 18 year old student from the Gaza Strip saw colours in the form of cream coming out of paint tubes and got to know canvas as a support for painting for the first time. During Hani's four years at art school, what he learnt was merely confined to painting technical matters thanks to two painters from refugee camps in the Gaza Strip, Kamel al-Mughanni from Gaza City and Muhammad Abu Sitta from Khan Yunis who had graduated from the Fine Arts College in Alexandria, who were his art instructors. In their classes he learnt all practical principles including the stretching of canvas and priming it, the thinning of oil colours and the variable methods of employing them on canvas. As to any academic classes in art history or art theory, they were inexistent. Over the four years, Hani had to settle for his instructors' personal dictates and the rudiments they improvised.

In the meantime, the legendary city of Nablus, which continued to be under Israeli military occupation until 1996, offered no stimulating artistic or inspirational activity for the art student from Rafah. It remained a culturally garrisoned city even after the withdrawal of Israeli troops from it. For Palestinians living in the West Bank and the Gaza Strip, it was Ramallah which was becoming the *de facto* administrative capital of the Palestinian National Authority (PNA) by the late 1990s. Here, artistic and cultural activities were booming after national and international institutions began to open new cultural centres in town and non-governmental organisations (NGO) pioneered in advancing funds to support local initiatives. With the return of many expatriates to start businesses there, the general atmosphere was radiant and full of promise.

Hani set his heart on moving to Ramallah following his graduation in 1999. But to earn his living he was obliged to work for a year as graphic designer with a local Nablus printing shop until the PNA Department of Education appointed him as art teacher in two neighbouring villages further north in the district of Jenin. The paintings he produced during his sojourn there represented the body of his first public exhibition in

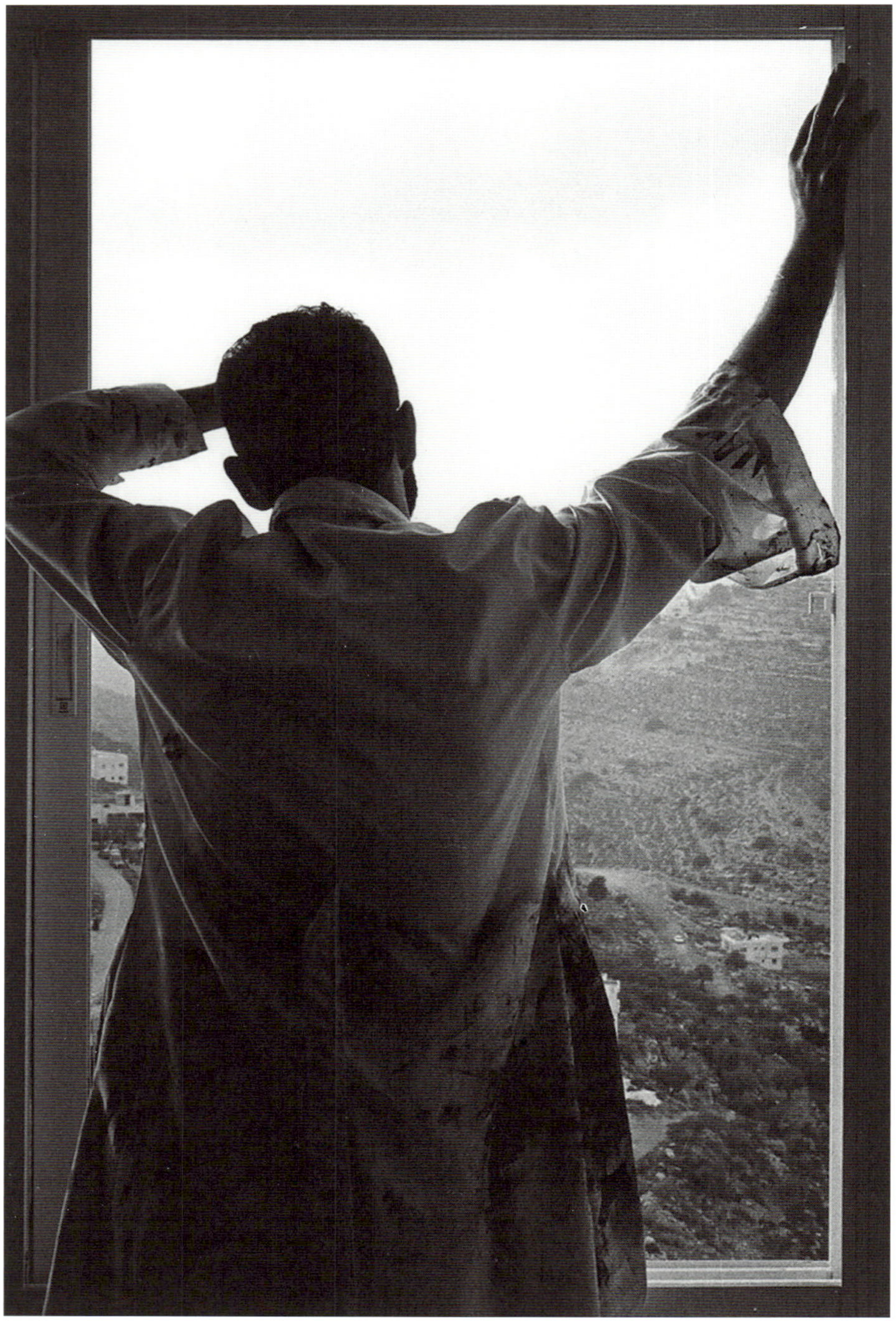

Artist at his home studio,
Ramallah, 2004.

Ramallah. It was co-sponsored by the French Cultural Centre and the AM Qattan Foundation which hosted the show. The occasion earned the 25 year old art debutant a gratifying success not only because a large number of the exhibition's paintings sold out but more importantly because his public exposure gained him a job as an art instructor at a local women's college in Ramallah. Hani lost no time in resigning from the village schools and moving to Ramallah.

Ramallah

During his student years in Nablus which were known as the 'Oslo Years', and after his move to Ramallah, the people's hopes for an end to the three decades of Israeli military occupation continued to be deferred and the Palestinian State failed to materialise as expected in accordance with the peace talks agreement. With the breakdown of the Israeli-Palestinian negotiations at the Camp David Summit in 2000, Israel extended its policy of closures by tightening its restriction on movement and reinforcing its military checkpoints throughout the occupied territories. In the meantime, Palestinian homes continued to be demolished, olive and fruit trees uprooted and lands confiscated to build further settlements on Palestinian territories, particularly around Ramallah and Jerusalem. In addition, a network of bypass roads was built which was confined to the use of Israel's settlers whose number had doubled since the beginning of the peace talks. Israel's colonial policies in the Palestinian territories under its occupation were all deemed illegal by international law. The discriminatory laws multiplied and the collective punishment the Palestinians underwent day in and day out seized them with a bottomless despair. Their bottled-up rage was about to explode at any moment.

The explosion finally erupted the day Ariel Sharon, the Israeli leader of the right-wing Likud Party set foot on al-Haram al-Sharif grounds in Jerusalem which encloses al-Aqsa Mosque, the third-holiest shrine in Islam. Uninvited and escorted by 1,000 armed police, Sharon who was an ardent supporter of the settlements sought to instigate controversy. When worshipers went out to confront him and his entourage with a hail of stones, the armed police responded with rubber bullets and live ammunition. Four worshipers were killed and over 160 were wounded. Within days, the Second Uprising, better known as al-Aqsa Intifada, burst forth throughout the Occupied Territories.

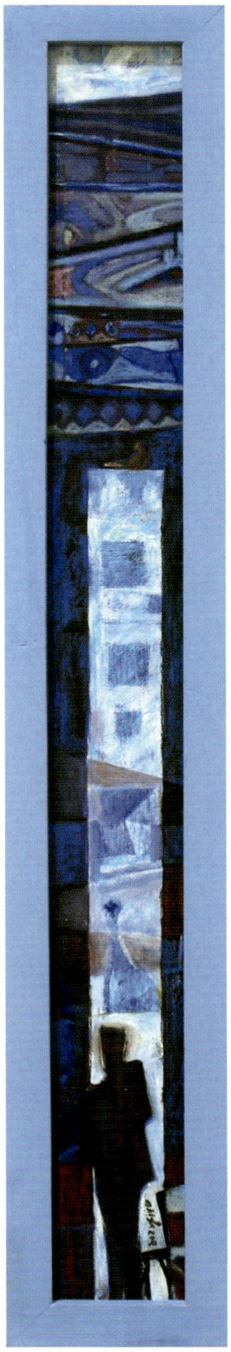

Door, 2002.
Oil on canvas, 90 x 15 cm.
Private collection, Beirut.

Like the first popular uprising, it started by employing non-violent methods spearheaded by marches and demonstrations staged at military checkpoints. But soon after the Israeli army waged fierce attacks on unarmed civilians of all ages, a campaign of suicide bombings by Islamist groups was unleashed. Armed groups associated with the mainstream Palestinian political leadership in Ramallah attacked Israeli army incursions and settlers. The spreading of violence brought the downfall of Ehud Barak, Israel's Labour prime minister, and Ariel Sharon who had been openly against the peace talks altogether was elected to replace him early on in 2001.

Within a year that witnessed the escalation of suicide attacks and the target killing of Palestinian national leaders, the Israeli army invaded the West Bank. Merkava tanks, war planes and helicopter gunships were employed to reoccupy all major cities, turning them into a massive open-air prison. It took no more than an hour for Ramallah to fall under siege and the bombing of the PNA headquarters to cut off Arafat's offices from the rest of the Palestinian government's compound, which was turned into rubble.

The recently-elected Israeli prime minister ordered the closure of all educational institutions and the cutting of electricity in all Palestinian homes, hospitals and public buildings. Sharon also banned movement by imposing curfews on a random basis and called for the detention of all suspected activists without a shred of due process. Hani Zurob was one of those suspects. During the first day in which Ramallah fell, Israeli troops stormed the apartment he shared with four other art graduates. Hani was arrested for being an 'illegal resident' and all his paintings and art supplies were destroyed. He was detained at Ofer prison for 53 days after which he was released as the prosecution failed in levelling an indictment at him. However, a deportation order was decreed against him.

With the widespread destruction of public buildings and private property and the vandalism of homes and offices by members of the Israeli army in addition to the death of over 3,000 Palestinians of whom the majority was civilian including some 500 children, the Palestinians were made to pay a heavy price. In contrast, however, and despite the surrounding death and destruction, Ramallah was turned into a hive swarming with cultural activities including stage performances, concerts, workshops, poetry readings and art exhibitions, each of which expressed its affirmation of life and bolstered the spirit of resistance against Israel's colonial policies and its military occupation of the West Bank and the Gaza Strip.

During the days and evenings in which curfews were lifted, Hani Zurob ventured out to attend plays performed by local talents at al-Qasaba Theatre, musical recitals organised by the newly established al-Kamandjati Association as well as concerts sponsored by the Edward Said National Conservatory of Music. In fact, days before his arrest in March 2002, he witnessed his most memorable poetry reading in Ramallah by national poet Mahmud Darwish who had never read anywhere in the Gaza Strip. Held at al-Qasaba Theatre which was filled to capacity, Darwish's reading was attended by a delegation of the International Parliament of Writers who travelled to Ramallah to express their solidarity with the Palestinian people. The delegation was headed by the 1998 Nobel Laureate Jose Saramago from Portugal and the 1987 Nobel Laureate Wole Soyinka from Nigeria. It included Russell Banks from the USA, Bei Dao from China, Breyten Breytenbach from South Africa, Juan Goytisolo from Spain and Christian Salmon from France.

The solidarity of international writers and artists who travelled to Ramallah during the Second Uprising was particularly uplifting to the people who stood up all alone to face Israel's war machine. Some international writers offered workshops on creativity within the context of living under the military occupation. Visiting artists created artwork that was displayed in Ramallah. One particular workshop that Hani deeply enjoyed was conducted by British art critic John Berger who travelled to Ramallah together with his Swiss friend the photographer Jean Mohr. Entitled Another Way of Telling in Palestine, the workshop was conducted at the AM Qattan Foundation.

For the first time, Hani Zurob was also exposed to contemporary art by international artists whose conceptual work created in situ reflected forms of expression that were new to him. In 2003 and 2004, the work of two artists in particular struck him for their simplicity in execution and daring originality. The first one was the creation of French artist and Berlin resident Aurore Millet Rienicke whose exhibition consisted of drawings executed with the tip of a red crayon directly on the white walls of the gallery space at the AM Qattan Foundation. The interconnecting lines running throughout the gallery rooms alluded to barbed wires.

The other project he particularly remembers was conceived by the German artist Thomas Kilpper. Sponsored by the Goethe-Institut in Ramallah, Kilpper was invited to lead a sculpture workshop in Jenin whose refugee camp had been completely razed during the Israeli invasion. Having lived through the nightly incursions of the Israeli tanks during his sojourn, Kilpper decided to create with a group of local teenagers a larger-than-life horse out of the debris of homes, the wreckage of cars and the twisted rods of scaffoldings. From a Red Crescent ambulance that was hit by an Israeli rocket grenade in which an emergency doctor was killed, the salvaged side of the ambulance formed one flank of the horse. The Arabic word for 'ambulance' continued to be legible in red on the horse's flank. Once completed, Kilpper and his Palestinian team of young workers secured the five-metre high sculpture on a farmer's tractor and they all headed to Ramallah. The 90 kilometre drive took 11 hours because the convoy had been stopped at every roadblock and military checkpoint by Israeli soldiers who had to assure themselves that this was no 'Trojan Horse' in disguise. Hani Zurob was among the crowds gathering in Ramallah to welcome the artist and his assistants and watch the parade of the farmer's tractor carrying Kilpper's horse. The scrap-metal body of the sculpture which recalls a rough embodiment of the horse in Picasso's *Guernica*—except that Kilpper's horse is standing up on all four legs—has since been installed in a square in Jenin to commemorate the resistance of its people during the siege.

Hani Zurob never missed seeing an art exhibition nor any other cultural event held in Ramallah. It was solely this hands-on education that neither his experience in Rafah nor his four years of art training in Nablus could provide. Following the success of his first solo exhibition there, acknowledgement of his emergence in the local art scene was confirmed when works of his were selected for an exhibition showing the ten finalists in the 2002 Young Artist of the Year Award organised biannually by the AM Qattan Foundation. During this exhibition, including experimental works inspired by his incarceration, was the first time he met with and saw works by Palestinian artists of his own generation who were born and raised in Israel.

Exhibitions mounted by fellow Palestinians from his own generation awakened his curiosity. They invited him to develop a critical eye and evaluate the differences he was seeking to express. Two particular exhibitions which included no artwork left a deep impression on him for their innovative spirit. The first titled 100 Shaheed: 100 Lives was curated by Adila Laïdi-Hanieh and held at the Khalil Sakakini Cultural Centre. It featured everyday objects that were held dear by each of the first 100 civilians killed during the Israeli invasion. A photograph of the fallen identifying the person along with a text next to each object narrated the personal anecdote associated with the exhibited object.

The second exhibition that captured his attention was held at the Municipality Hall. Titled Eyewitness and curated by an ad-hoc committee of women activists aided by local artists, the exhibition displayed a random selection of vandalised possessions and equipment from homes, offices and hospitals. The displayed objects included battered computer screens, ruined medical and sound equipment, domestic furniture and children's toys smashed to pieces. At the entrance, the banner across Ramallah's Main Street read "Like a phoenix we shall arise from the ashes. The best days are yet to come."

After having been re-conquered and beaten down to the ground as Palestinians have been following their Second Uprising, to continue upholding a spirit of defiance and never relinquishing hope in the future is a position that deserves explanation. Looking into what has been called 'a culture of resistance' allows us to understand how Palestinian art evolved in what had virtually been turned into a cultural ghetto since the Israeli military takeover of the Palestinian territories cut off the cultural bloodline of the region with the rest of the Arab world. More importantly, such grounds would offer us a bird's view of where Hani Zurob's work comes from.

A Culture of Resistance

The roots of what has been called 'a culture of resistance' in Palestine could be traced back to the first half of the twentieth century. It evolved out of the verbal arts exemplified in the nationalist poetry that was moulded in classical Arabic and the popular lyrics that were sung in colloquial expression. The patriotic tone of the verbal tradition was magnified in response to the Zionist threat that hung over Palestine's Arab natives during the British Mandate.

Soon after the 1948 fall of the country's coastal region and the ethnic cleansing of its people, other new forms of expression began to depart from the embryonic beginnings that first saw the light during the three decades of British rule in Palestine. Dominant among them was easel painting, whose nationalist iconography was inspired by the metaphoric imagery popularised by the verbal arts thanks to Isma'il Shammout (Lydda 1930–Amman 2006), who emerged from the Khan Yunis refugee camp in the Gaza Strip and led a whole generation of artists and dilettantes growing up in the refugee camps throughout the region. Their improvisations of his imagery expanded the repertoire of the national iconography he conceived.

Within two decades, Shammout's legacy was refuelled by a younger generation of trained and untrained artists who grew up in the West Bank and the Gaza Strip after the region fell under the Israeli military occupation in 1967. Their imagery, based in the Shammout school of painting, was equally induced by a nationalist poetry that surfaced during the period.[2]

The appearance of a whole collection of nationalist poetry came about soon after the fall of the rest of Palestine under Israeli military occupation. Ghassan Kanafani who coined the term *adab al-muqawama* or "resistance literature" published in Beirut a pioneering book on the subject which documented examples of a nationalist poetry that had been written between 1948 and 1966 by a young generation of Palestinians who had grown up within the Jewish State. Their poetry, which has never been known about in the Arab world, attained instant popularity from the Atlantic to the Gulf. The Arab intelligentsia, which had been let down by the crushing defeat of their states' armies within six days of their confrontation with Israel, found inspiration in a fresh and heroic poetry that surged from the heart of Palestine.

At the time, Palestinian natives surviving in Israel had lived since its establishment as third class citizens chafing under the rules of a military government that restricted their movement. The poets—whose collections when published had always been subjected to censorship with blank space left for missing verses—had often broken the military government's laws and dictates. Without obtaining travel permits they would secretly journey through back roads from one village to another to join some protest demonstration in which they would read their poetry intact and free from the censors. As a result, they would usually be arrested and detained, serving variable sentences without any legal process. Regardless of the quality of their poetry, which was generally uneven as its main thrust continued to be saturated with nationalist rhetoric and inveterate imagery, the political stand poets maintained was enough to elevate their status to being considered cultural leaders in their ghettoised community.

In the Arab world, the 'poets of resistance' were widely celebrated by the masses for restoring the pivotal role of the poet in traditional Arab culture. The poetry of Hanna Abu Hanna, Rashid Hussein, Tawfiq Zayyad, Salem Jubran, Samih al-Qasim and Mahmud Darwish infused an undying hope appealing to Palestinians everywhere. People living under Israeli military occupation in the West Bank and the Gaza Strip found in the chorus of their verses an embodiment of their own predicament and the voices through which to reaffirm their national identity.

The popularity of the Palestinian 'poetry of resistance' swelled during the 1970s, the decade that coincided with the widespread recognition of Palestinian nationalism after the Palestine Liberation Organisation (PLO) waged an armed struggle against Israel. Soon after the twelfth Palestine National Conference in Cairo, in which the PLO declared its goal for a "two-state solution", the UN General Assembly recognised it as the representative of the Palestinian people. The UN declaration was soon followed by an Arab summit meeting in Rabat in which the PLO was recognised as "the sole legitimate representative of the Palestinian people".

With the rise of the Palestinian national leadership on the political map of the region, visual expression by Palestinian talents growing up within the cultural ghetto of the occupied territories ebbed in concert with the ascent of Palestinian nationalist ideology and the emergent wave of popularity attained by the 'poets of resistance'. Just as much as easel painting in the post-1948 period developed out of the imagery evoked by the nationalist poetry of the period, so did the evolvement of painting in the occupied territories bask in the limelight of 'resistance poetry'. This time, however, the ground had been paved for all local talents by the pictorial repertoire established by Isma'il Shammout whose paintings were popularised through the wide diffusion of their reproduction in posters and postcards.

Thanks to the clandestine financial support advanced by the PLO Art Education Department in Beirut which was headed by Isma'il Shammout, a group of recent graduates from regional art schools living under the Israeli military occupation came together to play their part in moulding a visual representation of their national identity and collective aspirations. In 1973, the group together with local art amateurs and entrepreneurs established the League of Palestinian Artists. The mass printing of colour posters and postcards of a selection of their paintings reached public and private spaces throughout the occupied territories. Periodically, group exhibitions of their work were organised in different towns and cities to coincide with a social or national occasion. Always harping on nationalist themes usually dictated by the exhibition organisers, such themes included the honouring of the Palestinian child, the political prisoner and the village.[3]

In the absence of any art gallery, collective exhibitions of paintings were held in schools, churches, town halls, hotel lobbies and public libraries. Officially inaugurated by popular mayors, the opening of each art exhibition became a community event that drew ever-larger audiences from all segments of society. The overflow of attendants hardly left any space to view the exhibited works. But that was unimportant, for the majority of people who were unschooled in the appreciation of visual expression came in the first place to express their solidarity with their community's artists and celebrate what was viewed as a new cultural form of militating against the Israeli occupation. In time, the nationalist codes embedded in the paintings and the admiring crowds stirred the Israeli military authorities to impose censorship on all art exhibitions. Troops often stormed exhibition sites even after the exhibit's organisers had obtained official permissions from the Israeli military authorities. They confiscated paintings and ordered the public to leave. Artists were repeatedly subject to interrogation and arrest. The harsher the measures enforced on them, the more their audience drew parallels with the heroic experiences of the 'poets of resistance' and the more politically empowered the artists became within their ghettoised communities.

•

All that perturbation associated with art exhibitions took place over two decades before Hani Zurob showed up in Ramallah. It was during the 1970s and 1980s that the political empowerment of the leading painters had been anchored in the community for forging iconic images of Palestinian identity by which they promoted an 'art of resistance' steeped in the rhetoric of that period's popular 'poetry of resistance'. By the mid-1990s, the artists—now in their fifties—were holding the reins of a commodified art scene that was in concert with the new political realities on the ground following the Oslo Peace Accords.

In conformity with the Accords, Israel had allowed the surviving leaders of the PLO and their entourage along with a number of enterprising individuals to 'return' from their exile to what it called Area A of the Palestinian territories which fall under its military control. Limited to Ramallah and its environs, the once summer resort of a village had become the seat of what was later named the Palestinian Authority, a nominal government maintained by six security services while its jurisdiction was limited to civil autonomy. Some of the painters who used to be clandestinely supported by the PLO were now openly remunerated or directly employed by the Palestinian Authority. Just as the word 'liberation' was dropped from the nationalist rhetoric of the political leaders, so was the word 'resistance' dropped from referring to the art that continued to be produced by the leading painters who established the League of Palestinian Artists.

After the Israeli closure of the Orient House which had been since 1991 the official headquarters in Jerusalem of the Palestinian negotiating team to the Madrid Peace conference, and the confiscation of all its archives, provincial Ramallah turned into a so-called capital which began to simmer with foreign representatives. Thanks to the international aid flooding in, the town underwent a massive refurbishing and building programme offering new commodious villas to its officials chauffeured to work in their black sedans, high-rise housing and corporate buildings to promote commerce and tourism, as new suburban residential neighbourhoods were constructed to accommodate Palestinians allowed in from other parts of the West Bank to work in Ramallah. As some of its sidewalks continued to bear evidence of the tracks left behind by Israeli tanks, the international donations whose release is controlled by Israel covered all costs for repairing most public sites that were destroyed during Israel's invasion. Ramallah's main streets were now flanked with an array of cappuccino bars, trendy restaurants, fitness clubs, CD shops, luxury-car dealerships, designer boutique stores, along with other commercial attractions alluring to a whole new class of consumers.

The illusion of normalcy, stability and affluence earned Ramallah the title of a 'bloated bubble', as a whole pauperised world at its doorsteps continued to be ruled by Israeli roadblocks, military patrols and multiple checkpoints. Palestinians living in and out of the refugee camps never ceased to be consumed by daily distress, harassments and the menace of landing in one of Israel's military prisons at the whim of an Israeli soldier. While Ramallah's building projects were taking shape, Israel continued to demolish Palestinian homes in Areas B and C which were mandated under the Oslo Accords to remain under Israel's military control. In the meantime, more Palestinian lands were being illegally confiscated to accommodate new Israeli settlements.

With the proliferation of international Non-Governmental Organisations (NGO) funded by affluent nations and world enterprises, a young generation of ambitious professionals in Ramallah was lured by handsome grants and salaries into working on 'national identity' projects that posed no threat to the politics of the Oslo Accords. Meanwhile, after the closure of al-Wasiti Arts Centre, the only Palestinian art gallery in Jerusalem after all subsidy funds had been switched off, millions flowed in Ramallah to promote different fields of Palestinian culture and the highlighting of Palestinian identity. Cultural institutions sprouting all over town provided the veneer of a metropolitan city. In the field of visual arts, leaders of the old guard painters solidified their prestige as they continued to produce an art that sings the praises of national identity, cloaked in new and eclectic styles. In the meantime, they implicitly stood as gatekeepers deciding who the insiders and who the outsiders were to their domain.

From the exhibitions from his years in Ramallah that were most memorable for Zurob, none had been of works by any of the artists whose reputation was established on their adherence to the Shammout school of nationalist painting. Since his teens, he had been familiar with their paintings from seeing them reproduced in posters and postcards. Seeing their new work at close range in Ramallah had only confirmed to him how an art devoted to the articulation of a national identity in response to political agendas could well end up looking like clichés and tired iconography wherein the very spirit of a people's struggle and resistance had been dodged. Nowhere in their paintings could he detect a spontaneous brushstroke. He could only see how through their stylisations a distance had been created between the political message relayed in their art and the personal emotion of the artist at work. In the process, he noted how changes of individual styles were not a product of where an artist's inner struggle reached but how each artist craftily employed the same old template to produce new works.

With the exception of the non-representational paintings that were clumsy imitations of paintings by artists from the Arab world whose work was unknown both in the cultural ghetto of the West Bank and by the foreign patrons of local Palestinian art, all pictorial representations were loaded with codes and nationalist symbols. The most popular have been those paintings that emulated the photographic realism of Palestinian folk themes. In them, however, Palestinian identity was most often reduced to the idealised stereotype of a woman in her traditionally embroidered dress wherein all her personal traits have been stamped out.

For Hani Zurob, identity was not an abstract thought and its representation could not be generic, impersonal and divorced from the painter's self. He thought that national identity could only be experienced when one looks into another's face and recognises one's own self. Like a few young painters of his generation who sought to break away from what they considered the visual representation of a covert nationalist propaganda, he steered away from all populist forms of expression developed under the occupation. It was crucial for him to find a language through which to express the truth of his own being and give body to the experiences he lived. Having had no local artist to depart from, he was left to dig within his inner world to invent that language through which he could give birth to himself.

There were two artists who were Zurob's seniors who were different from their generation of painters and who helped him decipher his own language. They were Samir Salameh (Safad 1944) and Muhammad Saleh Khalil (Zarqa 1960), both of whom were born to refugees from 1948 and both had come to Ramallah following the peace agreement. Through their instructive critique of the work he produced, each of them contributed in his own way, cultivating the Gaza artist's curiosity to learn. As much as they became his mentors, they were friends with whom he was able to establish a special relationship.

Though Salameh and Khalil belonged to the same generation of the leading local artists, like Zurob they remained outsiders to the Ramallah art scene. For Hani Zurob, Khalil having studied in Dresden and Salameh having studied in Damascus and Paris opened up windows to the outside world to which they had been exposed during their years abroad. Being allowed access to their personal collection of art books, the young artist from Gaza was overwhelmed with joy. He read neither German nor French but the books' colour illustrations introduced him for the first time to view in his own privacy masterpieces of world art.

Having been deeply moved when he first saw the self-portraits of Egon Schiele in one of the books he borrowed from Samir Salameh, he felt elevated by his discovery. Seeing agony and passion in Schiele's naked and contorted figure, graphically expressed with directness and without any self-flattery, reconfirmed Zurob's belief in himself. His personal experiences in Gaza and what he went through during his own incarceration in Ramallah were more sufficient to speak of what was unique to him and what Palestine meant personally to him. He began to think that the very concept of originality in art could not be divorced from the artist's own body and identifying features. He wanted to look at a painting of his and be able to declare, "This is who I am!" The mirror set up in his studio began to look back at him. He trusted in it as he knew it could not lie to him. It was becoming the window through which he could verify a truth he saw nowhere in his environment. The mirror became as close to him as his own shadow. At the same time, it represented the only pictorial equivalent that embodied a living reality that he could touch with the very hands he paints with.

The earliest paintings Zurob created with the aid of a mirror were scoffed at. With bated breath he was accused of narcissism. Zurob, undaunted by his accusations, continued to experiment with paintings in which his own features were incorporated in his compositions. Neither his accusers nor the Gaza artist ever knew that ages ago one of the earliest authorities to establish a theory of art in the world that gave birth to the art of self-portraiture had written, "The inventor of painting according to the poets was Narcissus, who was turned into a flower, for, as painting is the flower of all arts, so the tale of Narcissus fits our purpose perfectly. What is painting but the act of embracing by means of art the surface of the pool."[4]

Under Siege

Paintings that evoked the accusation of Narcissism include those from the series Zurob titled *Siege*. They were all created after Ramallah had been re-occupied by the Israeli military forces; however, they were not about how Ramallah weathered the Israeli siege. The series was rather about how Ramallah's inflated mode of living pumped up by foreign aid had itself been assaulting and alienating the son of a pauperised people. To survive the world he encountered in Ramallah, he entrenched himself against what he experienced as a personal state of siege. Though the series included experimental abstract paintings with spontaneous brushstrokes whose gestural vitality recalled the freedom he exulted in as he painted political slogans on the walls of Rafah, the omnipresent subject in the series' figurative paintings centered on a naked figure suggesting the artist's own features.

At a time when the alienation of the Gaza artist in Ramallah was exacerbated by the restricted space within which he could move to avoid being arrested by the Israeli military authorities, the naked body rendered mostly in shades of blue appears disjointed and cramped up within its pictorial frame. Employing vigorous brushwork, body parts and facial features are sketchily delineated in black outlines or boldly reinforced over thick impastos of paint. Dashed with a limited palette of primary colours and accented by highlights in black and white, canvases are often dominated by the sharp contrast between a deep blue and a rich yellow as it were in reference to the colour contrast between Gaza's sea and the aridity of Ramallah's urban landscape.

In each work, the representation of the self manifests itself in different dispositions with body parts loaded with ambiguous references. Far from being symbolic as one familiar with the tradition of Western painting may tend to read them, each detail alludes to metaphoric associations

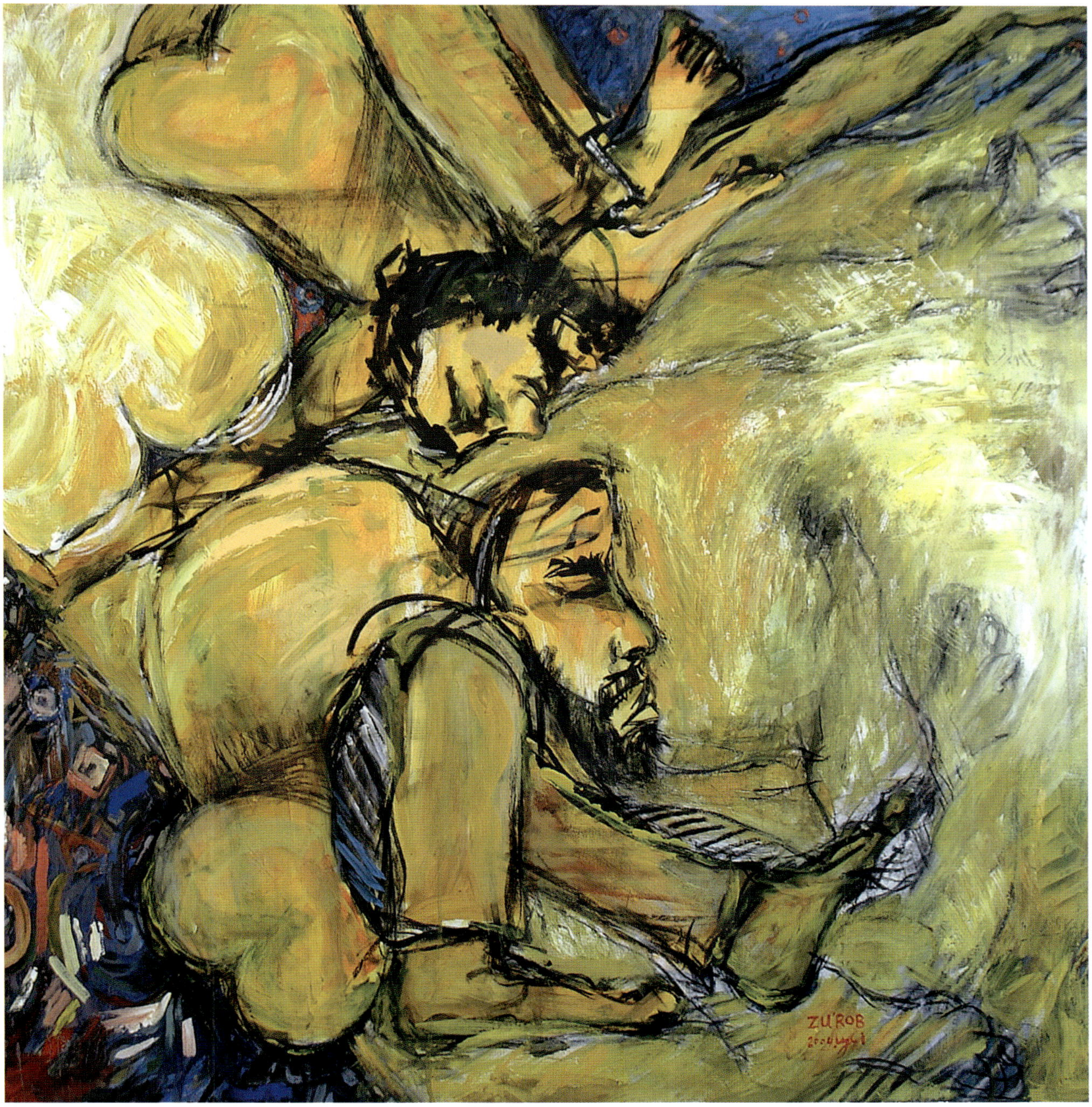

whose visual formulation stems from verbal expression. In that way, each painting represents an attempt to embody a meaning whose articulation unfolds like the cadence of a phrase in everyday speech. The mere description of some paintings unravels tangible clues.

In one of his earliest paintings in the series titled *Siege no. 3* which is saturated with yellow, body extremities float in all directions and the artist's countenance is suggested in two profiles placed on top of one another as each looks in a different direction. One arm turns into a foot and a second foot merges from the armpit as the seeming contour of buttocks assumes the shape of a heart.

Siege no. 3, 2004.
Acrylic and charcoal on canvas, 90 x 90 cm.

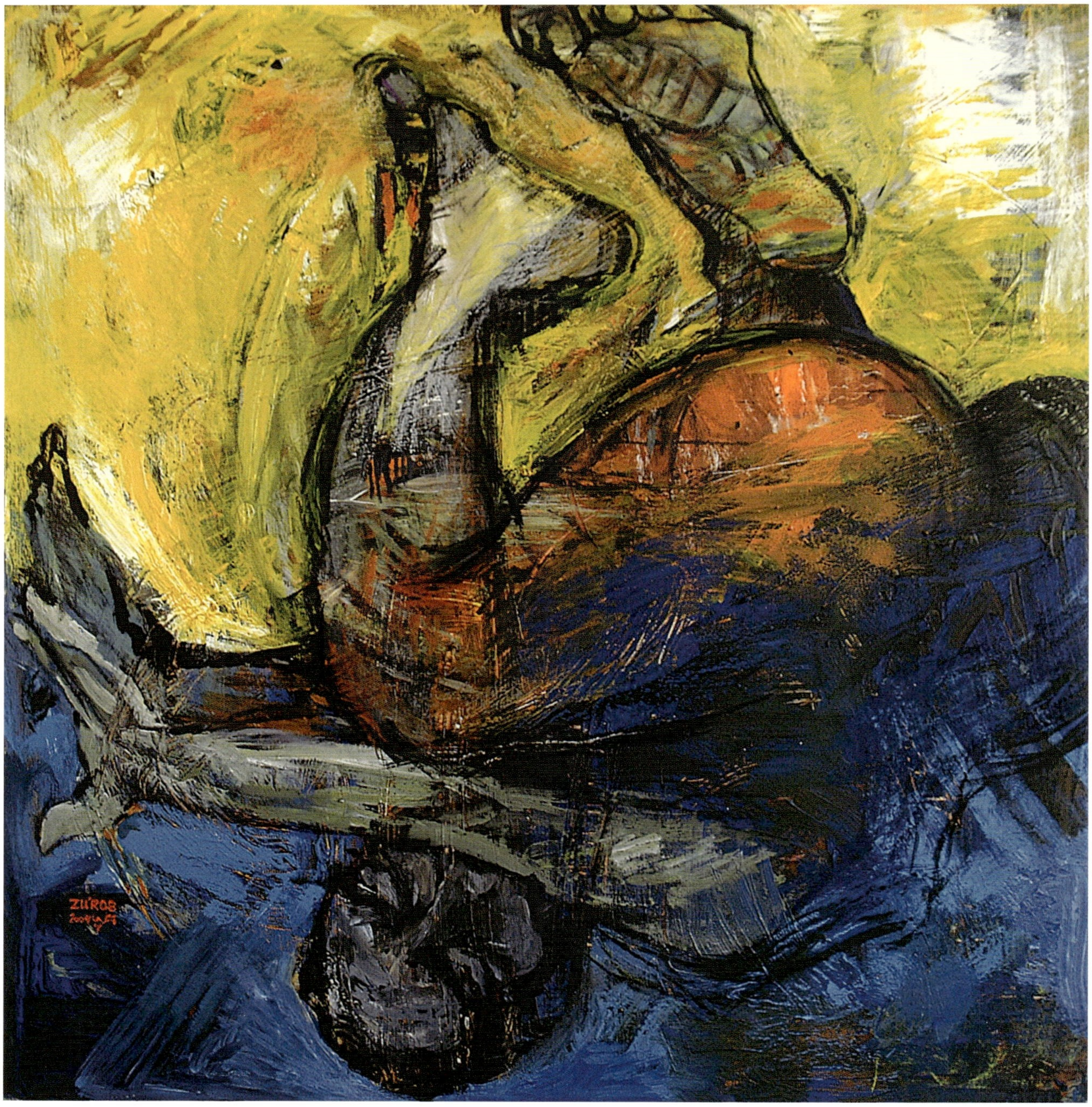

Siege no. 5, 2004.
Acrylic and charcoal on canvas, 80 x 80 cm.
Private collection, Jerusalem.

opposite
Siege no. 8, 2005.
Acrylic on canvas, 70 x 50 cm.

In a square painting titled *Siege no. 5*, the body, filling up the canvas, is viewed in a foetal position rotating around itself as it floats between a mustard yellowish sky and a surging wave of sea blue. With hands and arms tightly stretched out as in a swimming position, his bare feet are up in the yellow sky and his head is submerged beneath the blue. In other paintings, members of the naked body appearing distorted and dislocated are recomposed into intertwined parts and mangled limbs.

Siege no. 8 is a vertical painting wherein the standing figure in blue is arching forward with arms hanging down like forelegs of an ape. The artist's profile appears to grow out of the groin. At the borders of the

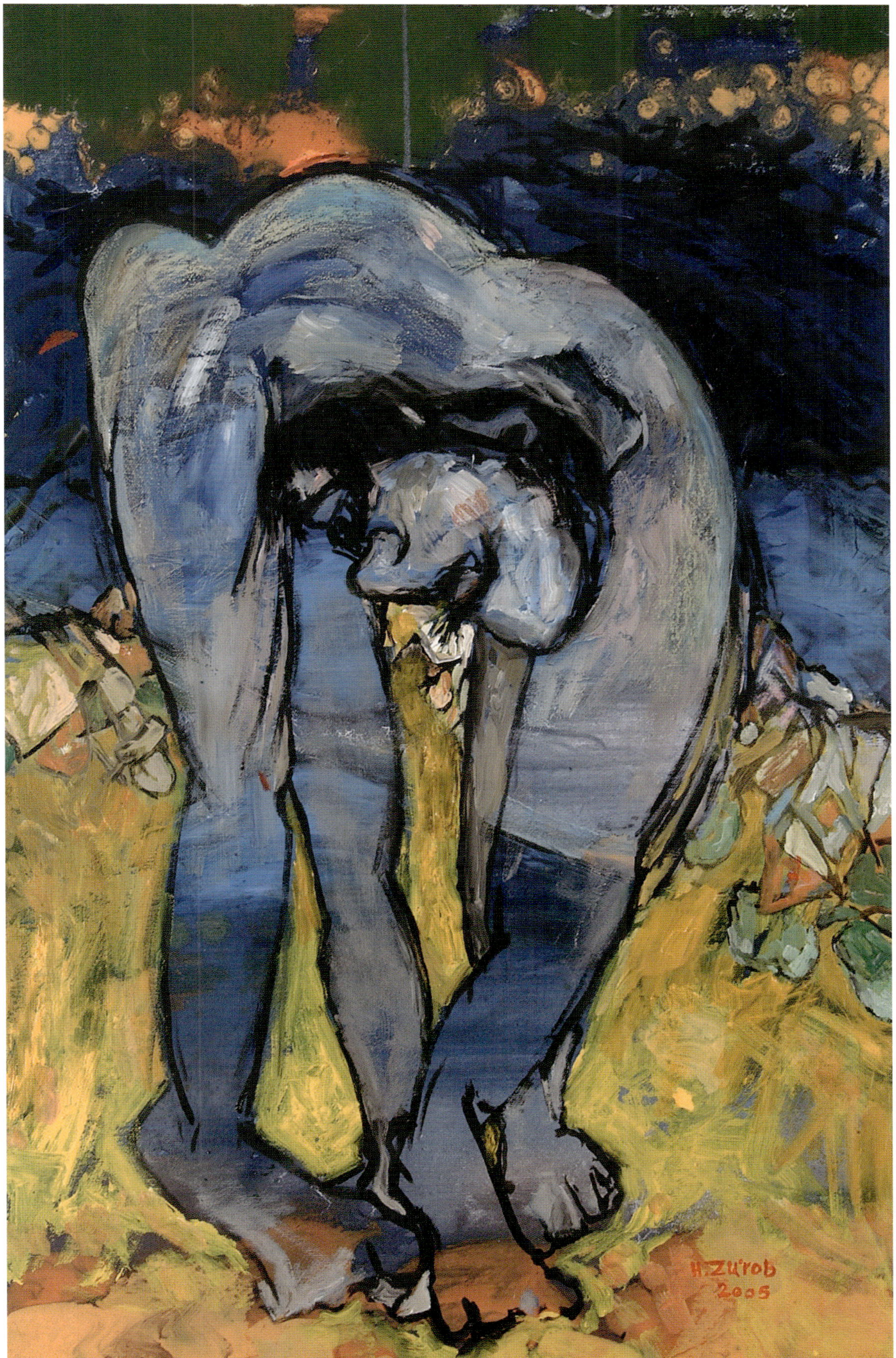
H.Zu'rob
2005

yellow grounds upon which the figure is standing, traces of a local village landscape curves upside down as if in a concave mirror. In contrast, the sky, marked with thick and wavy black outlines, looks more like an inverted sea ribbed with pebbles the colour of blood.

In a later painting in the series titled *Siege no. 11*, the mutilated body is viewed hanging upside down from what looks like a hook or a spinning wheel. Its mass is reduced to an inverted profile superimposed between reversed legs striding away from each other in mid air in a running position. The shape of a heart surrounding the head appears like a green halo punctured by spines to suggest a branch of a cactus tree, the wild plant which shares its name *sabr* in colloquial Arabic with the word meaning "patience". Against a lead-gray background, the entire weight of the composition's components all jammed together in the upper half of the painting precariously rests on a hanging arm with a hand tightly holding onto a bottle sitting at the edge of an angular base.

•

The predominance of the artist's self-portrait in profile in all the series' paintings calls for an explanation not only because self-portraits on the whole have been miserably scarce throughout the century-long history of modern Arab painting but also because portraits in general and self-portraits in particular have been central in Western art, albeit scarcely in profile.[5]

Since the beginning of the Renaissance in Italy, self-portraits have acquired a time-honoured status in Western art. The self-portrait collection at the Uffizi Museum in Florence conceived in the seventeenth century has long exceeded a thousand paintings. Today, nowhere outside the capitals in the Western world would one expect to see entire museums and national collections dedicated to portraiture comprising self-portraits as one finds in museums such as the National Portrait Gallery in London, the Portrait Gallery in Washington, DC or the Portrait Gallery at the Louvre in Paris. The reverence portrait painting commanded in the West may go back in its origin to the Christian world's belief in God's own incarnation, whereby the very personification of the invisible divinity was to find its visual representation in religious iconography.

Though the development of easel painting in Arab art germinated from the emulation of European models following the colonial encounter

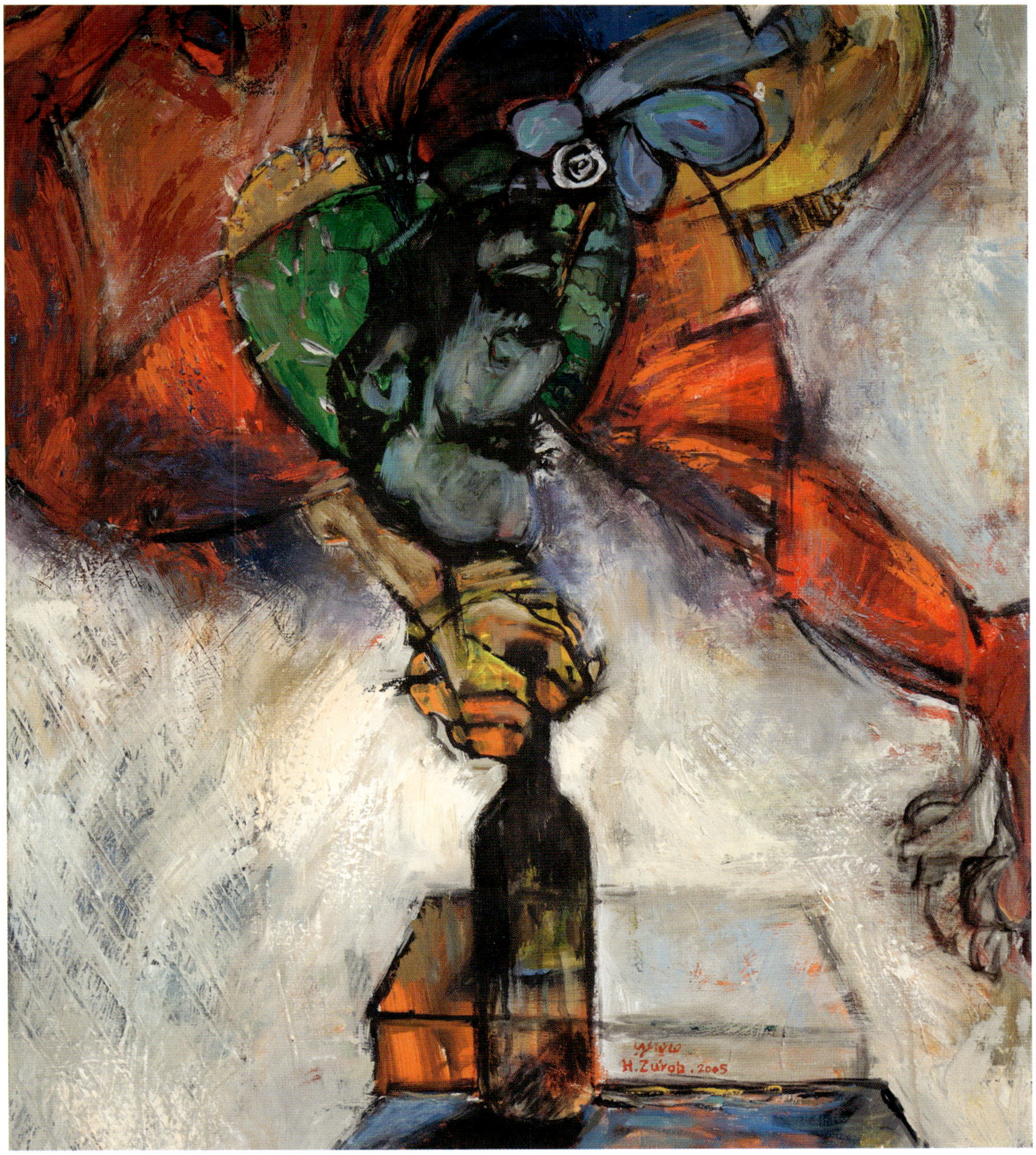

between Europe and the Arab countries of the Mediterranean, it was predisposed cultural and aesthetic modalities that determined what was borrowed and what was renounced by the Arab artist. Consequently, portrait painting in Arab art has never attained the status it occupied in the West and the paucity in self-portraits was a natural sequel.[6]

In the meantime, throughout the history of Western art, frontal and angled self-portraiture had been the artist's most intimate assertion of the self and the equivalent of using the first person pronoun in speech. In contrast, the less common self-portrait in profile has not been any less important; its equivalence in speech, however, may be compared to the use of the third person pronoun in autobiographic narratives. In

Siege no. 11, 2005.
Acrylic on canvas, 77 x 67 cm.
Private collection, Contemporary Art Platform, Kuwait.

this regard, the Renaissance polymath Leon Batista Alberti (1404–1472) offered an instructive illustration. His self-portrait in profile recognised among the earliest works in the European tradition was followed by an autobiography which was written in the third person.

As all self-portraits in Hani Zurob's painting series *Siege* delineate his profile, one wonders what qualities they share with the autobiographic writing in Arabic literature, written in the third person pronoun. Keeping in mind that in Arabic, unlike Western languages, the position of the third person pronoun in its masculine form (*huwa*) heads the list of all 14 pronouns; in what way could such a fact relate to the self-portrait in profile in Zurob's painting, imbued as it is with metaphoric associations rooted in verbal expression?[7]

In the Arabic literary tradition using the third person pronoun in autobiographic writings has not been uncommon throughout the last thousand years of the genre's history.[8] In the twentieth century, Taha Husayn's autobiography *al-Ayyam* (The Days) which has been considered "a highly innovative autobiography" and "a landmark in the development of modern Arabic prose", was all written in the third person pronoun.[9]

Husayn's literary device of employing the third person pronoun to achieve a measure of distance between the narrator and the event finds its analogy in Hani Zurob's self-portraits in profile. To realise them, the painter used to set up two mirrors at an angle to each other in order to capture the reflection of his own profile. Thus, the distance achieved through the two mirrors objectified for the artist his own features as much as the third person pronoun in verbal expression objectified the subject in the autobiographer's text.

The rare occasions when Taha Husayn resorted to using the first person singular happened during emotionally charged encounters the blind author had to face with the outside world. Such an occasion was reported when the narrator was talking with his nine year old daughter and the subject of his own blindness was likened to the blindness of Oedipus Rex. The introduction of the first person pronoun "I" in the mostly third person pronoun narrative in an autobiography has been referred to as "a doubling" of the narrative voice.[10]

Similarly, in Zurob's painting such 'doubling' may be found not in a painting in which the profile is repeated as in *Siege no. 3* but rather in the rare paintings in the series in which his face is frontally depicted. In such a case, the distance is breached as the painter confronts his viewer face to face.

Two paintings in Hani Zurob's series stand out owing to their frontal depiction of the naked body and to how the artist's features are not, as usual, defined in profile. The paintings' realisation coincided with separate incidents, both of which appear to have prompted the artist to veer away from using the two mirrors and opt instead to use a single mirror to paint himself facing his onlooker.

The first of the two paintings was *Siege no. 4* which was painted on the occasion of an invitation Hani Zurob received to participate in a workshop followed by an exhibition of the participants' work. The joint events were organised by the newly-founded Palestinian Association for Contemporary Art which was created by a group of locally established artists and art entrepreneurs after the Norwegian Ministry of Foreign Affairs announced its commitment to donate one and a half million dollars as seed money towards the establishment of a Palestinian art institution in Ramallah, later named the International Academy of Art Palestine. To constitute its curriculum, the Oslo National Academy was taken as a model and on its behalf Norwegian artist Henrik Placht was delegated as manager of the proposed project. Khaled Hourani who was heading the Art Department at the Palestinian Authority's Ministry of Culture was appointed as his assistant.

The principle aim of the workshop was to introduce young Palestinian talents to the wide spectrum of contemporary art in Europe while encouraging them to explore new methods of self-expression through the use of new media including performance, photography and installation. The exhibition held at al-Hallaj Gallery in Ramallah was organised to show the experimental work induced by the Norwegian initiative.

During the workshop Hani toyed with photographic experiments; as for the exhibition, he insisted on being represented in no medium other than painting. In response to the sponsor's inducement, however, he considered expanding the concept of his painting's frame and in the process turned its display into a form of installation. No wonder that the firm stand he took *vis-à-vis* the wishes of the exhibition's commissioner translated itself in what was to be the first painting in the series in which the artist's face is frontally depicted.

If the blue areas in all the earlier paintings of the series alluded to Gaza's sea, *Siege no. 4* which has been the largest canvas to work on up till then has all been painted in blue. With wide and sweeping strokes lashed spontaneously in different directions, the painting's background is smeared with thick layers of paint and diluted shades of a nocturnal darkness engulfed in black patches with hints of flashing light. As in an abandoned underground cell, the naked figure in the foreground saturated in blue is frontally captured in a seated position on a shapeless floor. The disposition of the body split between indigo and aquamarine together with the obstinate look of the sitter marks a presence that commands a sense of immediacy. Having placed a mirror slightly above his head, the painter must have looked so intently into it as it were to reach out through its imaginary depth where his viewer would stand. In the hand he painted himself with he is holding not a paintbrush but what looks like a writing tool the tip of which caps his signature. With his extended arm the writing hand is pressing against the ground he sits on. Through his concentrated gaze in a slightly upward direction, the Gaza artist seems to announce "I am here."

To emulate the space in which he worked, the painting was hung at the same level at which he painted it as he sat on the ground of his rented room. By hanging it at the end of a passage and close to the gallery's floor, the painting harboured the vague illusion that the ground in the painting could be imagined as an extension of the gallery's floor. What reinforced this illusion was how the narrow space surrounding the painting was turned into a site that expands the painting's frame.

Standing before *Siege no. 4*, the viewer could see on its right side succeeding footprints marked in blue on the gallery's floor. They evoked the impression that the naked figure had at some point stood up and slipped out of the painting by night and before his daytime audience showed up he sat back in his cell. Left behind at the end of the blue footsteps, the gallery visitor notes a brush dipped in a half-filled can of blue paint next to the artist's boots all drenched in blue paint.

The other work whose realisation coincided with another momentous occasion was *Siege no. 7*. It was completed soon after Zurob was offered a study grant to Paris. The offer beckoned that light at the end of the tunnel was finally seeping into his world. Vertical in dimension and higher than any canvas that preceded it, the painting's overall surface is blanketed with a profuse mixture of festive colours streaking a sky

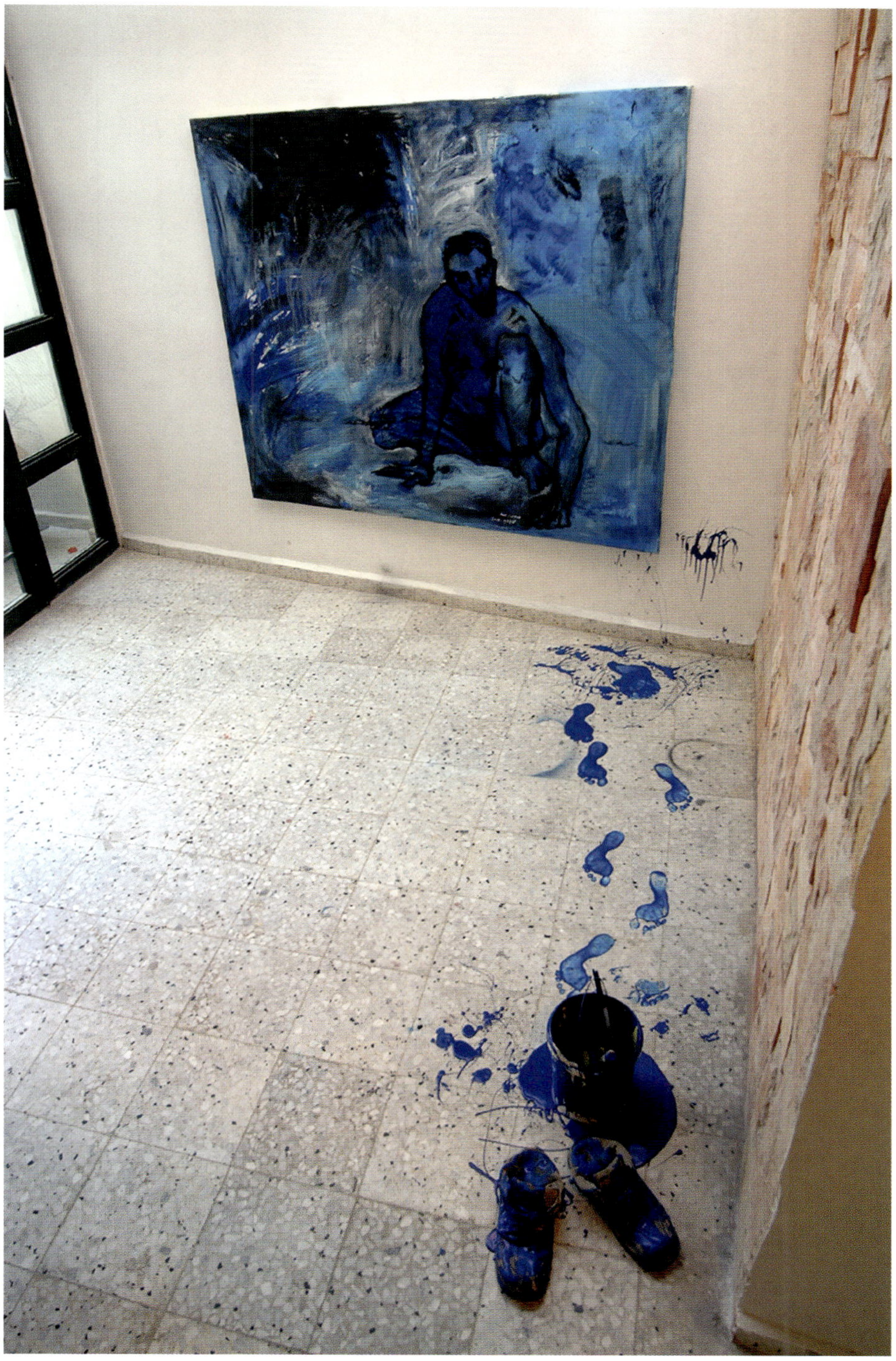

Siege no. 4, 2004.
Acrylic on canvas, 200 x 160 cm.

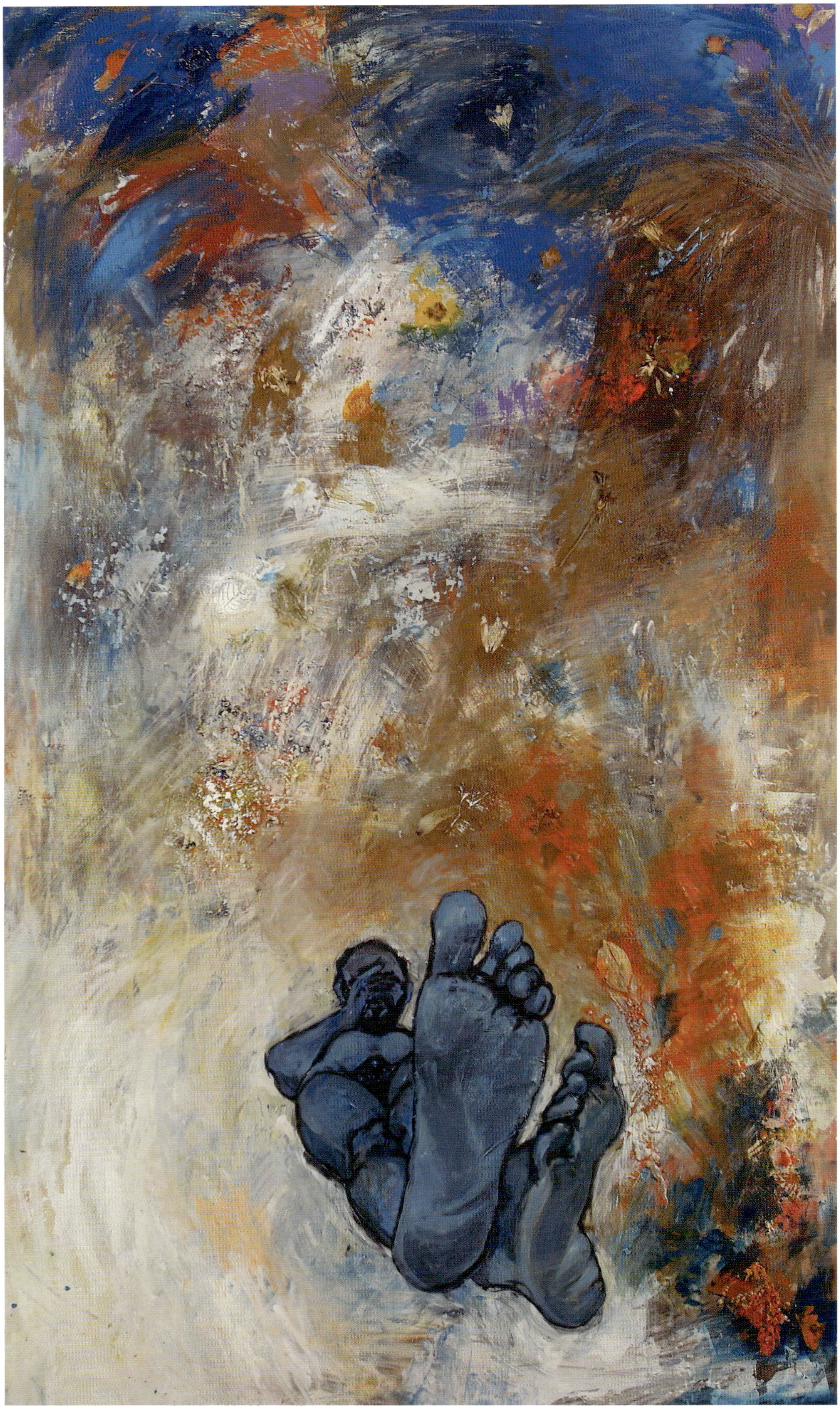

with smudges and vigorous brush strokes flashing out like fireworks. At the bottom part of what otherwise looks like a wholly abstract painting, we see the naked figure of the artist superimposed over the disparate background in a restful posture. Painted all in blue, the stretched figure is viewed floating in a foreshortened position. His face partly covered with one hand lies furthest from the viewer and the bottom of his bare feet dominates the foreground. The feet's domination recalls that of his boots drenched in blue that he had left on the gallery floor. With such unconventional modes of representing oneself, the Gaza painter seems to literally amplify a visual equivalent of exclaiming "my foot" to the art scene conjured up by Ramallah's cons and compradors!

•

Strangely enough, Hani Zurob's exit from the Israeli occupied territories was uneventful. At the Jordan River crossing, however, his interrogation by the Jordanian border authorities lasted for nine consecutive hours before he was admitted in to the country. It was already after midnight when he stepped out in the cold winter air to find one of his maternal uncles waiting for him. That was the first time they met as Hani had not been born when his maternal relatives left Gaza and sought refuge in Jordan following the 1967 war. Accompanied by his uncle they went to the house where all family members had long been sleeping.

That night Hani could not go to sleep. The excitement was overpowering. The following morning when he actually did see himself in the departure lounge at the airport in Amman, he was the first in line at the exit gate. He could not wait to fly. Still strained with the anxieties of the grilling interrogation he underwent the previous day, he was flushed with the thrill of taking off from the ground for the first time. Soon after he learnt how to buckle himself in his seat and once he began to see the hurrying clouds drifting below him, he felt he was all set to explore new horizons and find himself free to create art that is worthy of his life.

Siege no. 7, 2004.
Acrylic and dried flowers collage
on canvas, 201 x 117 cm.
Palestinian Art Court, al Hoash, Jerusalem.

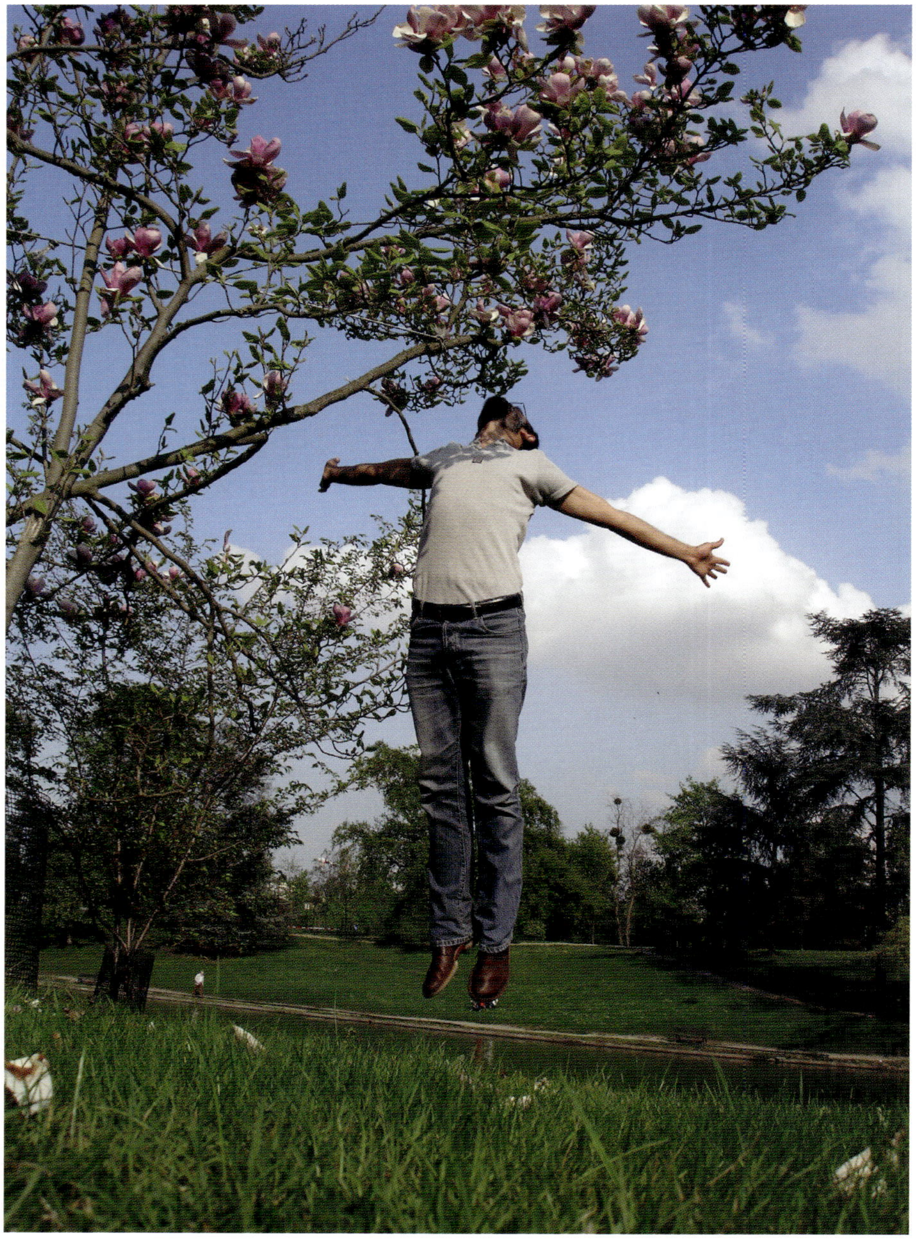

Artist celebrating his first spring at the Bois de Boulogne, Paris, 2006.

2.

Between Exits

Immeasurable was the freedom that Hani Zurob experienced as soon as he stepped out in the crisp cold air of February in Paris. Feeling free and safe to roam through spacious boulevards and across bridges at any moment of the day or the night was as foreign to him as the language he was hearing but could not speak and as alien as all the new scents he detected indoors and down in the Metro underground. Having been hurled overnight into the cosmopolitan hustle and bustle of the French capital may have been unsettling for a young man coming from Gaza, but the thrill of it all was nonetheless intoxicating. He could never have fathomed what it felt like to be unhindered anymore by military barriers and checkpoints no matter where he went throughout the city. The years of having to confine himself within a few kilometres around his Ramallah residence were finally over. He felt weightless. He could now drink in the silver greys of the city of light and stand as long as he pleased before a master's painting to enjoy the splendour of colours the 30 year old artist had thus far only seen reproduced in a friend's old book back home.

Once he settled in his studio at the Cité Internationale des Arts across the Seine, Zurob poured himself into his painting. The freedom in which he exulted was soon to find its way into his art. In the meantime, the very taste of freedom was getting mixed with the bitter realisation of being a total outsider in his new environment. Hope and despair kept alternating as he struggled to reconcile his dreams with what appeared to be insurmountable realities beyond himself. Painting became his

left
Siege no. 27, 2006.
Acrylic on canvas, 50 x 50 cm.
Private collection, Paris.

right
Siege no. 28, 2006.
Acrylic on canvas, 70 x 60 cm.
Private collection, Ramallah.

opposite
Sortie no. 2, 2006.
Acrylic, charcoal on canvas,
140 x 100 cm.
Private collection, Dakar.

primum mobile for being. With the financial security insured by his grant, he was able to dedicate long hours during the day and the night working on his art, a luxury he could never afford before. Within a few months he produced two series of paintings. *Sortie*, which was one of the first words he learnt in French, was the title he chose for the first series; *Barrage* (Barriers), which was the title of the second, was a word borrowed from the world he had left behind to refer to his sense of foreboding and apprehension as his six-month grant was approaching its end.

At first glance, the new set of paintings he created in Paris appears to be a continuation of the abstract experimental attempts he undertook in Ramallah soon after he learnt that the offer of an art residency in the French capital was about to become a reality. At that moment, the mere announcement was enough to prompt the besieged Gazan into abandoning his figurative mode of expression and plunge him into a venture that was to live up to that gleam of hope shimmering in the distance. A closer look at the paintings he produced soon after his arrival in Paris, however, reveals that the freedom he longed for and that he finally attained, along with his exposure to the new world in which he found himself and the turmoil that was fomenting within him, were all to bear equivocal traces on his new paintings.

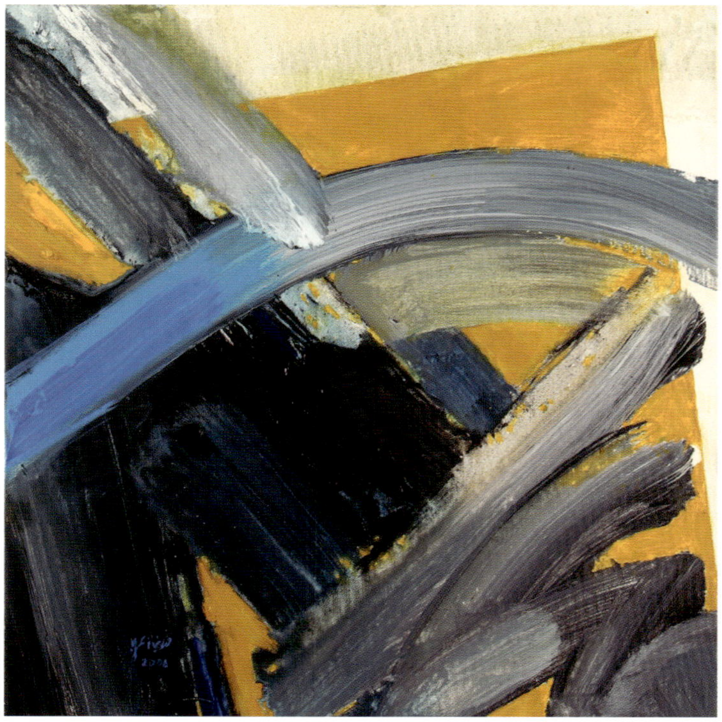

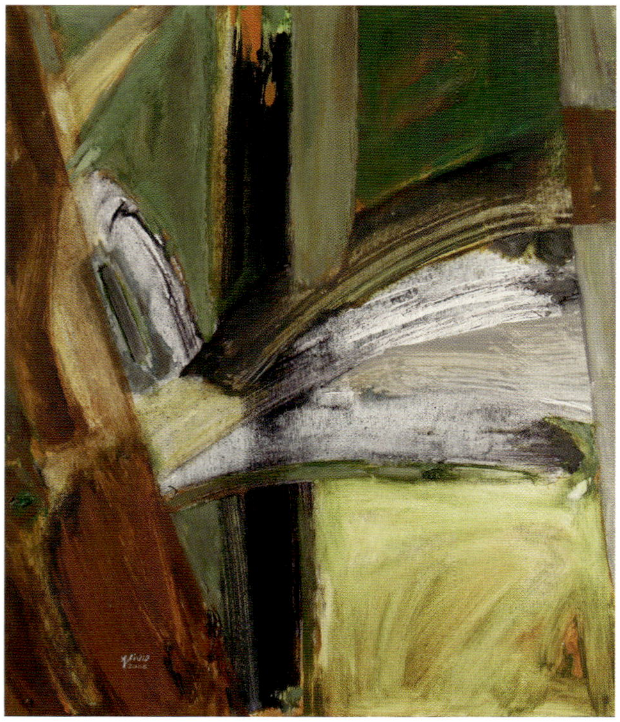

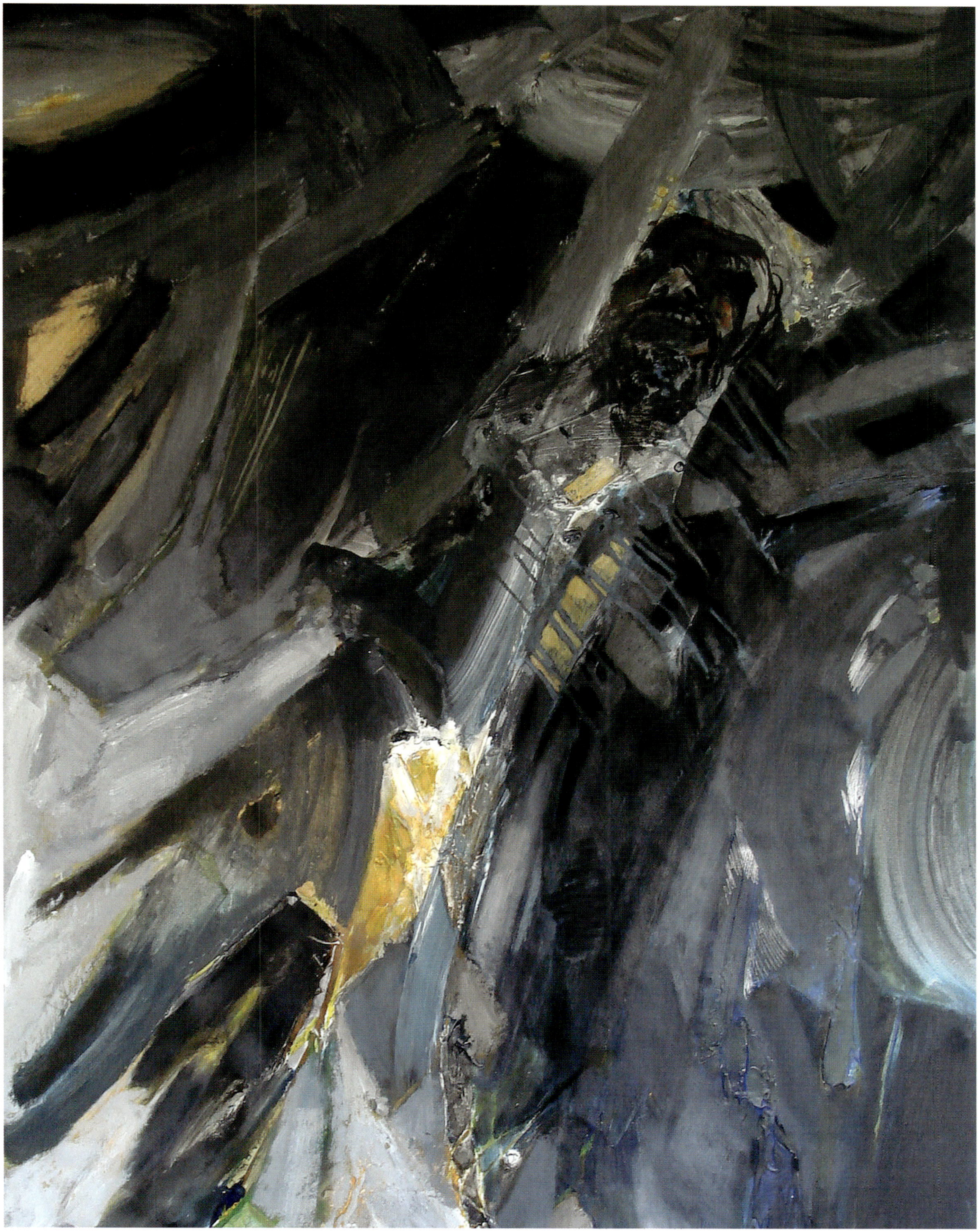

Perhaps Zurob's paintings *Sortie no. 0* and *Sortie no. 2* provide a cue to a preliminary reading of how the artist's plight during this critical period found expression in his first series of works. Being the earliest paintings he produced in Paris, they set the background that enhanced the creation of subsequent artworks. Additionally, each of these two paintings is embedded with signs that insinuate the artist's sense of being in between two perceptual states as manifested in the combination of different gradations of figurative and abstract formations in each work.

The bust of a male figure all in red with both arms thrown up and the mouth widely open is the subject of the first painting. It is executed with spontaneity, speed and sweeping brushstrokes that endow it with an overall abstract quality. In his second painting, however, the figure with raised arms seems drowned in a flood of frantic brushstrokes. The apparition of a bearded and blackened face screaming with bulging eyes emerges through violent swaths of paint diagonally dashed upwards in the direction of the man's ghastly features. Accents of underlying yellow markings punctuate the overwhelmingly grey and black layers of paint ebbing like the waves of a savage sea sweeping away the man's body.

As for the paintings in the rest of his *Sortie* series, they are devoid of any figurative reference. Each of their compositions however, which exults in a gestural mode of execution, is loaded with codes that are often relayed

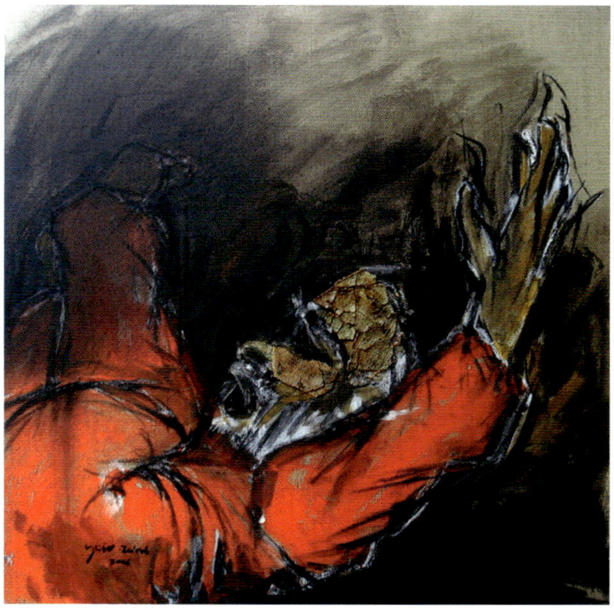

Sortie no. 0, 2006.
Acrylic, charcoal and avocados peel on canvas, 80 x 80 cm.
Private collection, Paris.

in the form of collages. By introducing the collage in these works, Zurob's *objets trouvés* do not only replace the figure, but their enclosure operates as associative relics of a lived experience in the same way the figure in his earlier paintings had operated as a representation of a narrative image.

The collage of found objects in the *Sortie* series include metro tickets he used between places he first discovered within the city, telephone calling cards he consumed to recover the distance between Paris and Gaza, shredded papers, supermarket receipts, even a bolt recalling one his father once bought for their house in Gaza, and gauze, which incidentally is a word originally derived from the place-name of Gaza. A fine silk fabric woven there has been imported to Europe since the thirteenth century.

•

Hani Zurob's struggle to forge his way between figurative and abstract expression lasted for years. It was as intense as his struggle to reconcile his sense of belonging with his experience of being a passing outsider

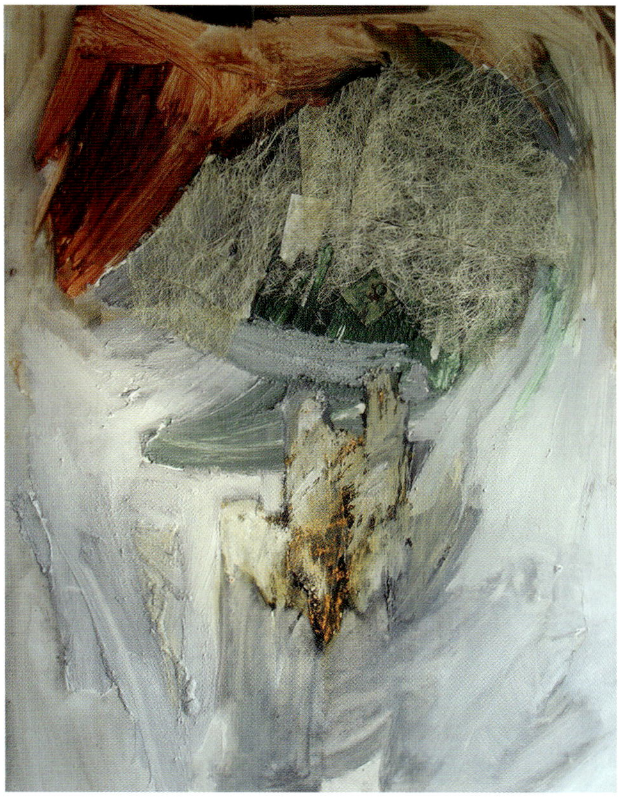

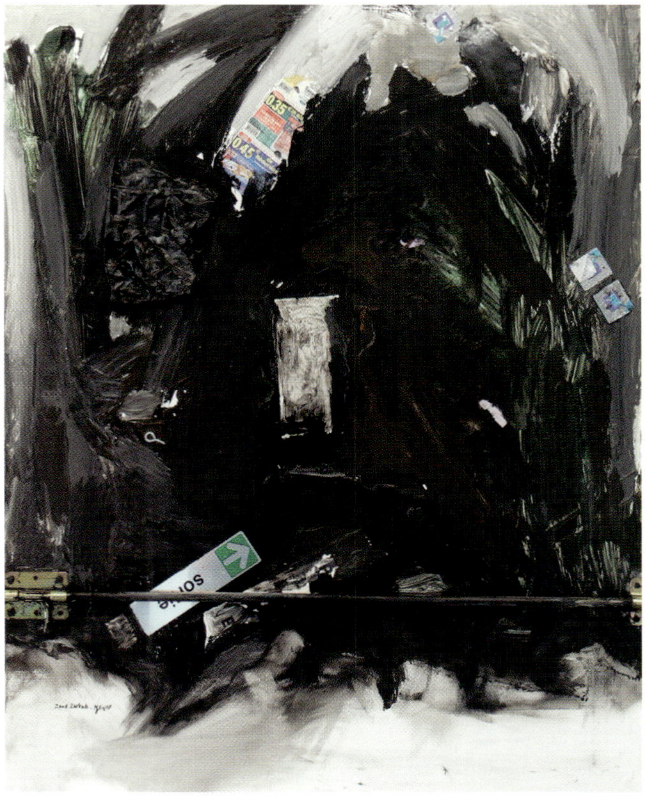

left
Sortie no. 3, 2006.
Mixed media on canvas,
116 x 89 cm.
Private collection, Paris.

right
Sortie no. 7, 2006.
Mixed media on canvas,
100 x 80 cm.
AM Qattan Foundation, London.

left
Sortie no. 8, 2006.
Mixed media on canvas,
80 x 75 cm.
Private collection, Paris.

right
Sortie no. 9, 2006.
Mixed media on canvas,
100 x 80 cm.
Private collection, Paris.

in a city that granted him freedom and opened up his eyes to a whole new world.

In time, the six-month grant period came to an end. But his scheduled return home to the spouse he left behind and to resume his duties as art instructor at the Women's Teacher Training College in Ramallah was barred by an Israeli order. Nobody at the Palestinian Authority headquarters in Ramallah could repeal Israel's order. The French consular official intervening on his behalf was informed by an Israeli officer that if Hani Zurob were to return home, he would no longer be allowed to reside back in Ramallah as the French official had been promised before his departure. He was told that Hani would be arrested at the airport and sent directly to jail for having lived in the West Bank 'illegally' according to the rules decreed by the Israeli military occupation authorities.

The Israeli change of mind coincided with the outbreak of bloody developments back in Gaza. After an Israeli blast killed a Palestinian and seven members of a family who were lounging on a Gaza beach, the armed forces of Hamas called off its 16 month old truce. A band of them using an underground tunnel carried out an attack on an Israeli army post

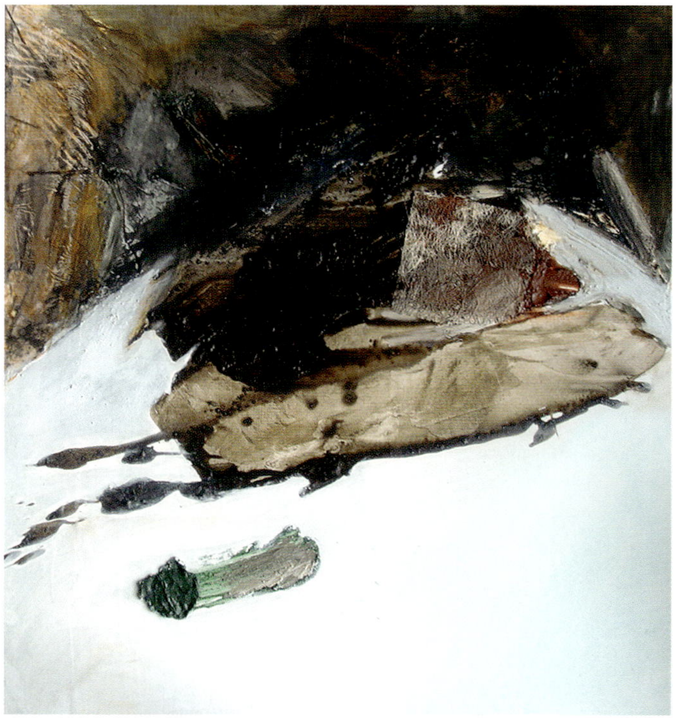

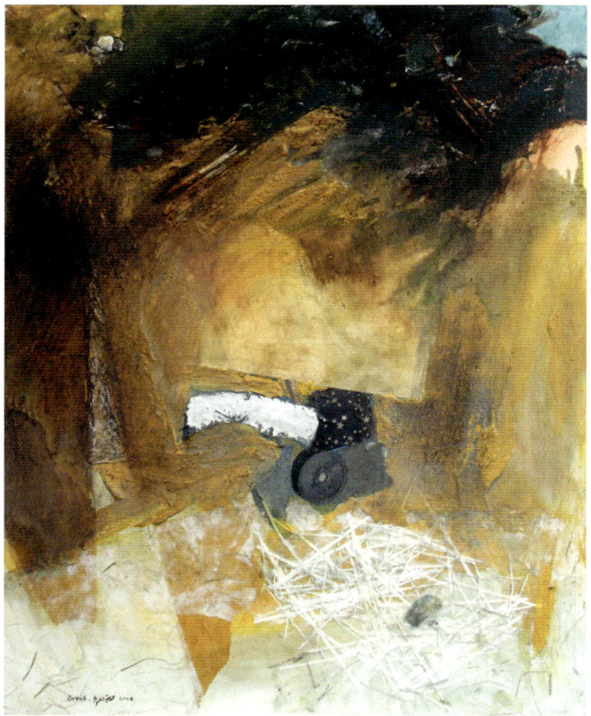

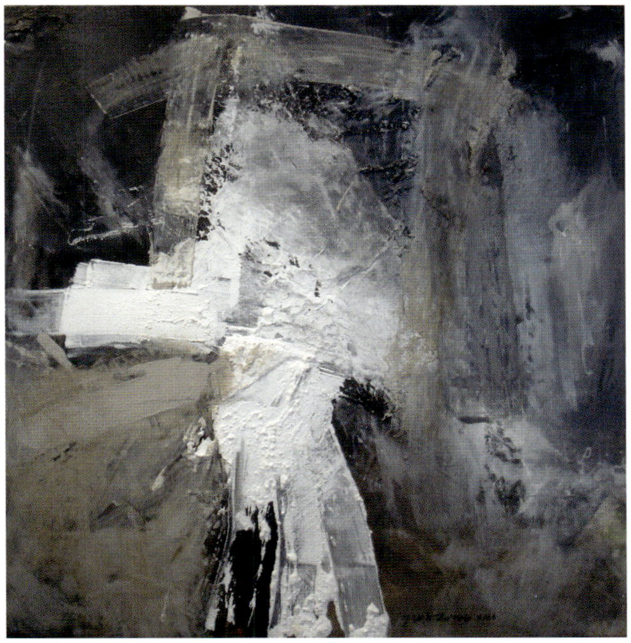 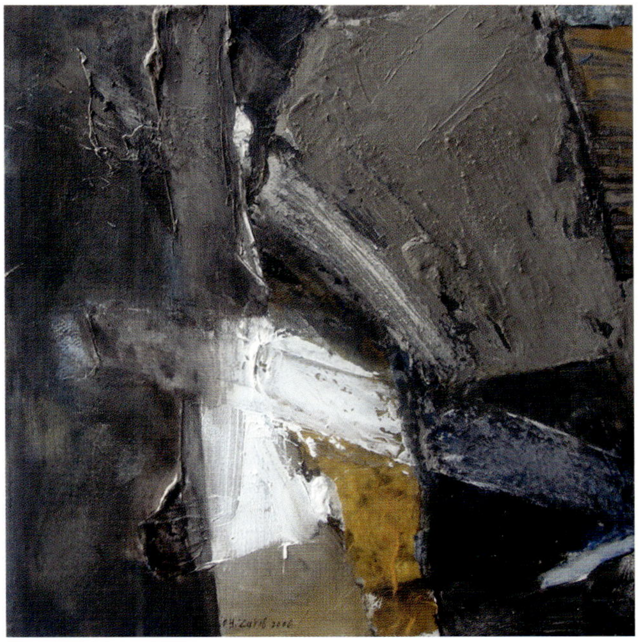

at the southern Gaza borders with Israel. Two Israeli soldiers were killed in the operation and one was captured as a hostage. Without delay, Israel retaliated by launching a military assault on the Gaza Strip killing 23 civilians and wounding over 75. Border crossings were additionally sealed off, barring all trucks carrying food, fuel and medical supplies into the Gaza Strip. In the West Bank, Israeli military authorities arrested and detained 27 Palestinian ministers who had won their nominations in a free election for their affiliation with the Change and Reform party of Hamas.

In Paris, the Gazan artist was left stranded with nowhere to go. Overnight, he was struck by a sense of homelessness that he had never experienced anywhere before. Seized by sleepless anxieties, entire days were spent running from one place to another meeting people who could help him find a way out of his predicament. Thanks to Arab colleagues, he was assisted in filling out the right forms enabling him to extend his sojourn permit and, eventually, bring over his spouse to France on a tourist visa. Consequently, the Cité Internationale des Arts offered him a temporary studio against a minimal rental fee which he could afford from sale of his works. Thus, Hani Zurob went immediately back to work. By the end of the year, the *Barrage* series was completed.

Throughout the summer that witnessed the prolongation of Israel's collective punishment of the civilian population in the Gaza Strip and

left
Barrage no. 3, 2006.
Mixed media on canvas, 70 x 70 cm.
Private collection, Paris.

right
Barrage no. 6, 2006.
Mixed media on canvas, 50 x 50 cm.
Private collection, Paris.

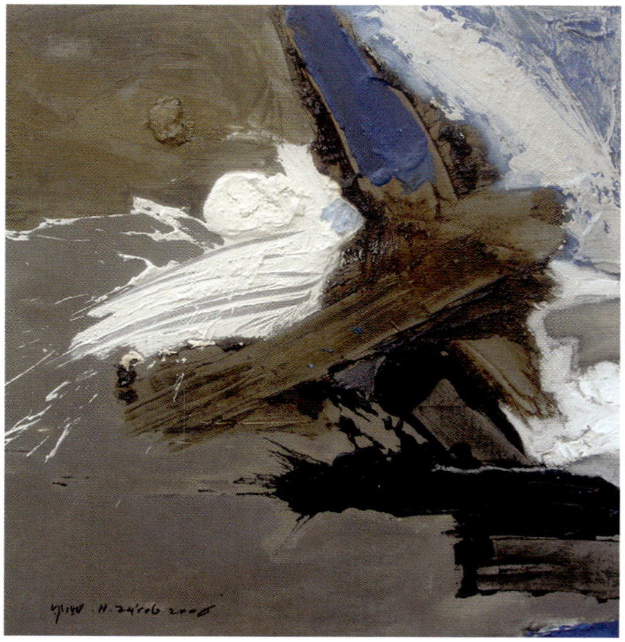 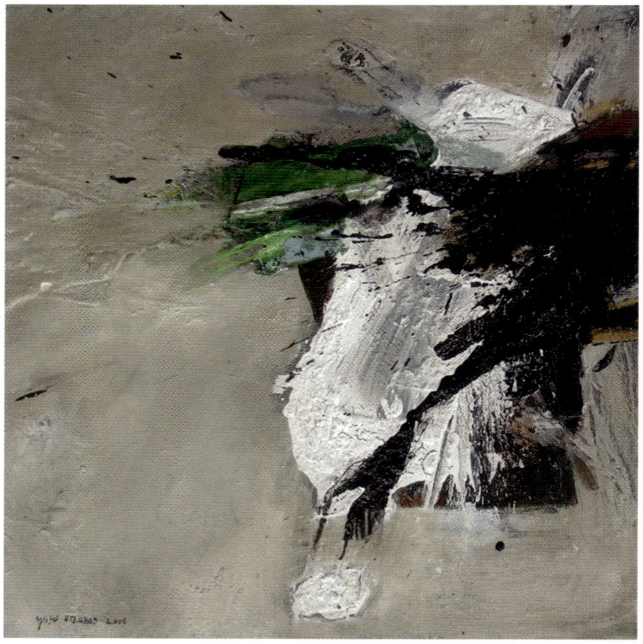

the waging of a full scale war on Lebanon, Hani spent most of his nights painting as his waking hours during the day were consumed by following up with developing news back home. While he had been intermittently feeling torn between figurative and abstract modes of expression, this time, he was absolutely certain that no painting language could express the intensity and immediacy of his anguish more forcefully than a painterly mode of abstraction for which free-flowing gestural brushstrokes might organically embody the emotional torrents of the day.

Preliminary sketches were not needed. Speed was an essential component of the painting process. With a loaded brush, he delivered bold strokes of paint on his support in a display of vigour and energy. Gestural flings of his brush were arrested mid-movement, leaving behind spattered paint and accidental flickers on thinly painted areas of his canvas. Dominated by ash and gunmetal greys, his series of paintings were often highlighted by swipes of white paint superimposed on inky black markings. Sporadic hints of saffron shades, aqueous green and steely blues alternate in punctuating each of the series' compositions.

Along with the wide brushes he used to apply his paints, all sorts of other objects were also employed to scrub and punch with including plastic cards, a kitchen spatula, his bare hands and fingers. Assailing his blank canvas turned into a sort of exorcism whereby the feverish

left
Barrage no. 7, 2006.
Mixed media on canvas,
60 x 60 cm.
Private collection, Brussels.

right
Barrage no. 14, 2006.
Mixed media on canvas,
60 x 60 cm.
Private Collection, Paris.

act of slapping thick layers of colour and moulding them in free forms exemplified the physicality of his emotive state, bringing forth a set of paintings charged with a palpable presence.

Around the same period in which Zurob had plunged himself into his experiments in Paris, verses written back home by Najwan Darwish, a close friend from Jerusalem, may best describe the state in which the Gaza artist was immersed:

> There,
> A language is trying to mend a land
> That it may embody the naked
> Waking up
> In this hallowed exile
> At the world's end.[1]

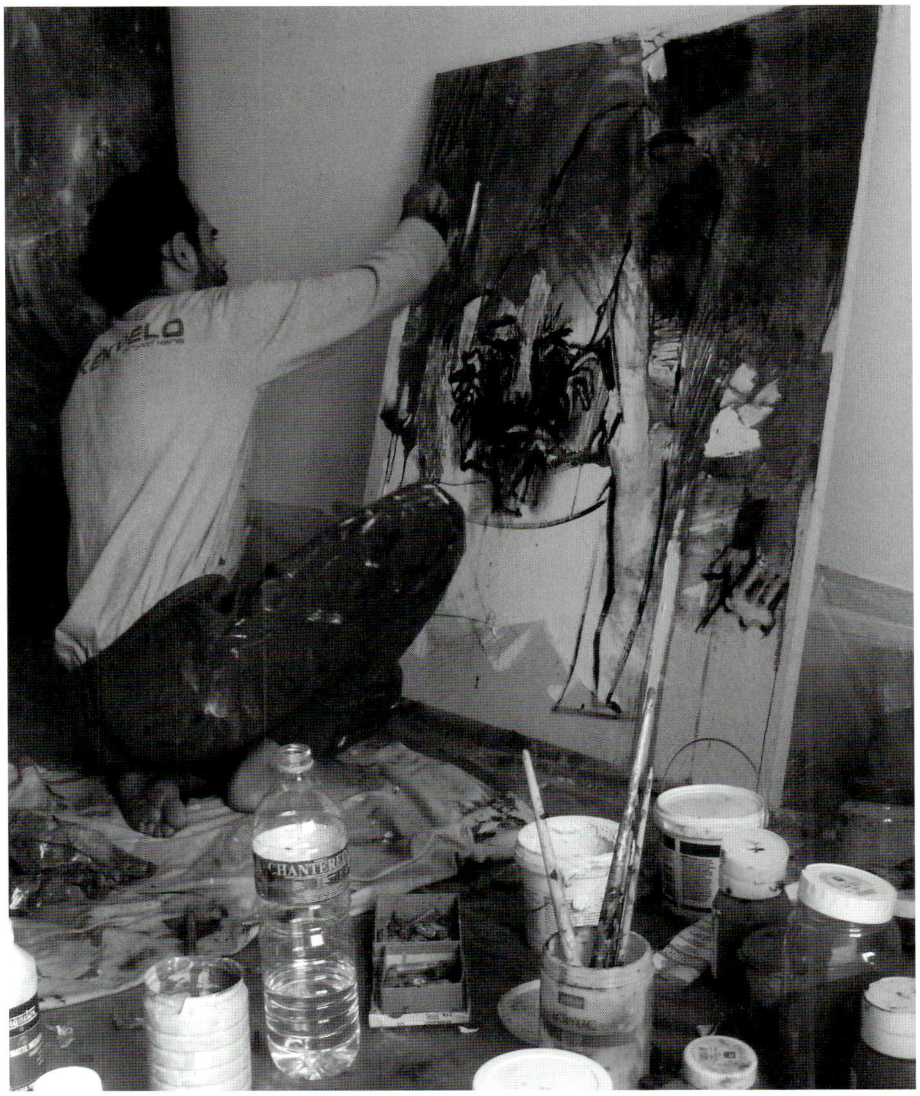

Hani Zurob at his home studio, Paris, 2007.

The bouts of painterly abstraction in which Hani Zurob was periodically engaged as a prelude or as a sequel to working on a figurative subject found an analogous example in a subsequent series he called *Projections*. Though it was produced during 2008, between two periods in which figurative expression seemed dominant in his subject matter, it stands out as a series of paintings whose execution method does not only find its roots in those of the *Barrage* series but it also enlightens the trajectory of his painterly quest. With a title that is his only one with a more abstract implication, the *Projections* series led the way for subsequent paintings in which figuration was to become fully integrated in his otherwise abstract space. *Projections* should be considered within this context before moving on to discuss a precedent series of paintings in which figurative formations overlap abstract settings.

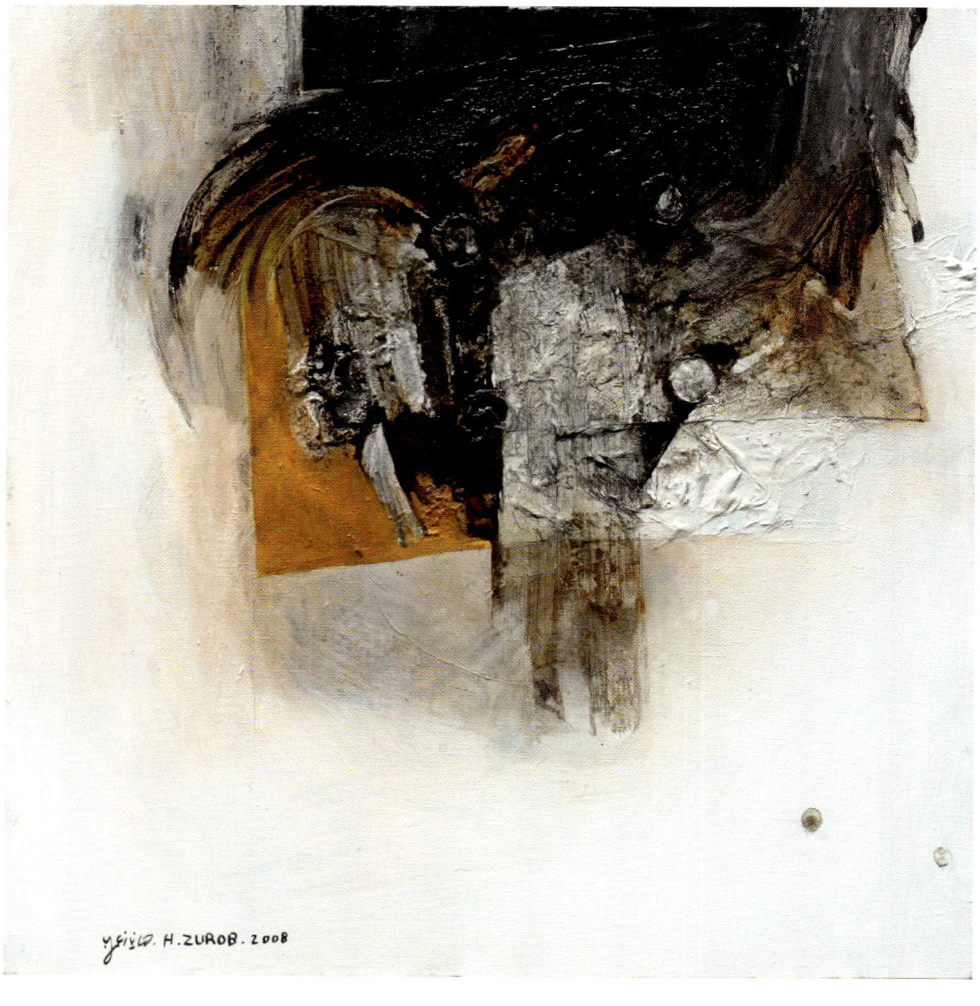

Projections no. 4, 2008.
Acrylic, henna, tar, pigments on canvas, 60 x 60 cm.

Just as the production of the *Barrage* series coincided with the outbreak of violence back home, the production of the *Projections* series coincided with the escalation of explosive developments in the Gaza Strip. Backed by Egypt, Israel tightened its blockade against all Palestinians living there. The year which had begun with the storming of the borders with Egypt in Hani's hometown of Rafah, when tens of thousands of Gazans crossed the borders to stock up essential foods and fuel, culminated with a full-scale war declared by Israel on the people of the Gaza Strip. Over 22 days, as the Strip remained under a wreckful siege, Israel dropped what amounts to 1,000 tons of explosives on the sliver of land considered one of the most densely populated places in the world. Homes, mosques, medical, educational and governmental institutions were turned into rubble. 1,400 Gazans were killed; many more were wounded and maimed for life.

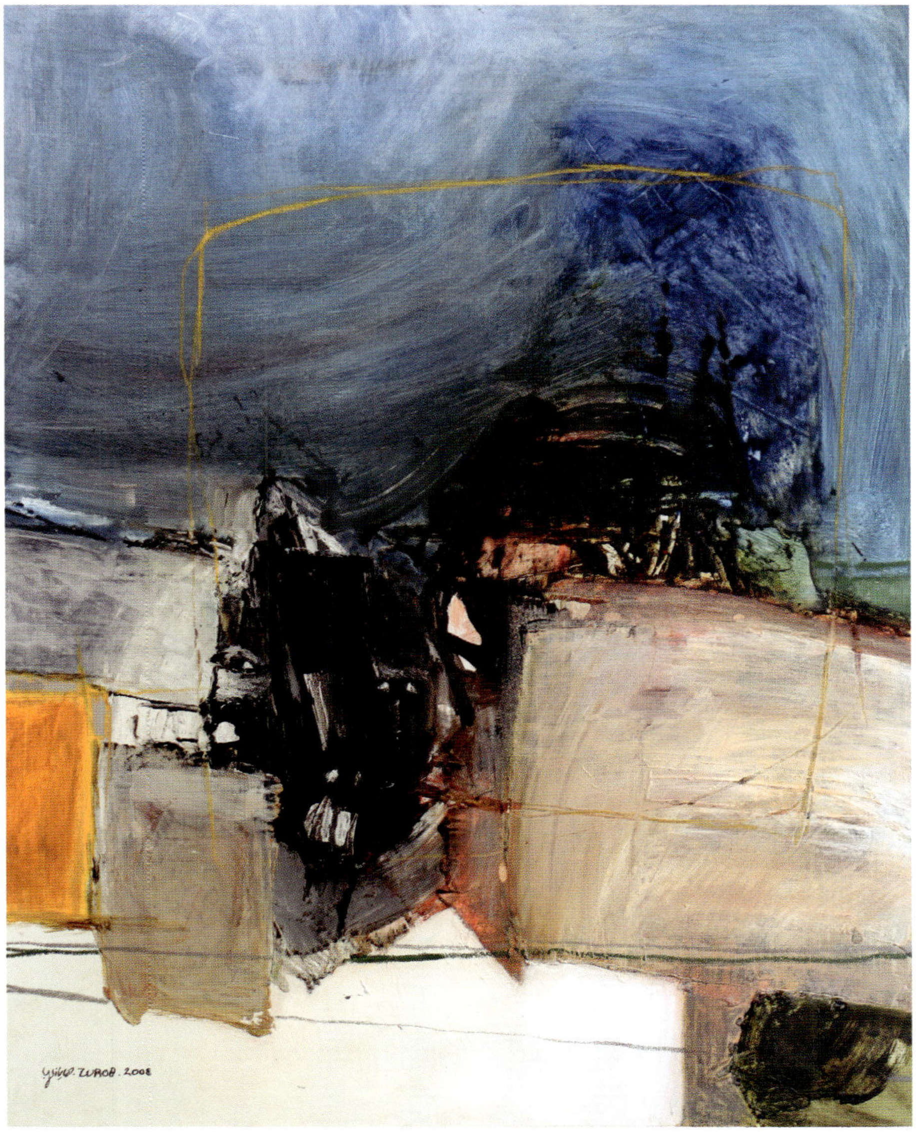

Projections no. 10, 2008.
Acrylic, pastel, tar, pigments on canvas, 120 x 100 cm.

In Paris, throughout the year, Hani Zurob maintained contact with family members in Rafah whenever internet phone lines were functioning. He lived through all the details of their and their neighbours' daily travails beset by the food and fuel shortages. His prime solace was derived from sharing news with friends from Gaza who were living in Paris or elsewhere and occasionally from doing the rounds of his favourite art galleries. Every day he made sure to stay updated with the Arabic news reports on *Aljazeera* channel and he read the daily *al-Akhbar* website. Most nights he turned to his painting.

Carrying on with living a life suspended between the two distant worlds of Gaza and Paris was a strain. The gap between the two places was getting ever more unbridgeable. Tension flared up particularly during critical periods endured by his friends and relatives back home. Were the experience of such tension to bear any traces in his abstract painting, it might have done so on a subliminal level and most probably each time it must have assumed totally different forms of expression.

In the *Barrage* series, for example, we may read the traces of tension in the vigorous brushstrokes which are loaded with colour and sweep across the canvas in every direction. The marks left behind convey a sensation of freedom. In his compositions, tension is mostly compounded the middle ground. On the other hand, in his *Projections* series, where his brushstrokes are not any less frantic, it is the spatial relationships between his tonal colour blocks, now more sharply contained within two main areas, which sustain the compositional tension accentuated by poignant contrasts between the blocks.

Assuming either square or vertical dimensions, each one of the paintings in the *Projections* series is horizontally divided in two distinct colour blocks with the upper block occupying a proportionately larger space as it is composed of tenebrous tones. Colour blotches with shades of dead leaves, scorched earth, tar and rust hang from above like some heavy cloud of darkness over narrow stretches of white space. Tension is generated through the unconventional gravity of each composition as the upper massive load seems in its descent to float above the more thinly-painted lower grounds. Contrasts disclosed between thin and thick layers in the upper part echo those between the darkness of the textured block above and the flat whiteness holding out in the strip below.

•

Marbles' War no. 7, 2007.
Mixed media on canvas,
200 x 200 cm.

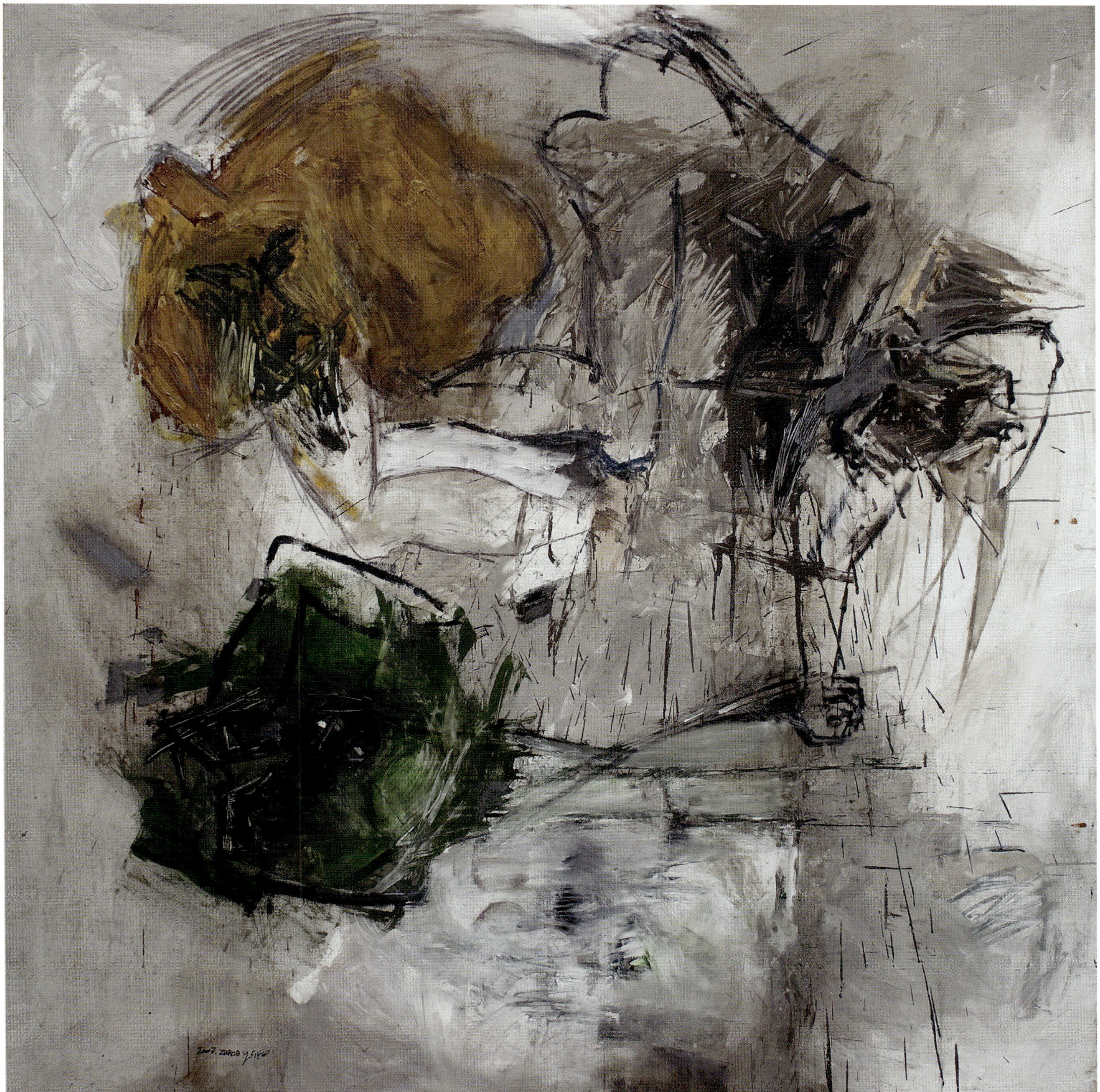

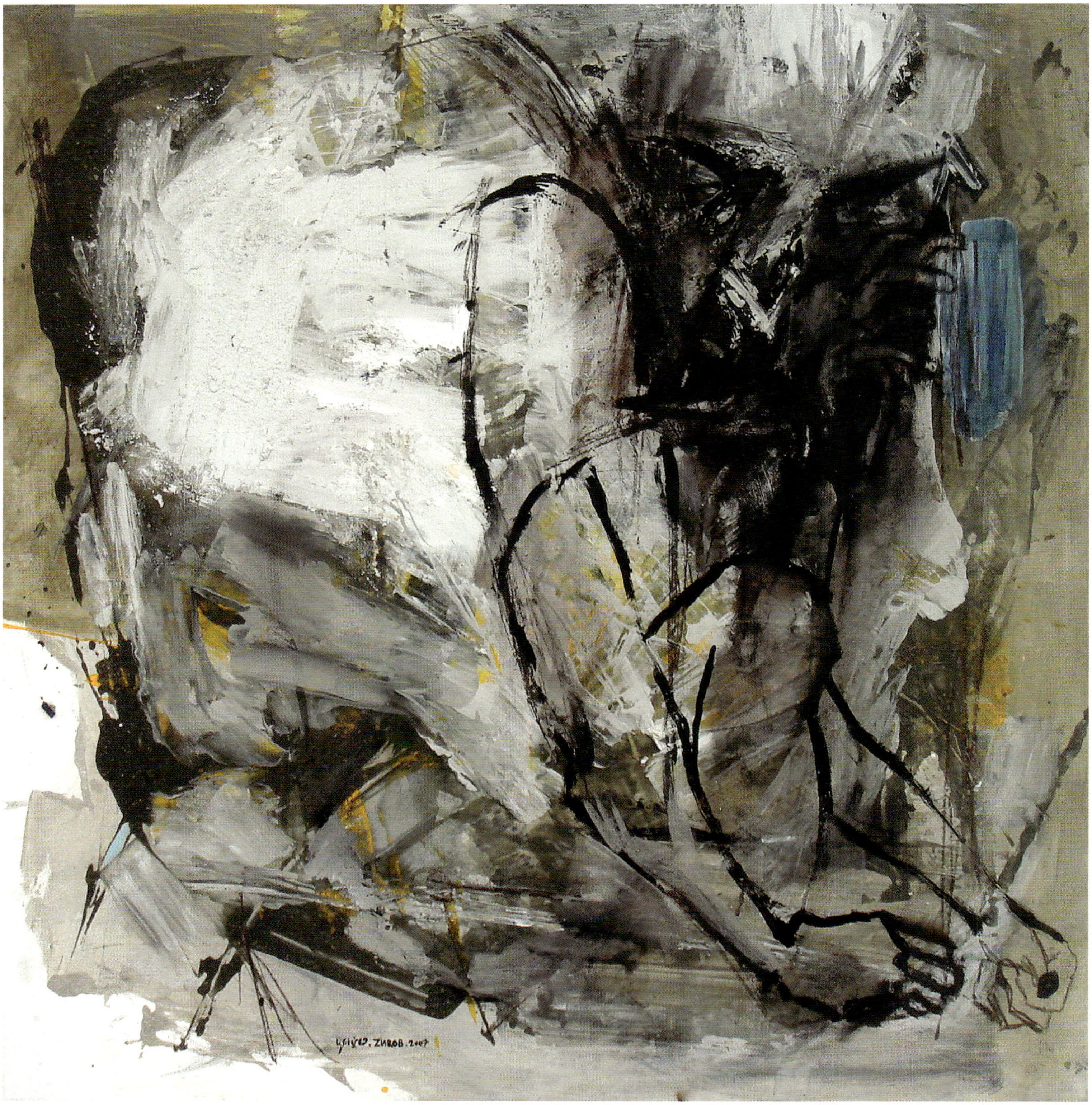

By the end of 2006, which coincided with the end of his rental period at the Cité Internationale des Arts, Hani Zurob was finally joined by his spouse Sabreen and managed to rent a small apartment on the third floor of an old apartment building in the 14th arrondissement of Paris. Despite all the practical shortcomings of the place, after his frequent displacements since he left his hometown of Rafah it was the first time in 13 years that the 30 year old artist felt he had a corner in the world he could call his own. The room at the end of the corridor was turned into his working space. There, Hani began work on a series of new paintings he titled *Marbles' War*: bringing together the words for his favourite childhood game and the state of belligerence in which he was living.

Associating the memory of a childhood pastime with the violence of a current situation is a curious way to identify a set of paintings. With the artist's inborn attachment to verbal expression, titles in Zurob's paintings have repeatedly represented a key subscript to understanding his art. That is why such a controvertible title cannot be lightly dismissed. To help us decode its meaning, however, the following words of Gaston Bachelard do not only offer a clue but they further suggest what may have motivated the artist in the first place to embark on this series of works soon after he moved to his new home.

Bachelard writes, "after we are in the new house, when memories of other places we have lived in come back to us, we travel to the land of Motionless Childhood, motionless the way all Immemorial things are". He adds, "the places in which we have experienced daydreaming reconstitute themselves in a new daydream, and it is because our memories of former dwelling-places are relived as daydreams that these dwelling-places of the past remain in us for all time".[2]

Thus, in the new "dwelling-place" it was Hani Zurob's unwitting "daydreaming" that must have triggered his imagination to bring together the world of the past as typified by his reference to his childhood game and the world of the present overshadowed by an ongoing war. The convocation of two distant meanings in his title was also to manifest itself in plastic terms as the artist employed a tangential painting method by which he sought to bridge the two distant corners of his world.

Formations associated with figurative and abstract expression were brought together—not as they were first combined through a blending process as in *Sortie no. 0* and *Sortie no. 2*. This time, the coming

Marbles' War no. 1, 2007.
Mixed media on canvas,
100 x 100 cm.
Private collection, Paris.

together occurred in the very conceptualisation of the painting series, whereby most compositions were based on the brazen superimposition of figurative delineations over free-flowing abstract formations.

With a background swept with spontaneously quick brushstrokes bursting with gestural energy, canvases are dominated by monochromatic tones alternating between ashen grey and burnt umber. Before drying, paint is vigorously scraped and scrubbed with hard-edged tools leaving behind scratches and textured markings evoking a weathered wall. Impasto blotches of white and black paint are smeared over the dried background and highlighted by random smudges of bronze and olive paint.

Superimposed over these free-flowing abstract formations, fragments of a squatted male figure are delineated with a thick brush in a stubbly black outline. One can detect an adult's thigh, a stretched muscular arm and a hand as it grabs what one assumes to be a marble just before it is flicked. The disproportionate head of a bearded man contorting the features of the artist come to light in different paintings to recall those of the screaming man in *Sortie no. 2* and what had been a constant constituent in compositions of the last figurative series the artist completed back in Ramallah. As it turns out, *Marbles' War* was not only the series that embodied an endearing memory but, in the process, it reconnected the artist with the last figurative works he completed on home ground and the series that eventually led him in succeeding paintings to reconsider the representation of the self as an integral component of his art.

It was the room in which he created this new batch of paintings that reawakened Hani's memory of the crammed space at the end of the corridor in his Rafah home. That was the first place he could call his own. There, during the long days of curfew, the boy used to lie down daydreaming among his father's old books, and the wafting scent of humidity and rat poison. Drawings he did on the floor were to become the embodiment of his daydreams. He recalls that it was only after the curfew was lifted and schools were opened that he spent all his time after school hours playing marbles in the sandy alleyways of his neighbourhood.

An observation made by John Berger after he visited a refugee camp on the West Bank very much like the camp in which Hani was raised sheds further light on the series of paintings that brought Hani back to figurative painting. Berger wrote that in the camp he saw "three boys squatting and playing marbles in the corner of an alley". He noted "the dexterity with which the boys flick a marble with one thumb, the rest of the body motionless, is not unconnected with the familiarity of very cramped spaces".[3]

Haunted by the memory of the home in which he was raised as much as by his fear of being doomed to oblivion in the art metropolis that is Paris, Hani Zurob doggedly pursued his painting. Superimposing figurative delineations over gestural painting embodied his sense of living at one and the same time in both places. Perhaps the ultimate sign summing up his shifted experience manifested itself in the manner in which his new paintings were signed. Unlike his earlier signature, which was solely in Arabic, the Arabic lettering now appears diminished next to the spelling-out of his name in Latin letters.

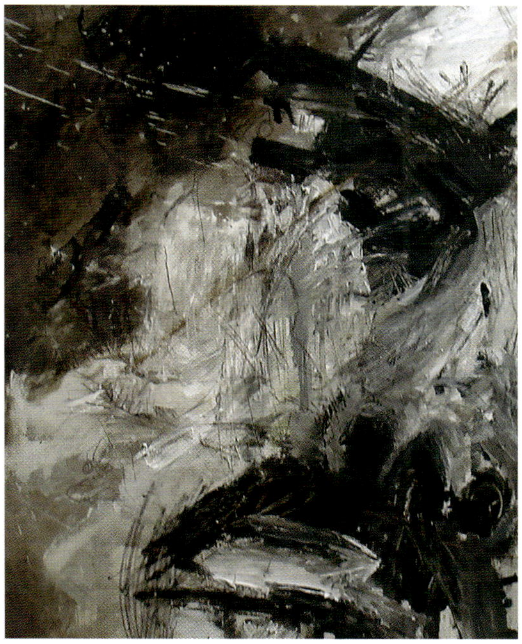

Marbles' War no. 8, 2007.
Mixed media on canvas,
200 x 200 cm (detail).
Private collection, New York.

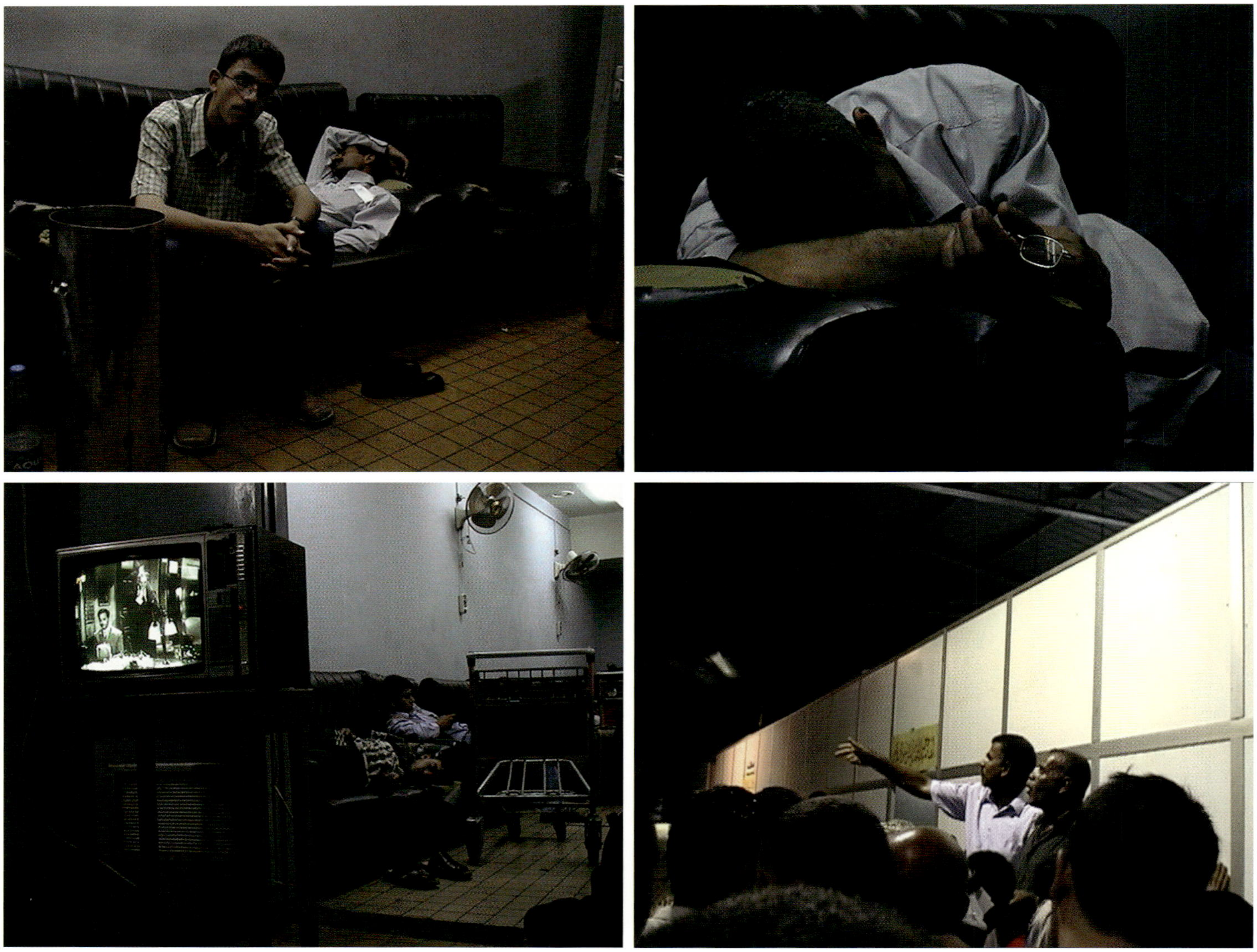

Taysir Batniji

Transit, 2004.

Video 6 minutes 32 seconds.

3.

Standby

The Rafah Crossing

Hani Zurob's hometown of Rafah became the site of the Palestinian gateway to the world in 1998 when the Yasser Arafat International Airport opened up south of the city. Within four years, however, all hopes for flying in and out of the Gaza Strip were shattered when, under the pretext of security concerns, Israeli warplanes bombarded the control tower in 2001 and military bulldozers completely destroyed the runway. In the years to come, as the Israeli siege of the Gaza Strip was tightened with Egypt's full compliance, the city of Rafah, divided since the 1978 Egyptian-Israeli Camp David Accords, was to become the only site of access for all people going in or out of the Gaza Strip.

In 2004 the Paris-based artist Taysir Batniji (Gaza 1966) documented the experience through which Palestinian travellers like himself go in their attempt to cross over to their homes in Gaza. Defying the Egyptian authorities' ban on filming or photographing any detail of their passage, he created a video with a camera hidden under his jacket. Titled *Transit*, the video is mainly composed of a series of still shots. Erratically punctuated by pauses of a black screen, the images are flashed as if in a slide show tracked by the clicking sound of a slide projector. The images' stillness, their unhurried appearance and the regulated clicking sound set a monotonous pace charged with the anxieties of marking time.

Most shots capture waiting passengers huddled around their bulky bags and luggage carts as they languish in a barren waste under a blazing sun or as they wait in basement rooms of the Cairo Airport. It is there that Palestinian passengers, unauthorised to enter Egypt, are taken right after they land to spend the night, during which they are kept under strict surveillance in the all-night glare of fluorescent light. On a good day the waiting lasts around six hours. But as all entry allowances are arbitrarily restricted by the whims of the Israeli military authorities, at times the waiting lasts as long as a week. Dispirited and drooped in fatigue amidst unsanitary conditions, some passengers are photographed as they collapse, over their baggage while others look apprehensive, waiting for their travel documents to be returned with a stamp allowing them to cross the Rafah border.

Batniji's video of still images concludes with a clip showing the commotion and sounds of a crowd of men surrounding two Egyptian officials, each of whom is holding a stack of passports. They take turns in yelling out names at the crowd. Once an individual identifies himself, the passport is hurled in his direction. Suddenly, as passports whirl over the heads all sound is cut off from the tape as the animated scene continues for a few seconds before it is cut off and the screen turns black.

Since 1967, 'waiting' has claimed a central role in the life of the Palestinian generations who have grown up in refugee camps throughout the region or under military occupation. It is not confined to waiting for a passage through a military checkpoint or for an official stamp on a travelling document. It goes back to 1948, following the mass expulsion of Palestinians from their homes. The waiting started with standing in line for the UNRWA distribution of food and temporary shelters, for a job to secure survival, for questioning by military and security Arab and Israeli officials, for a son or daughter's release from an Israeli prison, or for a visa to immigrate abroad. Unsurprisingly, the subject of 'waiting' has permeated the history of Palestinian literary and artistic expression. Batniji's essentially silent video speaks louder than words. It is perhaps the most loaded six minutes and 22 seconds of artistic expression to document the subject during the first decade of the twenty-first century.

Waiting II, 2009.
Acrylic, oil and tar on canvas,
73 x 60 cm.
Private collection, Paris.

Waiting

Within a year of his first experience of flying that landed him in Paris, Hani Zurob had created the series of paintings he titled *Standby.* The

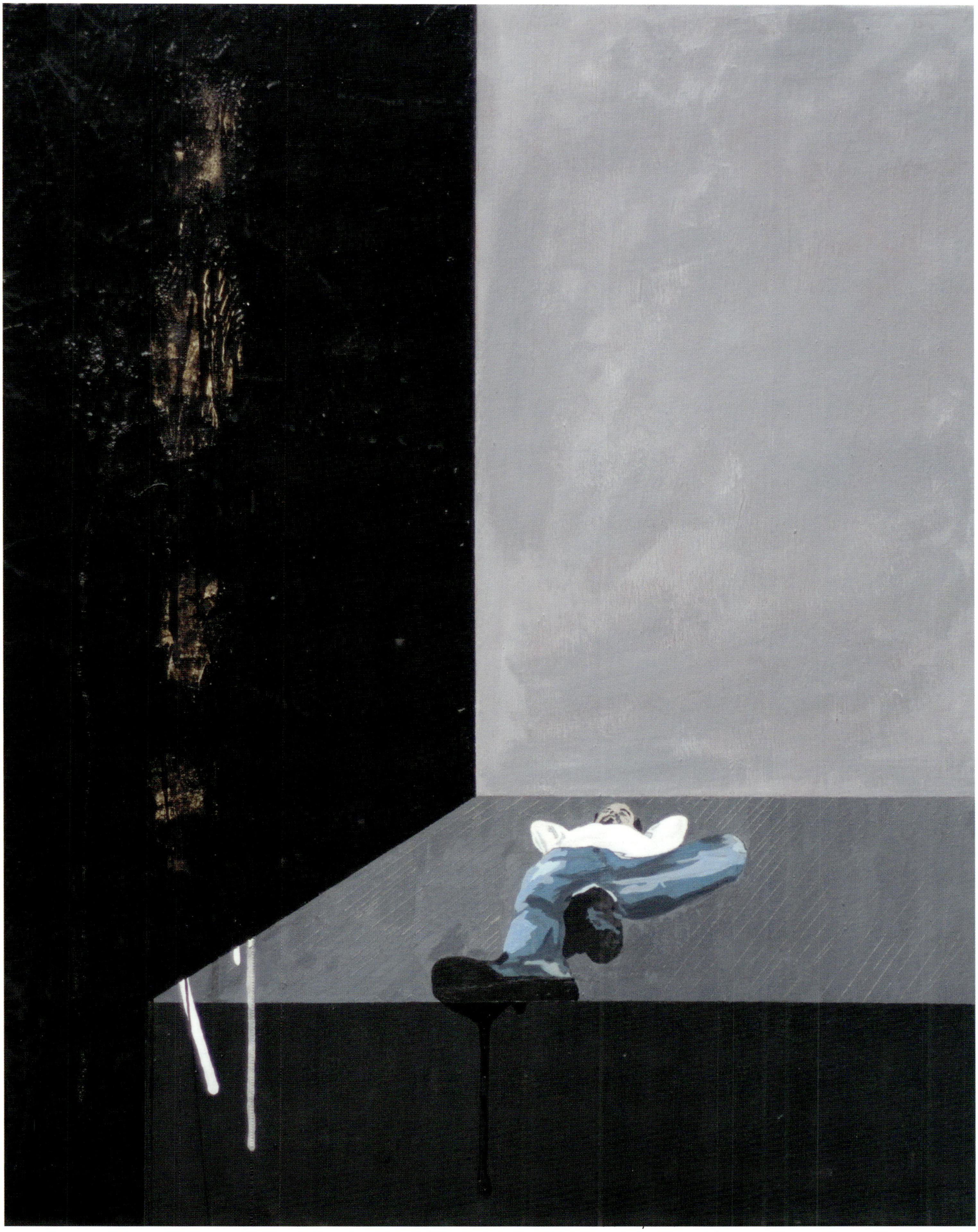

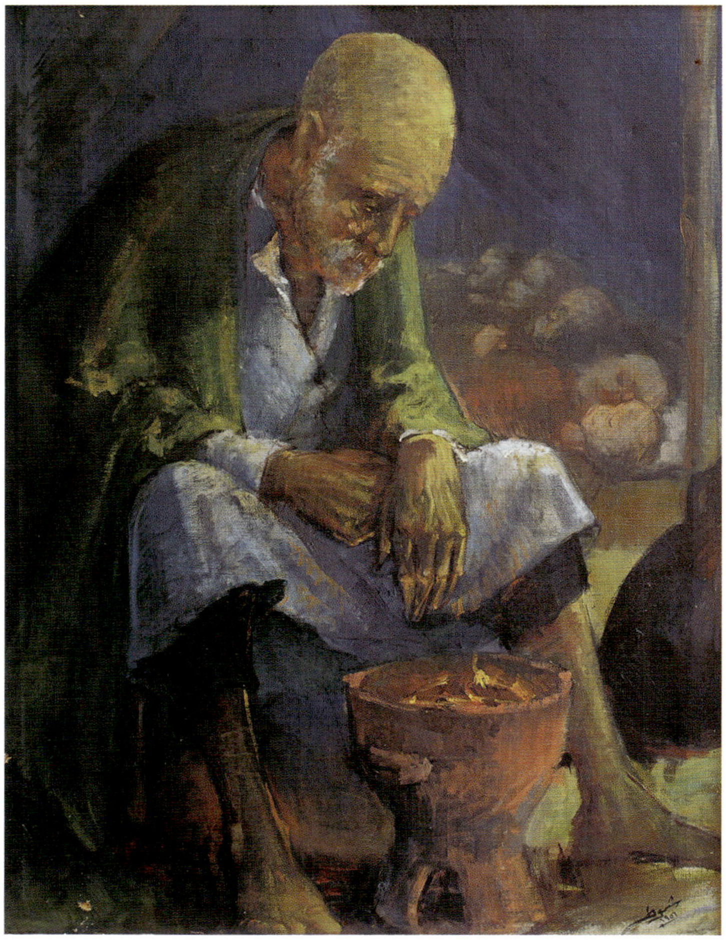

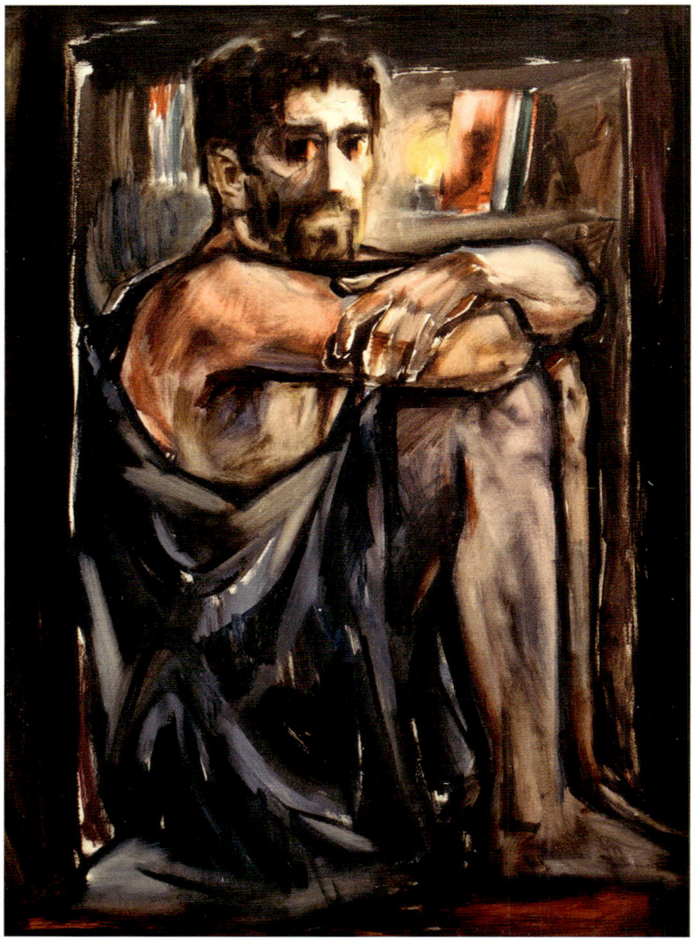

left
Isma'il Shammout
Memory and Fire, 1956.
Oil on canvas, 100 x 80 cm.

right
Isma'il Shammout
Waiting for the Dawn, 1987.
Oil on canvas, 102 x 76 cm.

word, implying the passing of anxious time waiting, summed up for him an experience that is only too familiar to Palestinians everywhere; its subject has repeatedly been depicted in Palestinian art.

In the post-1948 history of Palestinian painting, Isma'il Shammout was the leading figurative artist to emerge from a Gaza refugee camp soon after the fall of Palestine and for whom 'waiting' was a recurring theme. Two of his paintings created over 30 years apart are worth noting in this context. The figure's disposition in each of them recalls that which Zurob unknowingly sought many decades later to give expression in order to the same subject.

The first Shammout painting created in 1956 and entitled *Memory and Fire* brings us face-to-face with an image of a seated old man cloaked in the trailing garments of a peasant. Engulfed by what appears to be a winter night, he is seen barefoot and bent over an earthenware brazier within a tent. Looking lost in thought, he stares into the embers before him whilst a row of children is seen sleeping on the ground behind him.

Three decades later, Shammout painted another canvas he titled *Waiting for the Dawn*. The painting represents an unclothed and unshaven young man wrapped in a sheet and seated on the ground with folded arms over his knees and tightly pressed against his chest. He appears caged by the incised delineations of the rectangular pictorial frame. As his body faces the right side of the canvas, his head is turning sideways to look straight at us.

Through Shammout's bodily disposition of the human figure captured in two nocturnal sites and combined with metaphoric titles, we are persuaded to read two contrasting states of 'waiting'. The figure's disposition in the first painting, as its metaphoric title suggests, attempts to give form to the sense of loss and set the *mise-en-scène* wherein recollection of the past and anxieties about the present are being contemplated by what appears to be a landless and aging peasant following his expulsion from his native village.

In the second painting, again thanks to the metaphoric hints in its title, the artist seeks to express—by means of his disposition of a barely-clothed young man—a totally different state in a refugee's life. Here, the young man appears impatient and vexed with anger. Holding himself tightly in what looks like a foetal position, he confronts us with a piercing

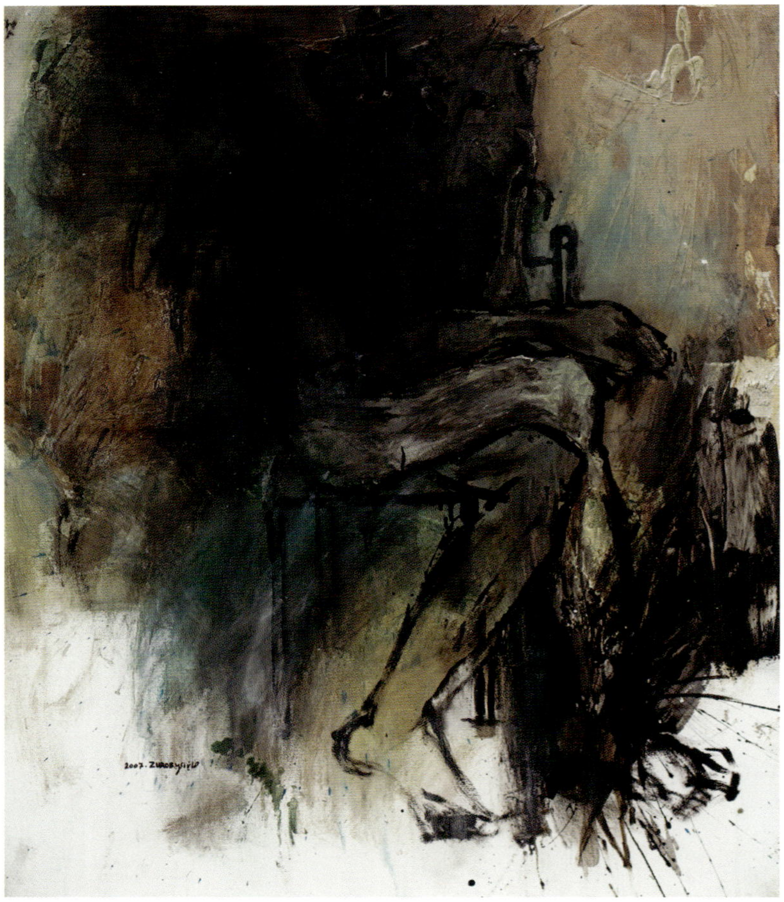

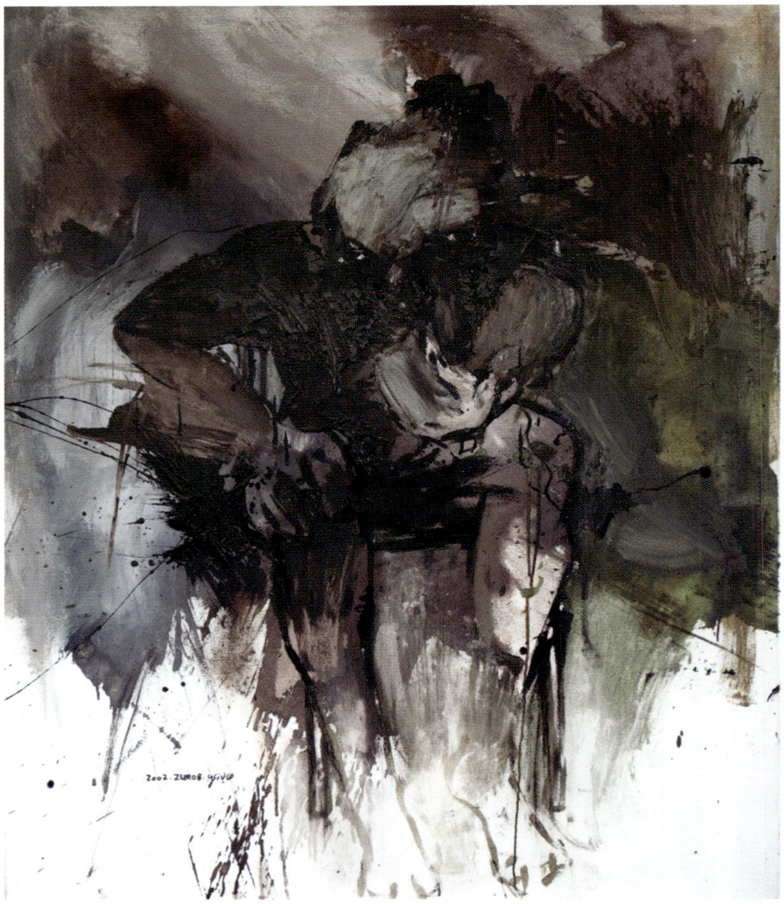

look and burning eyes that proclaim his faith and hope in the daybreak that looms in the background after a long night's wait.

As for Zurob, the subject of 'waiting' in his *Standby* series is moulded in a pictorial language that is foreign to Shammout's rhetoric and narrative style that made him popular among his people. Though all paintings by the two artists representing the same subject share similar dispositions, namely that of a seated male figure within a space shrouded by the illusion of night, Shammout's expression of 'waiting' comes to light in the form of an iconic figure whose stable positioning connotes withdrawal and apprehension in the painting of the old man, hope and the determination to resist in the painting of the young man. In contrast, in every one of the first eight paintings in Zurob's series, the subject of 'waiting' reflects a dilapidated state of despair and unrest.

Standby no. 1 and
Standby no. 2, 2007.
Mixed media on canvas,
120 x 100 cm

Depicted frontally, Hani Zurob's figure of a naked young man has been quickly sketched with a nearly dry brush leaving details unfinished.

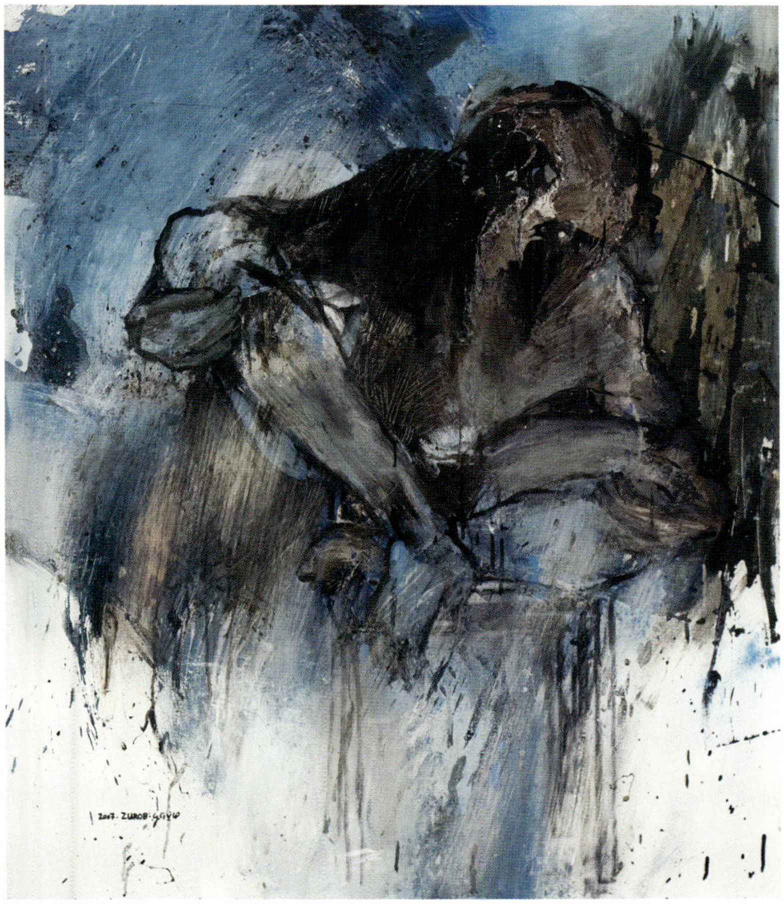

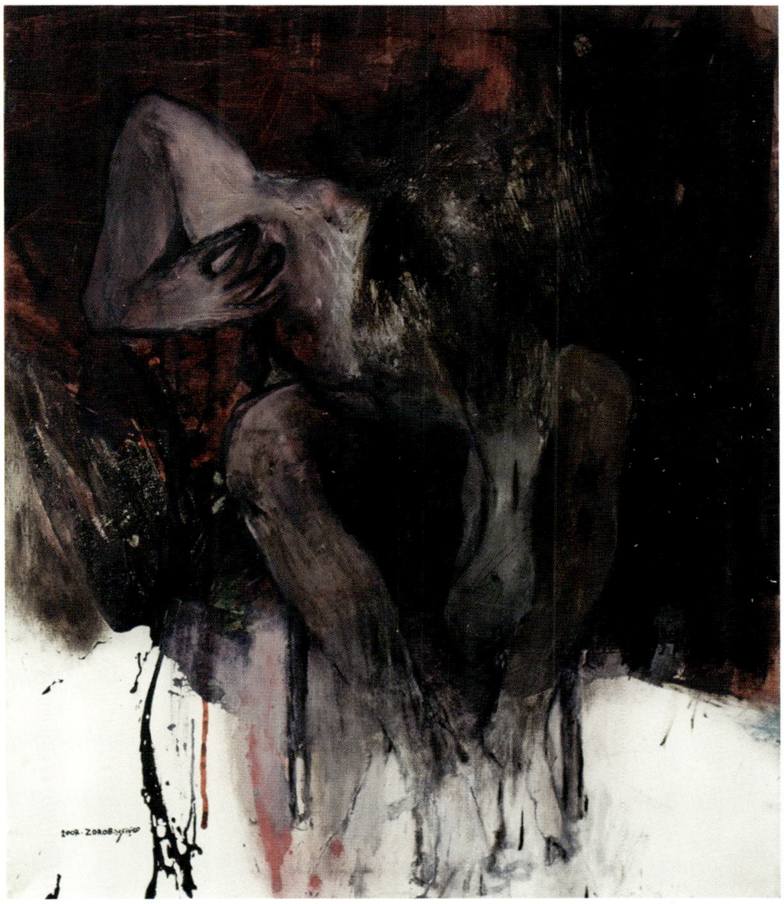

Each painting, rendered in a spontaneous painterly and tactile fashion, captures what looks like the same person in a different seated position. The upper parts of the large paintings are assailed with a barrage of sweeping brushstrokes loaded with successive layers of paint with colours alternating between indigo blue and magenta, henna ochre and black. The bottom stretch of each painting is left blank save for occasional smudges and drops of spattered paint that tarnish the white canvas. Features of the seated figure are totally obscured by splashes of an impenetrable black. Only in *Standby no. 2* can we detect the white of two eyes emerging from the darkness to reveal an agonised look fixed on us. In each painting, the man's different position appears to capture a convulsive movement.

How Zurob differs from Shammout in his interpretation of the same subject is not simply a matter of style. The difference is most sharply discerned in how each artist implies time in his painting. In Shammout's metaphoric works, the artist claims to represent two historical moments lived by two

Standby no. 3 and *Standby no. 4*, 2007. Mixed media on canvas, 120 x 100 cm.

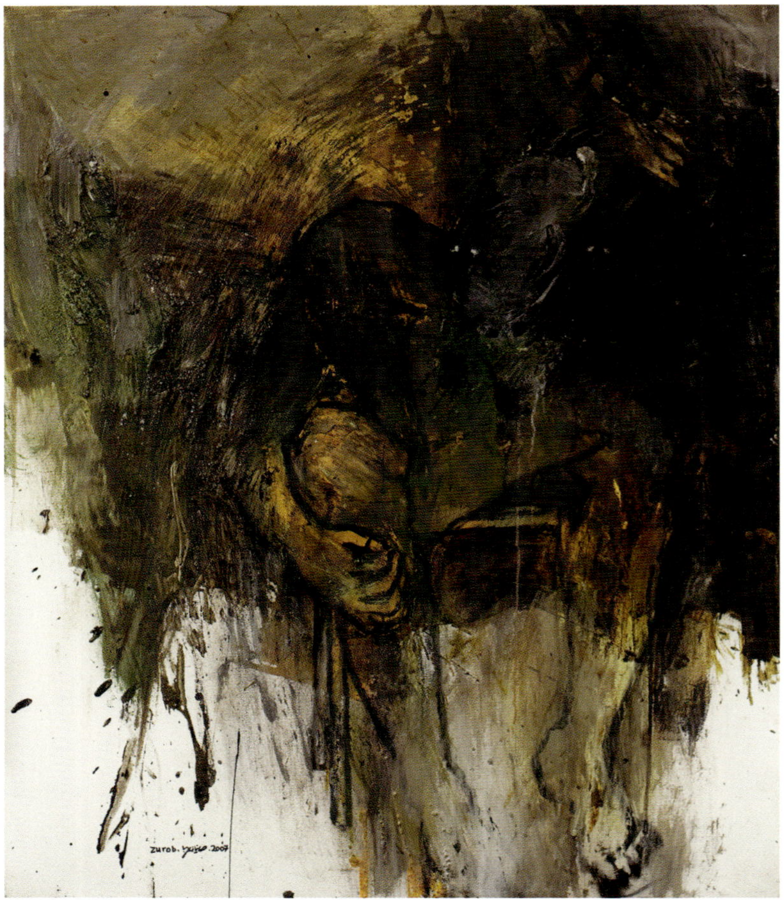

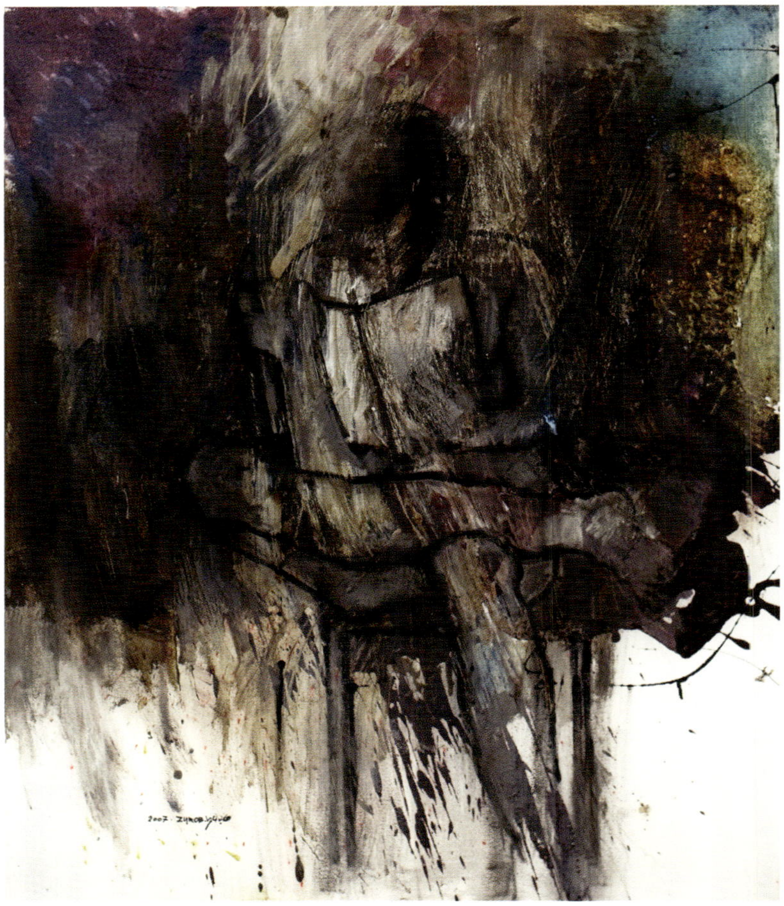

generations of Palestinian refugees each of which is associated with a different time of day. In contrast, in Zurob's series, which is not any less metaphoric, time unfolds in what appears to be the incarnation of a bodily movement. Each painting in the series, sharing identical dimensions with the others, seems to represent a sequential instant of a movement actuated by the same person as if it were captured on a filmstrip.

Unsurprisingly, on every occasion of the series' display, the artist insisted on having those numbered from one to seven—a number that has always been connected with periodicity—to be hung jointly together in a continuous horizontal row. With each painting touching the other in the order they were created, the row of seven paintings set in the direction from left to right reads like a line of text in Latin letters. While each painting in the series represents a different bodily movement, which does not clearly show whether the person is about to stand up or to continue sitting down, bringing together stasis and motion within a single frame,

Standby no. 5 and *Standby no. 6*, 2007. Mixed media on canvas, 120 x 100 cm.

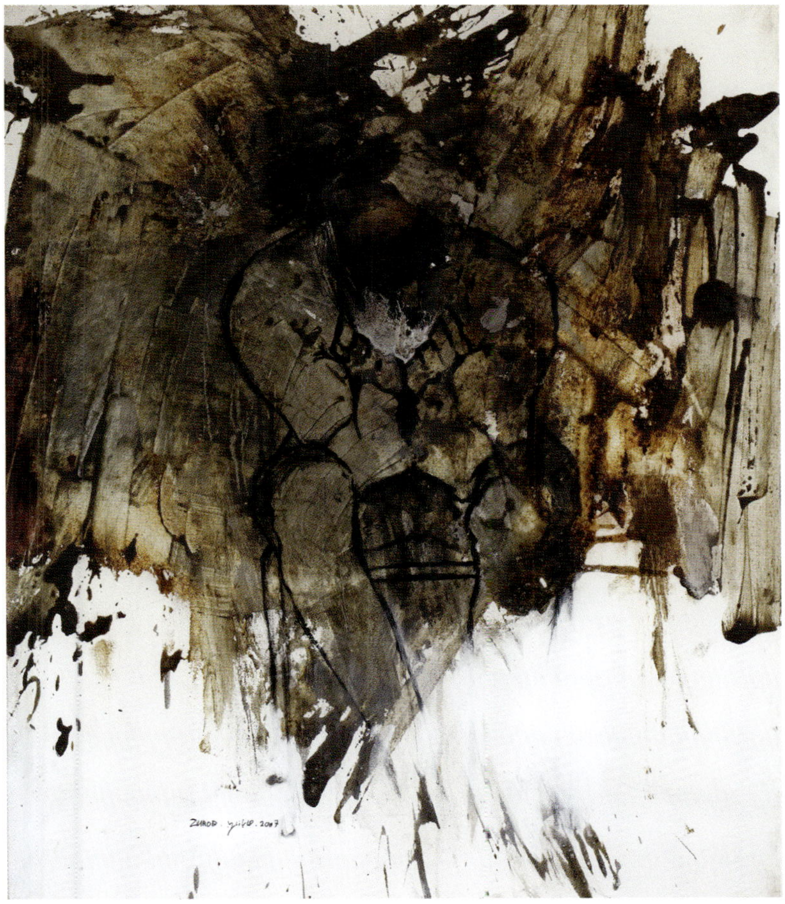

each image translates the transitory state and agitation that standby travellers usually go through.

Though Zurob may share with Shammout and his followers a fondness for employing metaphors and allegories whose articulation was first expressed through images popularised by Palestinian national poetry, his employment of such borrowings takes a radical departure from his predecessors. The title of the *Standby* series is a vivid illustration. The series exhibition was meant to coincide with the sixtieth anniversary of Palestine's fall marking the sixtieth year of waiting for a people to return home.

The Self and the Other

Standby no. 7, 2007.
Mixed media on canvas,
120 x 100 cm.

One of the most distinctive characteristics to note in this series, which echoes an avocation cultivated in earlier series in which the key figure

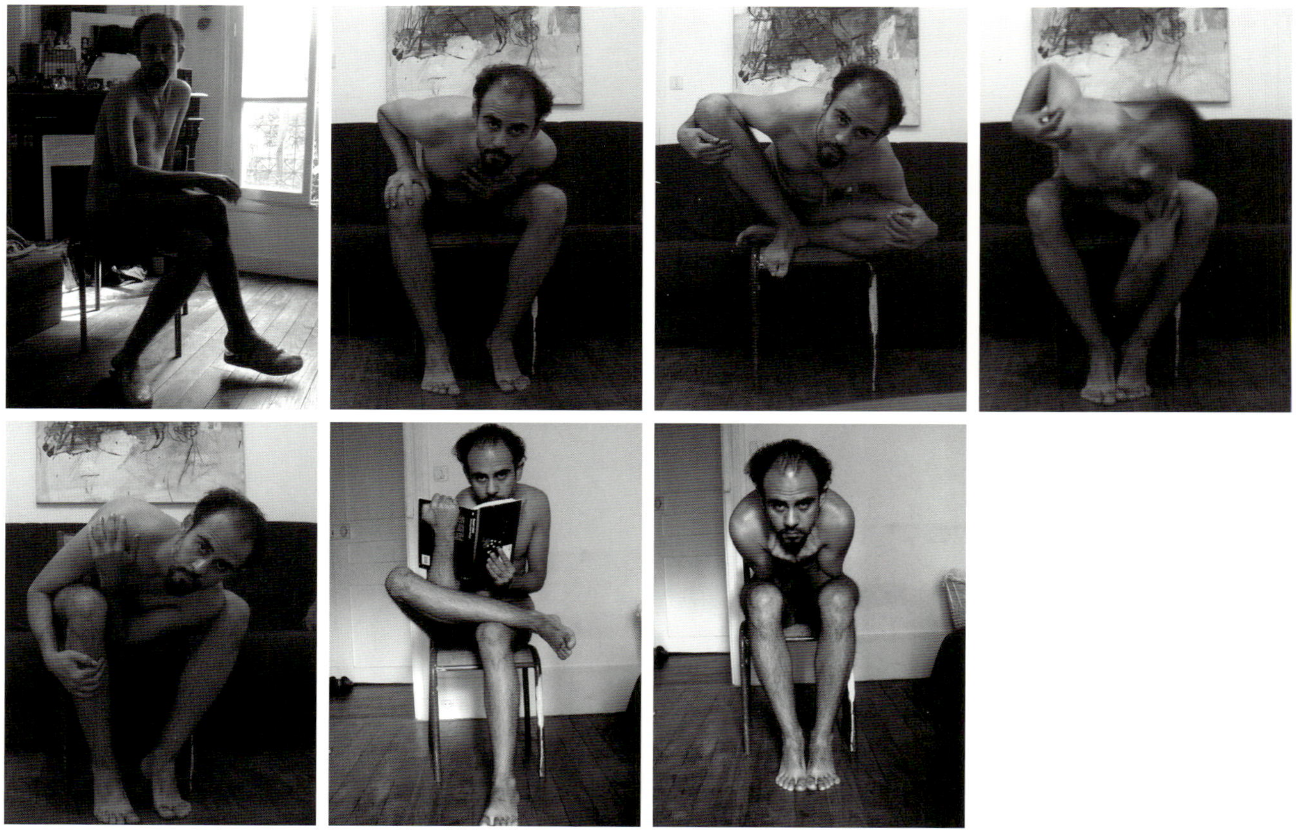

The artist photographing himself for the Standby series, Paris, 2007.

reflected the artist's own features, is the fact that the person pausing as a model for the *Standby* series was none other than the artist himself. The paintings were accomplished by using snapshots he took of himself seated in different positions. When asked "why paint yourself?" Hani answered "I am more familiar with my own body than I am with any other's." Then he added, "when it comes to any Palestinian sentience, the self and the other are one and the same especially as it comes to the experience of waiting".

Thus, by turning a personal standby experience into a metaphor and by sitting as a model to represent this metaphor, Zurob took an unprecedented step towards crystallising a Palestinian collective experience in art. Far from Shammout and his school of thought whose principle aim was to stir the viewers' empathy and rally support for the national struggle, Zurob sought through his art to channel the fluidity he senses between the self and the other.

In this series of works, the artist's self is experienced as another in himself as much as all others surviving the same destiny are experienced through the self. That is how the Gaza artist's painting comes closest to revealing the poet's voice in his art. "I do not ask the wounded person how he feels,/ I myself become the wounded person", wrote Walt Whitman. "For every atom belonging to me as good belongs to you"..../ "Translucent mold of me it shall be you!/ Shaded ledges and rests it shall be you!..../ Vapors lighting and shading my face it shall be you!..../ Hands I have taken, face I have kissed, mortal I have ever touch'd, It shall be you...."[1]

Faces are the central subject of the remaining paintings in the *Standby* series. Frontally depicted and viewed together closely lined up in a horizontal grid, each one of the paintings appears from a distance as a mere blob of stark blackness exploding amidst each canvas. At a closer range, features figured and disfigured emerge from beneath thick layers of a black opaque pigment splashed and smeared onto the support. Executed with tremendous speed and vigour, daubing the black pigment leaves behind harsh markings and shades that are accentuated at times by a bluish henna dye, at other times they are imbued with hues of coffee and burnt wood. Now and then, eyes seem to peer at us from the depths of the blackened face and the illusion of jagged teeth may be traced through the blurred features of some other face. As the contours surrounding each face are left unpainted, the plain white of the canvas is seen from a distance as a halo encircling each face. At a closer look, haphazard spots of some accidental drippings of the opaque black pigment appear hardened as liquorice drops, and one sees in the surrounding whiteness a margin of breathing space that serves as the whiteness needed for the legibility of words on a page.

Reading behind the obscurity common to all faces of the seated figure and to the blackened faces in the series' last ten paintings, one glimpses at what could possibly make the features of the artist's self and those of the other interchange amidst all this illusive obscurity and defacement. To do that, it is most befitting to begin by exploring the possible experiential and metaphorical associations the artist may have affiliated with the very substance with which his works were created, namely tar, the semi-fluid opaque black petroleum product akin to asphalt.

Tar

Called *zift* in colloquial Arabic and *qitran* in classical Arabic, a word from which the French word *goudron* derives, tar was first employed in Palestinian art by Naji al-'Ali (al-Shajara 1937–London 1987) who was raised in the refugee camp of 'Ain al-Hilweh in Lebanon. Before becoming the political cartoonist whose biting sarcasm earned him widespread popularity throughout the Arab world, al-'Ali was an aspiring painter. In an exhibition he held in Beirut in the mid-1970s, all his paintings, depicting characters from his camp's environment, were created on plywood boards with tar he appropriated from the construction sites at which he was employed as a menial worker.

Al-'Ali's unconventional employment of tar was not only because he could not afford to buy paint but also because he wished that the very substance employed for painting communicate the dismal state that the word *zift* connotes in colloquial Arabic. The word's metaphoric employment further represented the cynical comment with which he challenged his peers who at the time aspired to attract oil-rich patrons during a period that was buoyed up by the oil boom.[2]

The undaunted Palestinian cartoonist was assassinated on a London street for having named names in his cartoons of the Arab and Palestinian political leaders who went along with what was being termed the 'peace process'.[3] Overnight, al-'Ali's assassination turned him into a heroic legend throughout the Arab world.

After three decades had been spent hearing about a 'peace process', a whole lifetime for the Gaza artist, it was high time for him to put to the test the medium that his favourite Palestinian artist had employed. After all, the 'dismal state' that the word *zift* represented to al-'Ali seemed to have been perpetuated into an incurable state for Zurob. *Goudron* was not to be found in Maison Marin, his favourite art supplies store outside Paris, but in construction warehouses within the city.

"Every painter paints himself" is a dictum that goes all the way back to Cosimo de Medici; but looking outside the Western tradition of portraiture, to apprehend how the self and the other could be simultaneously implied in each portrait in the series of obscure faces by our Palestinian painter, it is necessary to bring to light the artist's experience and personal associations with the bituminous substance he painted with and follow that with the cultural significance associated with its blackness.

Standby no. 10, 2008.
Mixed media on canvas,
120 x 100 cm.

The earliest memory of tar that Hani Zurob retains goes back to 1988 when the popular uprising against the Israeli military occupation was

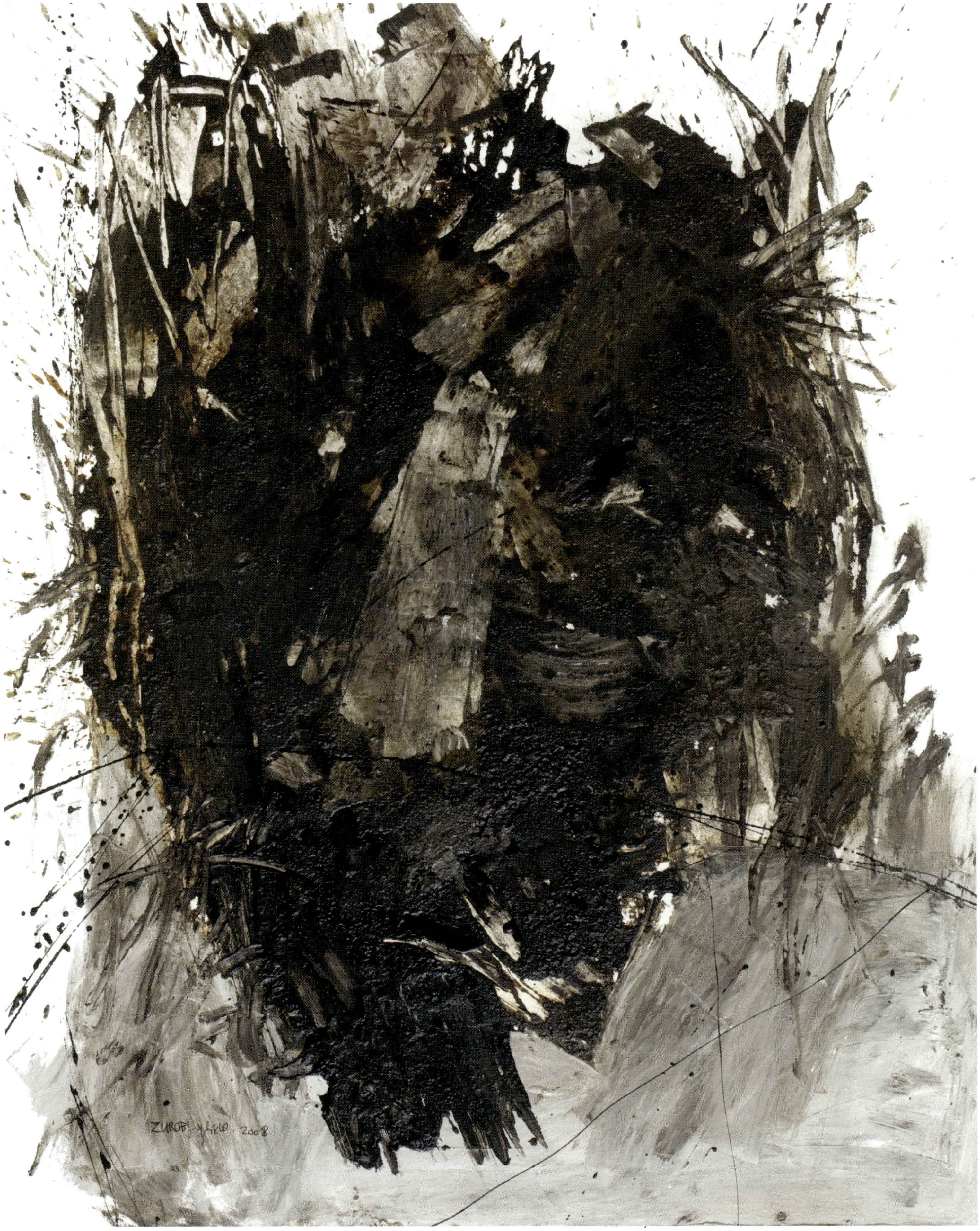
ZUROB
2008

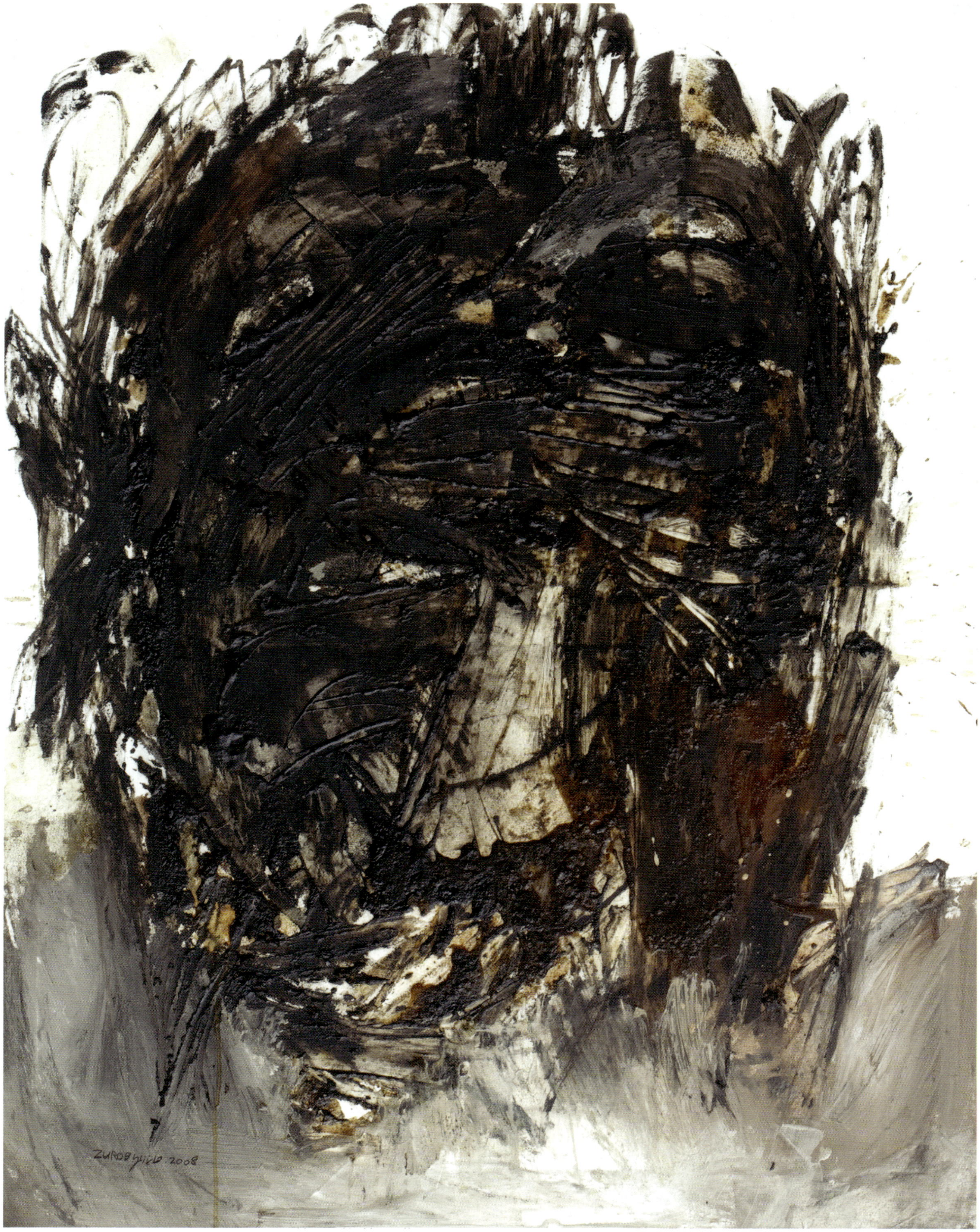

in full swing. During one of the frequent curfews the Israeli forces had imposed on Rafah, he remembers a particular curfew lasting for "40 days and one night". The morning the curfew was lifted he went outdoors with everybody else and saw how all the walls and doors of his neighbourhood had been totally besmeared with tar including the trunk of the date palm tree at the end of the road. Under the blinding sunlight the entire town looked drowned in pitch-blackness. It was Israel's punitive measure to deter the underground leaders of the Uprising from writing political slogans and messages on their doors and walls.

Turning left out of their doorway, the orange grove of the Barhoum family was no longer there. All of its trees had been bulldozed. The viscous pitchy liquid hosed on every surface had already hardened over the soil and the tree remains. For the boy, the nauseating smell permeating the air everywhere was equivalent to the stench of death. Soon enough, the date palm tree died and within a few years the family owners of the orange grove built a concrete apartment building on their piece of land.

There was a second occasion that Hani Zurob's life was once again marked by tar. It was during the outbreak of the 2002 popular uprising when the Israeli forces invaded and reoccupied Ramallah. Classified as an "illegal resident" according to the Israeli military occupation laws, he was arrested. Along with a whole group of young people, he was detained for 53 days at an outdoor military camp outside the city known as the Ofer prison. As the camp tents were already packed with young and old men, he and other late arrivals were left to sleep their nights on freshly asphalted grounds of the recently expanded prison. Nothing was provided for a bed. His shoes served as a pillow. Night and day the foul smell of hot tar was suffocating. Again, the nausea it induced deprived him from craving any food. Perhaps the famished condition he yielded to was what Rimbaud meant when he wrote "My hunger pangs are bits of black air."[4]

As for how the colour black is regarded in the artist's native culture, like all other Mediterranean cultures, Arabs mainly associate black with death. The association is summed up in the colloquial Palestinian women's curse *sawad aleik* literally meaning "may you be in black". It is a curse of death women hurl as a bad omen echoing the more renowned Biblical curse dubbed "the Mark of Cain". Black also has another metaphoric connotation in popular usage which appears to literally congeal Zurob's faces in black. When one has a close relation who commits a disgraceful act, one's face is said to be "blackened" (*iswad wajhoh*). It is through the correlation and

Standby no. 12, 2008.
Mixed media on canvas,
120 x 100 cm.

overlapping of these cultural associations and metaphorical connotations of black that we can best appreciate Zurob's faces and the concealed features of his seated figure.

The slow escalation of death on one hand and the growing offenses of national dignity on the other have been the twin experiences of common Palestinians following their political leadership's signing of the Oslo Peace Accords in 1993. Since then, and unceasingly, death has been exacted from land, sea and air on a pauperised civilian population besieged in the Gaza Strip. Israel's protracted genocide there continued neck and neck with its ethnic cleansing on the West Bank where it continued to dispossess people of their homes and properties in order to build the Apartheid Wall, the illegal colonial settlements and clamp thousands of Palestinians of all ages in jail without the right for a trial.

In the meantime, the representatives of an acquiesced Palestinian regime in Ramallah queue up to pay lip service to national rights as they went on entertaining false hopes in a so-called 'peace process' after the 'process' has been going on for three decades without yielding anything new other than the proliferation of a national disaster. That is what 'blackens the face' of every Palestinian maintaining any sense of dignity and self-respect. The twin significance of black is all embodied in the way Zurob employs tar.

The same substance with which Israeli forces effaced Arabic words from the walls of Rafah in the hands of its native artist was turned into a creative instrument for putting down an experience in black and white. By transforming tar into an expression of resistance, the essence of his experience is thus sublimated into images, which are enraptured with a tactile sensation. The horizontal chessboard display of the faces purport to the interplay between one face and the other the way his seated figures horizontally hung closely together read like a verse or a line of text. Dots, whirls and strokes as employed in the creation of words make up the obscured and interchanging features of the self and the other. It is the inky black in his series of paintings that accredits them as improvised substitutes superseding the writing of his experience.

Since paper was invented, black, the very colour of the eye's pupil, has been the means by which human thought has been documented. But after spending close to two years among the Palestinians, Jean Genet, reflecting back while writing of his experience, wondered in his last book, *Prisoner of Love*, if "these black marks add up to reality... [when]

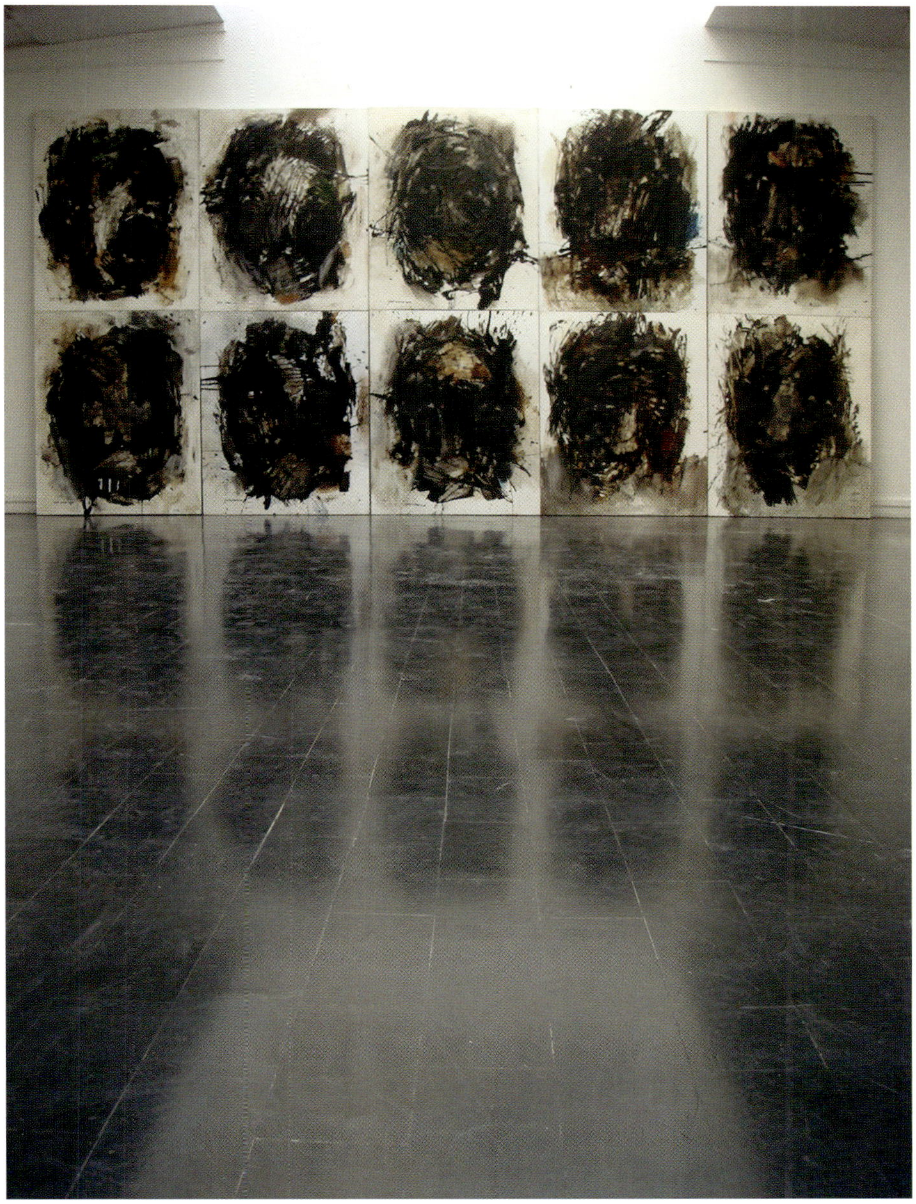

Standby nos. 10–20, 2008.
Mixed media on canvas,
240 x 500 cm.

whiteness may all possess more reality than the signs that mar them." He asked, "Is the white page, and every little blank space between the words, more real than the black characters themselves?"; then added "if the reality of time spent among—not with—the Palestinians resided anywhere, it would survive between all the words that claim to give an account of it…the space between the words contains more reality than does the time it takes to read them."[5] Hani Zurob's painting abides within white space.

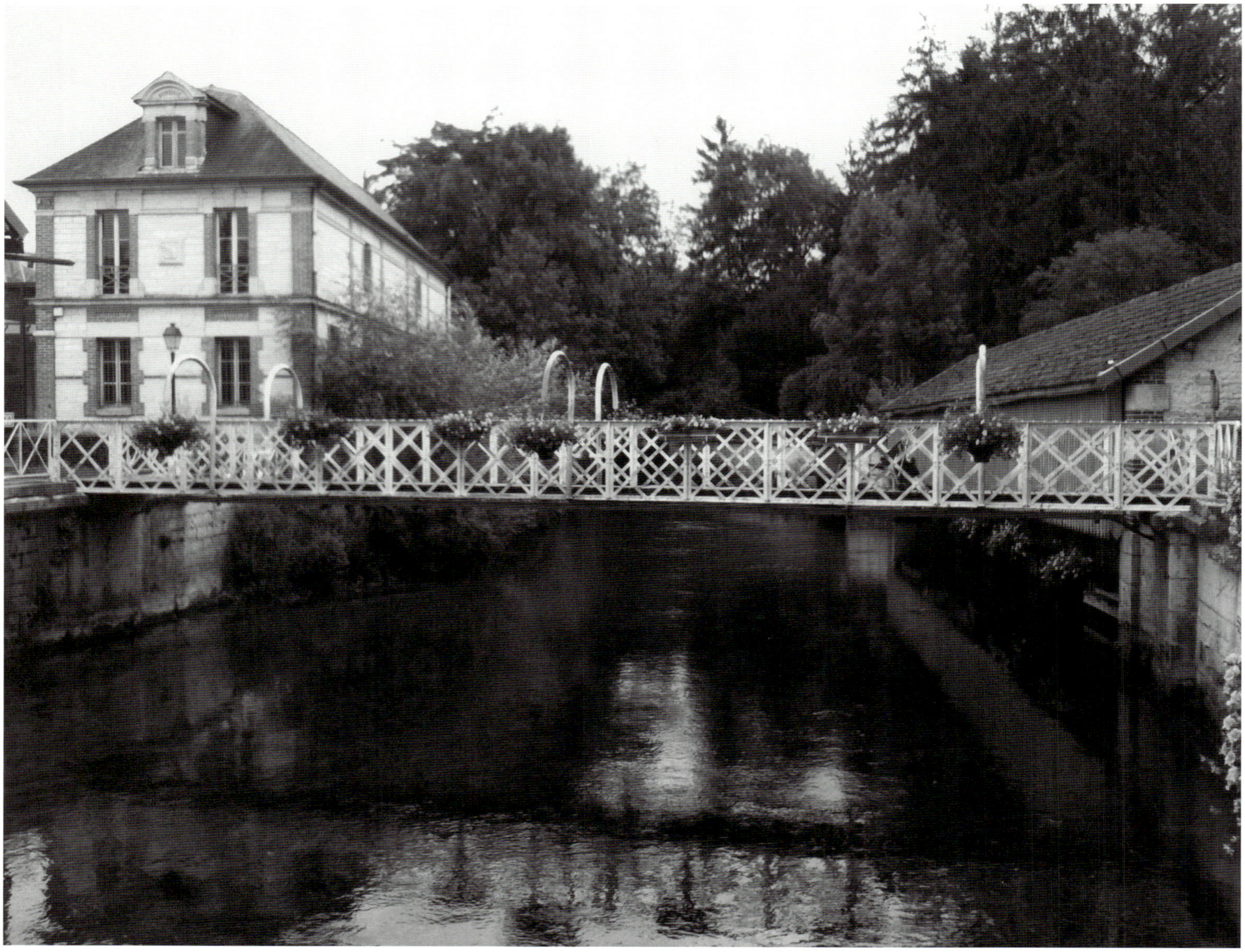

Bridge across the Ource River,
Essoyes, 2009.

4.

Mirrors

In 2009, Hani Zurob won the Renoir Grant that comprised an offer to spend an eight-month art residency in Essoyes, the native village of Renoir's wife where the French Impressionist created many of his paintings in the garden atelier of the house he bought there in 1895. It is in the village's cemetery where Renoir was buried along with his wife and their children Pierre, Jean and Claude.

Members of the jury recommending Zurob for the grant included Sophie Renoir-Doisne, the great granddaughter of the painter, Lionel Pissaro, the great grandson of Camille Pissaro, and Maya Widmaier Picasso, daughter of the twentieth century artist. It was through the Renoir Association, created in 1986 by Evangéline and Claude Renoir (son of Pierre) to perpetuate the legacy of the old master, that the grant was offered. The Gaza painter was the first Arab artist to receive it.

Located in the Champagne region, Essoyes is nestled in the valley bordering the river Ource, a tributary of the Seine. For over four centuries, the region has been renowned for its sparkling wines and particularly for its production of Chardonnay and the Pinot Noir wines. The living space and studio offered to the resident artist overlooks the river. It is a stone's throw from Renoir's old house, soon to be turned into a museum.

Hani and Sabreen enthusiastically welcomed the opportunity of a sojourn in Renoir's village, especially after the working space in their

Paris apartment has been gradually reduced since the arrival of their son Qudsi, now two years old. For Hani, having been raised in a region that is one of the most densely populated regions in the world and after spending three years learning the ropes of survival and conviviality in the cosmopolitan and multi-ethnic French capital, Essoyes, with its native inhabitants counting less than 700 individuals, exhorted a startling change and challenge.

With their limited knowledge of French, Hani and Sabreen had usually been chilled by the general indifference they occasionally encountered in their daily communications in the big city and looked forward to being out among country folks. But they did not fathom that over and above their lack of language proficiency, the shorter days of winter there and the long months of snow would only reinforce their isolation from the closely-knit community outside their temporary residence. After being accustomed to a relatively secluded life in Paris, their communication with others in the Essoyes community was further diminished to a bare minimum.

What was to exacerbate Hani's seclusion, which was to leave a distinctive mark on the paintings he produced during his sojourn there, was the incumbent absence of Sabreen and their child. Since her arrival in France, Sabreen had been obliged every six months to take a trip back home. As a native of Jerusalem she—like all of the city's Arabs and their offspring—was no longer recognised as a citizen of her city of birth since Israel annexed the Old City and its environs in 1967. They were reduced to "permanent residents" and were thus granted by the Israeli authorities identity cards designating their status as such. But as Israeli demographic policies never ceased to advocate a Jewish majority in Jerusalem, over the years, Israeli law enforcement authorities seized on all sorts of technical pretexts to revoke the identity cards while confiscating more lands in the ever-expanding municipal boundaries of a Greater Jerusalem. That way, more than 4,000 Jerusalem Arabs overnight found themselves unwelcome strangers at home. To avoid having her identity card revoked and thus lose her right of residency in Jerusalem, Sabreen has been taking the trip twice a year back home where she usually spends at least two months with her family. Since Qudsi's birth she has been taking the baby boy with her. Whole days passing by all alone in Essoyes during the darkest winter months without talking to anyone provided Hani with ample time to reflect on his experience as a total outsider in his French environment. His reflections were soon groping for expression in his paintings.

Over a number of weeks since Sabreen and Qudsi left, Zurob worked on a large painting that belonged neither to the preceding *Standby* series nor to the subsequent *Flying Lesson* series, most of which was produced during his sojourn. The painting stood in a category all of its own, grappling with deep-seated existential questions that had plagued him since he first began sensing the state of being cut off in Essoyes. The questions he wrestled with obviously revolved around the theme of the self and the other. This time, however, these questions did not relate to the interchanging fluidity between his self and the collective other as propounded in earlier paintings but they focused instead on how the awareness of the self may come about through the eyes of others as Paul Ricœur dissertated.[1]

Rare in its horizontal dimensions, *Untitled* represents a seated male figure surrounded on all four sides of the canvas with the dense black of solid tar. Unlike the seated male figure in his *Standby* series whose features were repeatedly obscured by darkness, here, engulfed by the dead of night, the man's face appears chalky and overexposed under a glaring spotlight. The man's features clearly define the likeness of the artist.

In contrast, through the nebulous gleam spilling off the light flooding his face, we see the bent figure of the artist naked, a hand gently holding each knee. The spreading of his legs exposes his genitals. His right arm, bathed in a red light, seems to analogically reflect an infrared light detecting the degree of his body heat. Above him, there is mechanical apparatus holding three surveillance video cameras set up at different heights as if to monitor bodily movements from different angles. It seems as if at the moment he reached the pictured position an automatic flashlight burst in his face.

From the viewer's perspective, the seated artist is beheld bowing deep down and looking up at us. In this position he looks like having been caught off guard in a private moment in the bathroom. The body movement suggests that he might have suddenly heard footsteps outside. Or, having suspected the unexpected presence of a person behind his closed door he bent forward in this position to look up through a crack in the shutters or through the door's keyhole. His peering look meets ours. Thus, the painting confronts us with questions of who is really covertly looking at whom and who as a result is embarrassed, if at all, the viewer or the viewed?

The fleeting moment that Zurob unknowingly captures in this painting brings to mind the example Sartre cited in his analysis of "the look" *vis-*

à-vis "the other". Once the subject of the spying eye behind a keyhole realises that the object of looking is looking back at the onlooker, self-awareness is reawakened accompanied by a sense of what Sartre calls "shame".[2]

In a similar context, the painting further recalls another example provided by Derrida. In his attempt to answer the question, "who am I?", the French philosopher opened his argument with the sense of embarrassment he experienced one day upon emerging from the shower when he found himself being looked at by his cat.[3]

In both examples, the self-awareness being brought about as a response to another's gaze illustrates how the subjective observer in Sartre's example, and the object of observation in that of Derrida, can overcome 'shame' or embarrassment upon recognising that the other, be it human or animal, shares equal grounds with the self whereby the reciprocity of gaze brings together the two counterparts in an inter-subjective relation with each other.

This painting, the first that Zurob created in Essoyes, is a self-portrait representing in every way what Derrida had described as "subject, object and signatory", yet the artist named it *Untitled*.[4] If he were to name it "self-portrait" it would have classified it within the traditional genre of painting which apparently was not the artist's intention. What he sought to express here was a more complex matter; namely, his experience of suddenly realising that he is the quintessential Other in Essoyes, where he felt that all his comings and goings, as well as his most private moments, seemed to be surveyed by the community.

The surveillance apparatus of video cameras triggering the flashlight in the Gaza artist's face is a key code in the painting that brings in an allegorical dimension borrowed from the world where Sabreen and Qudsi happened to be at the time. With the hazy shape of a heart spotted in red floating in space between the right monitor and the artist's face and the shape of a second heart spotted in white and green placed in the foreground covering the end of his right leg, a link is implied between the world of Essoyes and that of the city that witnessed the birth of his partner in life.

Throughout the Old City of Jerusalem, the Israeli authorities have installed surveillance video cameras. Every road and corner, alleyway, entryway and desolate square is monitored round the clock. At night, the glaring light

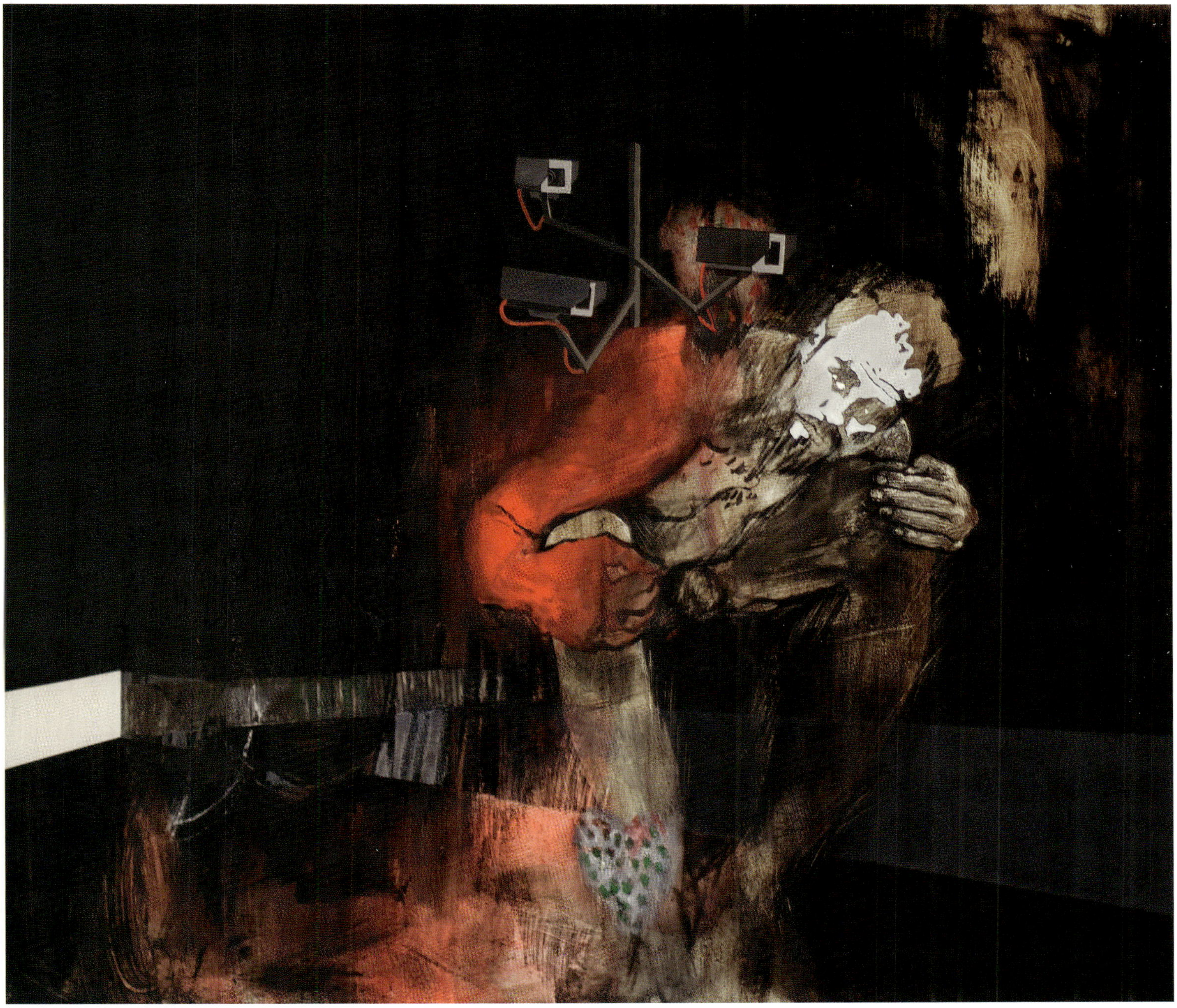

Untitled, 2009.
Acrylic, oil and tar on canvas,
100 x 120 cm.
Association Renoir, Essoyes.

blazes the city's ancient stones. For the Arab natives, since their part of the city had fallen under the spying eye of a video surveillance system, home has turned into what feels like an open-air prison. While the gates and prison guards of the West Bank and the Gaza Strip are visible everywhere, those of the Old City of Jerusalem remain invisible. In Essoyes, the sense of being constantly watched by the community represented for the artist a similar form of prison governed by invisible guards.[5]

To appreciate how the imaginary apparatus of surveillance in the painting relates to the punitive system actually installed by Israel, it is worth remembering Michel Foucault's seminal study analysing the visibility and invisibility of prison guards. According to Foucault, the inmates' experience of the threat of punishment by invisible prison guards is not any less brutal than that experienced by visible guards. To illustrate his point, he discusses the Panopticon prison, originally conceived by an eighteenth century Englishman. Architecturally conceived as a circular prison building with a central tower built in its inner court, the Panopticon prison includes individual cells with a single window overlooking the tower. Prisoners are thus separated from each other while a single supervisor in the tower is capable of watching what goes on in each cell. According to Foucault, power relation is thus established on the tension of being "visible and unverifiable" whereby "the inmate must never know whether he is being looked at at any one moment [but that] he must be sure that he may always be so".[6]

With that in mind, the viewer may now see how the observed 'prisoner' in this unconventional 'self-portrait' of a painting seems to communicate without words:

> I may be the object of your gaze just as much as you are of mine. The encounter of our gazes is what makes each of us conscious of the other. Now that your gaze made me aware of my own otherness, I know that I can never be able to see you from where you are seeing me. But through my naked exposure, I present myself to you as one who has nothing to hide. Being seen from anywhere in the outside world is part of being considered a responsive subject in it. That is how painting grants me freedom from the prison you confine me in.

By the end of his residency in Essoyes and as a token of thanks and appreciation of their hospitality, Hani Zurob offered the Renoir Association the choice of retaining any one of the paintings he created during his sojourn. All members of the Association favoured the choice of *Untitled*.

•

Heritage is the title of the first painting in which one of the earliest photographs of Qudsi was incorporated. Created in Essoyes during the child's absence, it was certainly a key work that ultimately led Zurob into the conceptualisation of his *Flying Lesson* series. As for the photograph, it was originally taken on a beach in Normandy over a year earlier. On that summer day away from the bustle and pollution of Paris, the sight and scent of the sea which had delightfully awakened the artist's childhood memories of Rafah was to throw Qudsi into a fit of panic as it was the first time the child had seen the sea. The photograph was captured as the crawling child was rushing away from the surging waves.

The father was intrigued by Qudsi's fear of the sea. He remembered how in Rafah he used to walk with family and friends over four miles in the sand to reach the sea. A day spent out on the beach represented the peak of joy and bliss to be found away from the congested space and indoor gloom of life in the refugee camp. In what is Zurob's only attempt at a landscape, *Heritage* assembles an assortment of images summoned from his memory of his long hikes to the sea and juxtaposed with the photograph that captured his child running away from it.

Apparently the view, encapsulating sand in the painting's foreground with a rock-ribbed hill on the sides topped with the silhouette of trees against the early morning sky, was the last view Zurob remembered seeing just before reaching the sea bristling beyond the woods. Looking at the scene the artist recalled from his walk *towards* the sea now combined with the photograph that was taken as the child was running *away* from it, we note how in the reciprocal movement in opposite directions the distance in time between the two events has been erased. In the process, nowhere is there the attempt at a spatial illusion of depth in the naturalistic scene. In fact, the trees in the background appear closer to us than the sands in the foreground.[7]

Though the peripheries of the painting look static and naturalistic, the structure surging behind the crawling child suggests the movement of abstracted bodies intimating splinters and fragments of what looks like a world in shambles. In jutting planes, we spot bits and pieces of

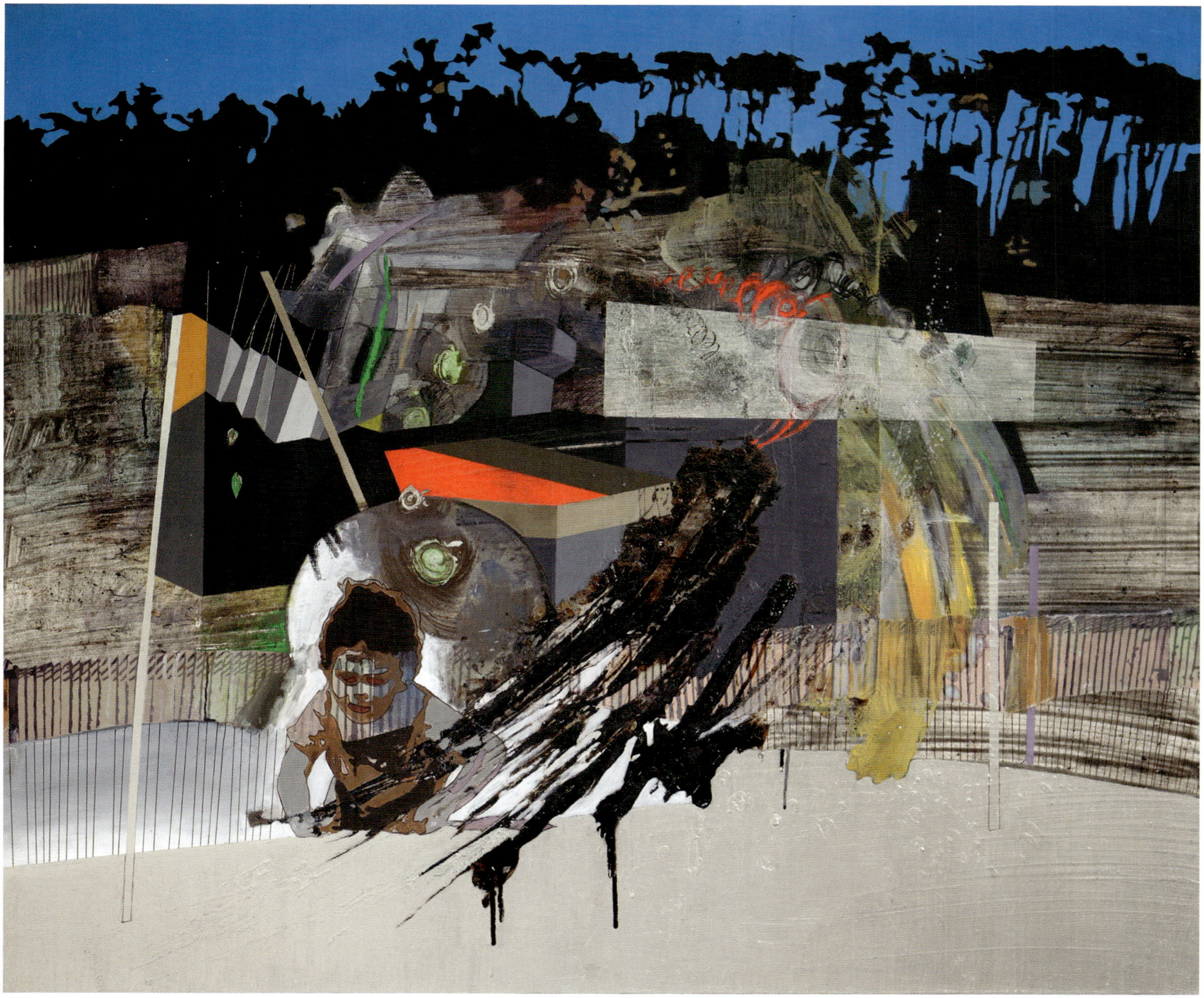

Heritage, 2009.
Acrylic, oil, pastel and tar
on canvas, 100 x 120 cm.
Private collection, Paris.

recognisable objects including fences, corrugated tin, elliptic utensils and shapes reminiscent of a crumbling wall, cement blocks and a hanging staircase. Dumped together and bulging out in a chaotic state with the weight of the silhouette of trees above, they all seem like a tidal wave advancing towards us in contrast to the rocky hill and sands that appear to be receding. The crawling child appears to be running away from all this chaotic structure. As in the Arabic language when the past tense is used to mean the continuous present or the future tense, here time present and past overlap.[8] A past moment remembered from the artist's childhood is contiguous with a recent present captured in the photograph of his child. The sands of Gaza and of Normandy are interchanged at the tips of the child's hands. The fierce waves of the Atlantic that scared Qudsi off turns into thick brush strokes loaded with tar sweeping away the remaining traces of the artist's childhood home. The ensuing wreckage jammed into what now looks like a forbidding landscape appears to reflect Edward Said's thought when he wrote, "each Palestinian structure presents itself as a potential ruin".[9]

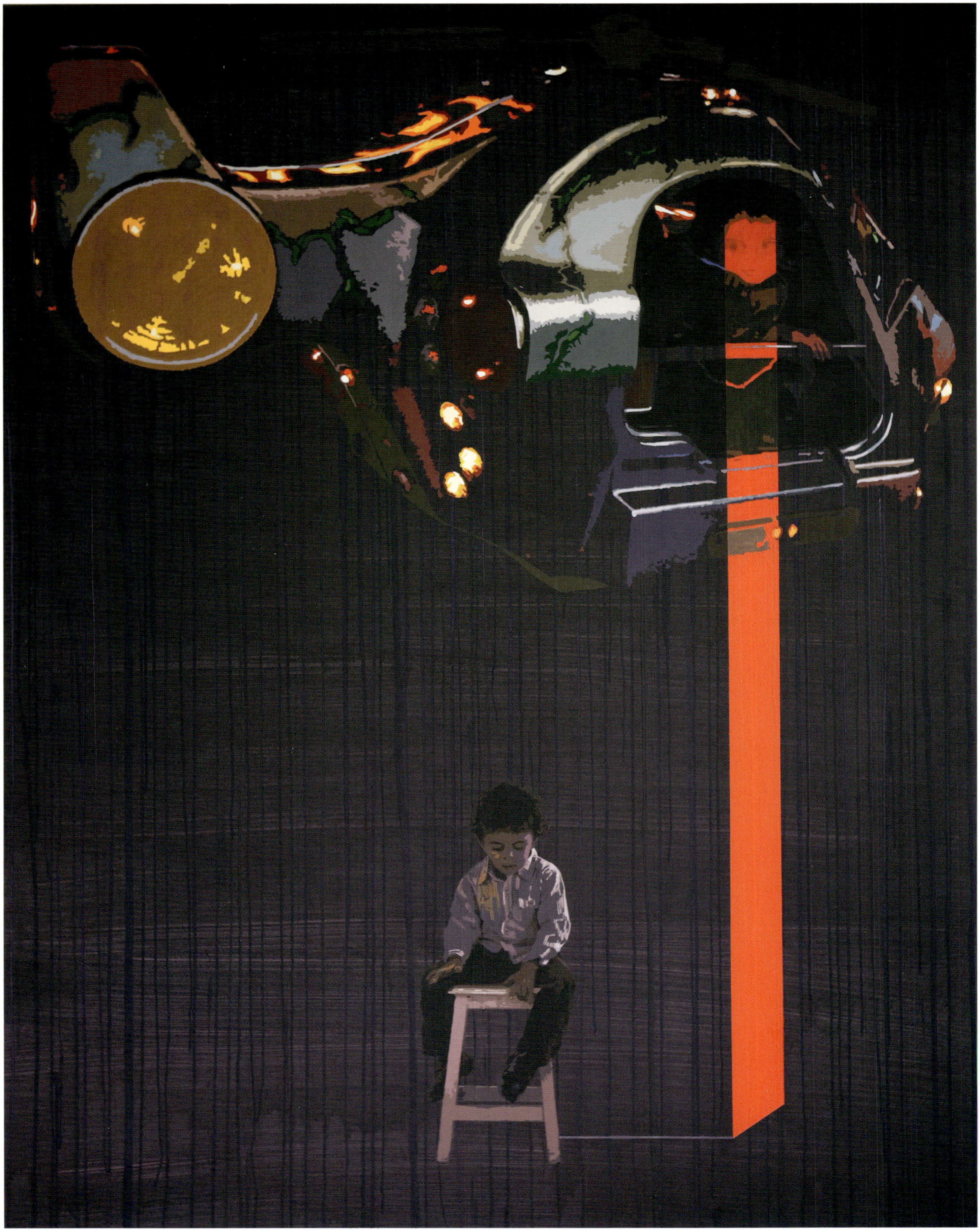

5.

Airborne

Leaving the Ground

Hani Zurob embarked on the painting series *Flying Lesson* soon after his return from the airport where he accompanied Sabreen and Qudsi who were heading to Jerusalem. In his isolated state back in Essoyes, it was the snapshots that he and Sabreen had taken of their son at the airport and in their Paris apartment which he found himself going back to again and again that triggered the idea of the series.

Unknowingly to the Gaza artist, it was in Essoyes that Renoir had created all the canvases he painted of Claude, his youngest son, who was born there. In the temporary absence of his own son, Zurob sought to recapture in this series not only what that absence meant to him as a father but more importantly to consider the broader significance of the boy's flight in the context of his own palpable experience of exile. One cannot help but think that because the very word "lesson" in the series' title implies expectation of a subsequent act, suggesting training and exercise or the initiation of a process that envisions a more advanced stage of knowledge, its implications infer *time*. In contrast, the word "flying", which implies the penetration of *space*, takes on a metaphoric significance representing a boundless step in some rite of passage between two distant points whose associative meanings are beyond what is simply meant by the contemporary convenience of air travel.

Flying Lesson no. 8, 2011.
Acrylic and pigments on canvas,
200 x 160 cm.

To grasp the significance of what Zurob sought to express through the metaphor of 'flying', it is worthwhile considering the cultural background and the contextual setting in which he operated. To bring that into play, the following pages scan how 'flying' figured in traditional Arab culture, how this subject and its affiliations has more recently assumed expression in works by fellow Palestinian artists and finally how connotative associations of flying have been revived in popular mythmaking. By bearing in mind these three interrelated areas, we gain a bird's eye view of the grounds in which Zurob's originality unfolded.

The subject of flying occupied a prominent role in the Islamic spiritual tradition as well as in Arabic secular literature of science and the fantastic. The one and only miracle in Islam that was cited in the Holy Qur'an was one of flying, namely that of the Arab Prophet's Night Journey (*al-Isra' wa al-Mi'raj*), which is believed to have been undertaken on a winged stallion named *al-Buraq*, a word deriving from *barq*, meaning "lightening". The journey proceeded from his place in Medina to Jerusalem, and from its Holy Rock he ascended into heaven wherefrom he returned to Medina before dawn. Over the centuries, this supreme mystical experience of the Prophet generated an extensive body of literature and its image occupied a central position in Islamic miniatures and popular arts.[1]

By the ninth century Abbas Ibn Firnas of Cordova was credited for being "the first man in history to make a scientific attempt at flying".[2] In the field of philosophy, it was through the image of the "Flying Man" that the tenth century Islamic philosopher Avicenna communicated the nature of self-consciousness and how the soul possesses an innate awareness of itself. The philosopher's description of his "Flying Man" portrays a suspended man born full-grown with eyes closed. He would be "moving in the air or void, in such a way that the density of the air would not touch him that he might sense it. And his limbs would be, as it were, spread out in such a way that they would not come together or touch one another." He proceeds "in full wakefulness to knowing that the being of his soul is other than the being of his body. Indeed he does not need the body in order to know the soul and perceive it".[3]

While Avicenna's hypothetical "Flying Man" furthered religious studies and metaphysical treatises in the Islamic tradition concerning the distinction between soul and body, in Western culture it was viewed as a thought experiment that prefigured by six centuries the Cartesian notion of the self upon which both Sartre and Derrida elaborated the concept earlier summed up in Descartes' notorious proposition, "I think therefore I am."

As for the field of fantastic literature, the *Thousand and One Nights* whose earliest Arabic manuscript goes back to the second half of the thirteenth century, the tales including episodes on the "Flying Carpet" and on Sinbad the Sailor being carried off by the *Rokh*, a gigantic bird capable of carrying elephants, continue to inspire science fiction writers and charming audiences of all ages throughout the world.[4]

Homo Viator

In contemporary Palestinian art a number of visual artists have been haunted by the subject of flying. In their works, each artist has found different means and forms of expression to imply individual metaphoric connotations often initiated by the artist's life experience. Over the last six decades, their work has varied from employing the most representational form of expression to the most abstract conceptualisation of the subject. A brief discussion of some of their works will contextualise Zurob's rendering of the subject.[5]

Among the post-1948 generation, Ahmad Na'wash ('Ain Karem 1934) stands out as one of the earliest artists who alluded to the subject of flying. He was 14 years old when all the inhabitants of his village outside Jerusalem were forced to run for their lives under a hail of bullets. Growing up in a refugee camp in Amman, his paintings have never ceased to be crowded with frail gesticulating human figures that float in the void. Flatly

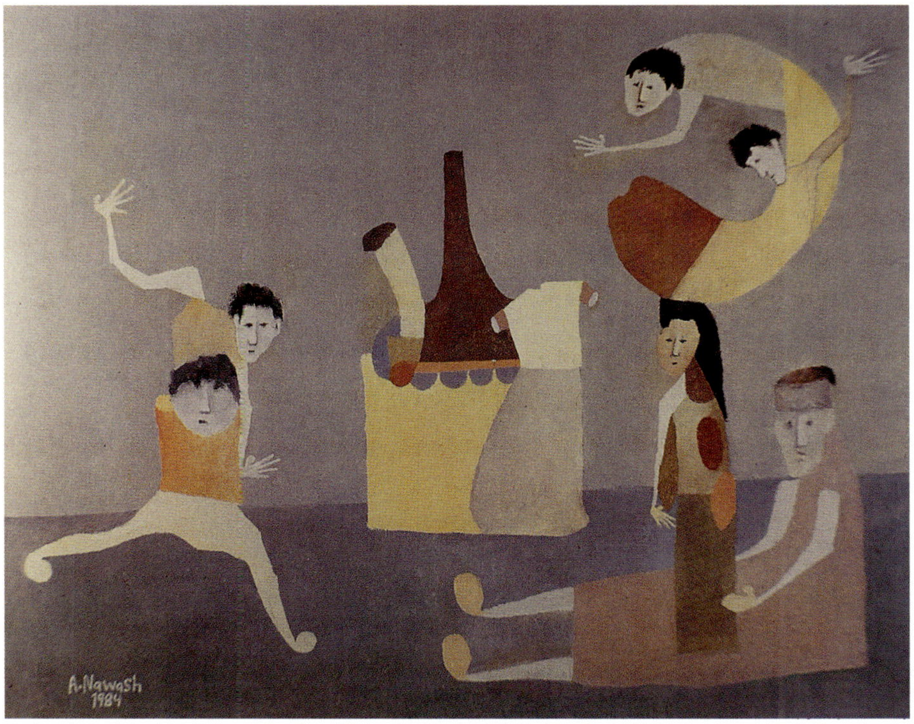

Ahmad Na'wash
The story of my Country, 1984.
Acrylic on wood, 72 x 93 cm.

rendered, they all look like marionette characters in a surreal world. Some are dismembered as they defy gravity while others are repeatedly seen flying in mid-air.[6]

From the generation who were born in refugee camps and who grew up under the Israeli military occupation, two specific artists' earliest paintings drew upon the subject of flying. In the early 1980s, Taysir Barakat (Gaza 1959) painted a dream world in which he improvised on scenes of barefoot children flying in roseate and balmy skies above their humble dwellings. By the decade's end, Jawad Malhi (Jerusalem 1969) included flying figures in dramatic paintings charged with the symbolic portrayal of death and rebirth. With the advent of the twenty-first century and the international spread of media arts including video, installation, performance, photography and digitally-generated imagery, a number of Palestinian media artists have explored the subject of flying.

Speaking of today's artist as "*homo viator* whose passage through signs and formats highlights a contemporary experience of mobility, displacement, [and] crossing", Nicolas Bourriaud described "fiction as vehicle and the journey as a kind of drawing".[7] A number of Palestinian media artists belonging to the same generation have employed fiction in their address of flying and journeying. Works by three artists in which the subject is manifested through fiction will be briefly described before works by two other media artist whose work may not directly fit under the same rubric but nevertheless falls under what Bourriaud calls an "aesthetics of expeditions" based on "composition by journey".[8]

In 2006, Khalil Rabah (Jerusalem 1961) created an installation titled *United States of Palestine Airlines, London Office*. It represented what looks like an impeccably sanitised fictional travel agency with a large model aeroplane carrying a fictitious name with a fictitious logo, both of which are free from any Arabic wording on the model of the fictitious national airline. The desolate and lifeless place dressed up in white is furnished with empty sofas, empty display cabinets, several non-functioning clocks and a world map with anomalous colour arrangement. The message communicates without further words the impossibility of flying to Palestine, a country defragmented in the artist's imagination into a "united states".

In contrast to Rabah's static installation, in 2008 Larissa Sansour (Jerusalem 1973) released a lively five-minute video entitled *A Space Exodus* that is full of magic and tongue-in-cheek humour with a political bite. Inspired by Stanley

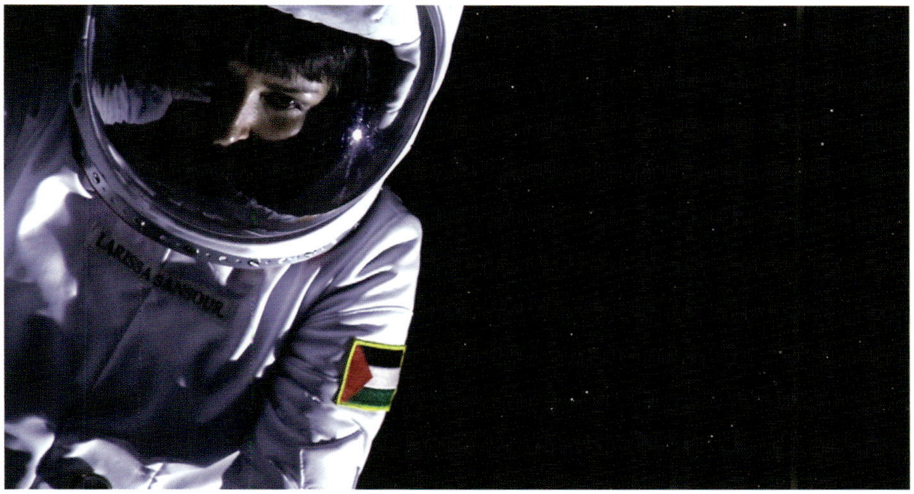

Kubrick's *2001: A Space Odyssey*, we see the *homo viator* artist sporting her astronaut's suit and journeying to the moon where she ultimately plants the Palestinian flag. Summoning state-of-the-art technological imagery and concocting the low gravity of her galactic environment, the Palestinian woman astronaut seen bouncing lightly on the moon surface to the Arabised version of the musical score of the 1968 science fiction film disorients and tickles the viewer. Israel may indeed wish the moon could be the place to send all Palestinians to, but as Sansour unravelled a glimpse of that dark universe she also offered her viewer the weightlessness of freedom.

Between the grounded air traveller imagined in Rabah's installation and Sansour's astronaut penetrating outer space, the subject of flying has also been pursued in key films by Elia Suleiman (Nazareth 1960). In fact, some of the most spectacular episodes of his surreal and wryly humorous films include vignettes relishing variations of flying.

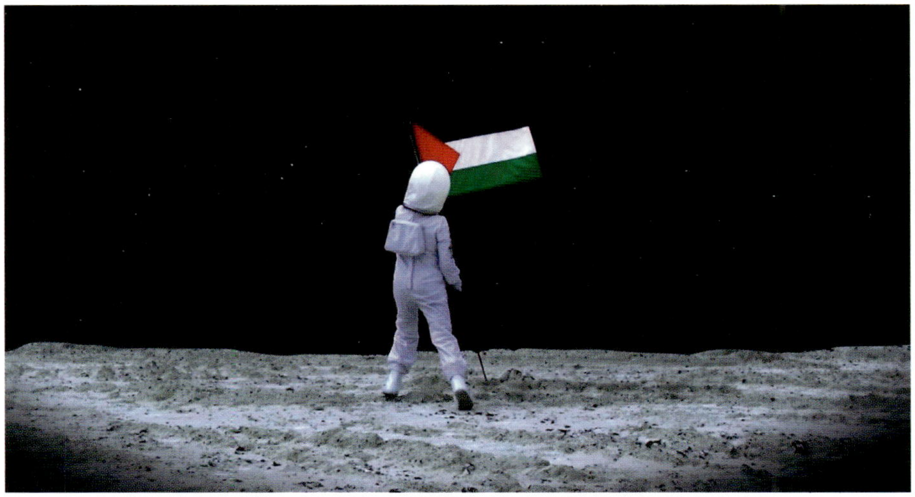

Larissa Sansour
A Space Exodus, 2009.
Video 5 minutes 24 seconds.

In his 2002 *Divine Intervention*, a red balloon adorning the smiling face of Yasser Arafat is released by Suleiman, who plays the leading role in the film. The balloon bouncing off the Apartheid Wall gently flies up into the open sky. Israeli soldiers wrangle among themselves, not sure whether to shoot the balloon down or await instructions. In the meantime, the balloon unabashed continues its flight over the Old City of Jerusalem and finally settles over the Dome of the Rock.[9]

In a concluding episode of the film, the woman protagonist impersonating 'divine intervention' appears as a Palestinian ninja wearing the *kafiyyeh* peasant headdress popularised by the national freedom fighters. Versed in martial arts, she is endowed with the superpowers of the mythical Zen warriors. With the speed of a whirling tornado she suddenly flies vertically upwards in mid-air to dodge a hail of bullets whistling by and takes on every one of the Israeli soldiers who had been using her image as a target on a firing range.

In his 2009 film *The Time that Remains*, Suleiman, whose deadpan satirical gags have been likened to Jacques Tati and Buster Keaton, is seen facing the Apartheid Wall and holding on a jumping pole. He takes a gigantic leap above the Wall that is three times the height of what the Berlin Wall was. The leap was rendered with the grace of an athlete and a long shot shows him flying unscathed over to the other side.

While Rabah's installation on the subject of flying may be classified in terms of what art critic TJ Demos refers to as a "monologic" fictional work wherein the viewer remains a passive observer, Sansour's video and Suleiman's films, drawing upon the same subject, employ all the digitalised wizardry of science fiction imagery available to present 'dialogic' works in which, in Demos' words, "exile becomes a shared experience between artist and viewer alike, suggesting the basis of an emergent political construction".[10]

Recovery of Distance

An imagination that is unbound by conventions, whereby smiles and laughter may be shared with the artist as well as with other viewers liberated by the farcical absurdities of fictitious scenes, is perhaps one of the artist's finest tools of resistance. Yet, when Emily Jacir (Bethlehem 1970) takes on the subject of flying, or rather the impossibility of flying home for far-off exiled Palestinians, she confronts the subject head on, with an imagination that is free from fiction. Simultaneously, she recalls how even Palestinians living on home grounds are not allowed by the Israeli military authorities to move freely within their country of birth. Her mock of such absurdities along with her indulgence in the ugly details of reality give birth to a 'dialogical' art of resistance, which is fired by an imagination imbued with pure poetry.

Two works of hers created over the two-year period 2002–2004 complete each other. One is an installation that invites a smile at an absurdity and the other is a series of 32 photographs with text documenting the grim realities of Palestinian exiles together with their compatriots who continue living at home.

Inspired by the luggage conveyer belts that are found in the arrival halls of airports everywhere, Jacir designed a sculptural installation composed of stainless steel and a rubber belt operated by a self-acting motor. Her model appears identical to a regular conveyor belt and runs like one, except that it assumes a circular form. Any luggage placed on it would only turn around in a vicious cycle. The key code to this absurd-looking conveyor belt unfolds when the viewer approaches to observe it at a closer range or to read its title. The motor automatically switches on and the rubber belt begins to turn around. Proximity between the body of a human being and the machine triggers a response that earns the work the title *Embrace*. With this single word, the viewer is reminded how the anticipated embrace of a missed person at the end of an airport conveyor belt is precluded here, as is the case with Palestinians who cannot fathom flying home.

In 2002–2003, Emily Jacir sought through a project she titled *Where We Come From* to act on behalf of fellow Palestinians who were prohibited from making the trip home and stand for her besieged people living under Israeli military occupation who could not move freely within their homeland. Becoming a naturalised US citizen allowed her according to Israeli immigration laws to travel back home only on a tourist visa. With such an opportunity, she is also permitted to cross Israeli military checkpoints with less dehumanising complications than would impede native residents living under Israel's military occupation. Thus before flying from New York on her expedition she had one question in mind to ask each of the participants in her art project. "If I could do something for you, anywhere in Palestine, what would it be?"

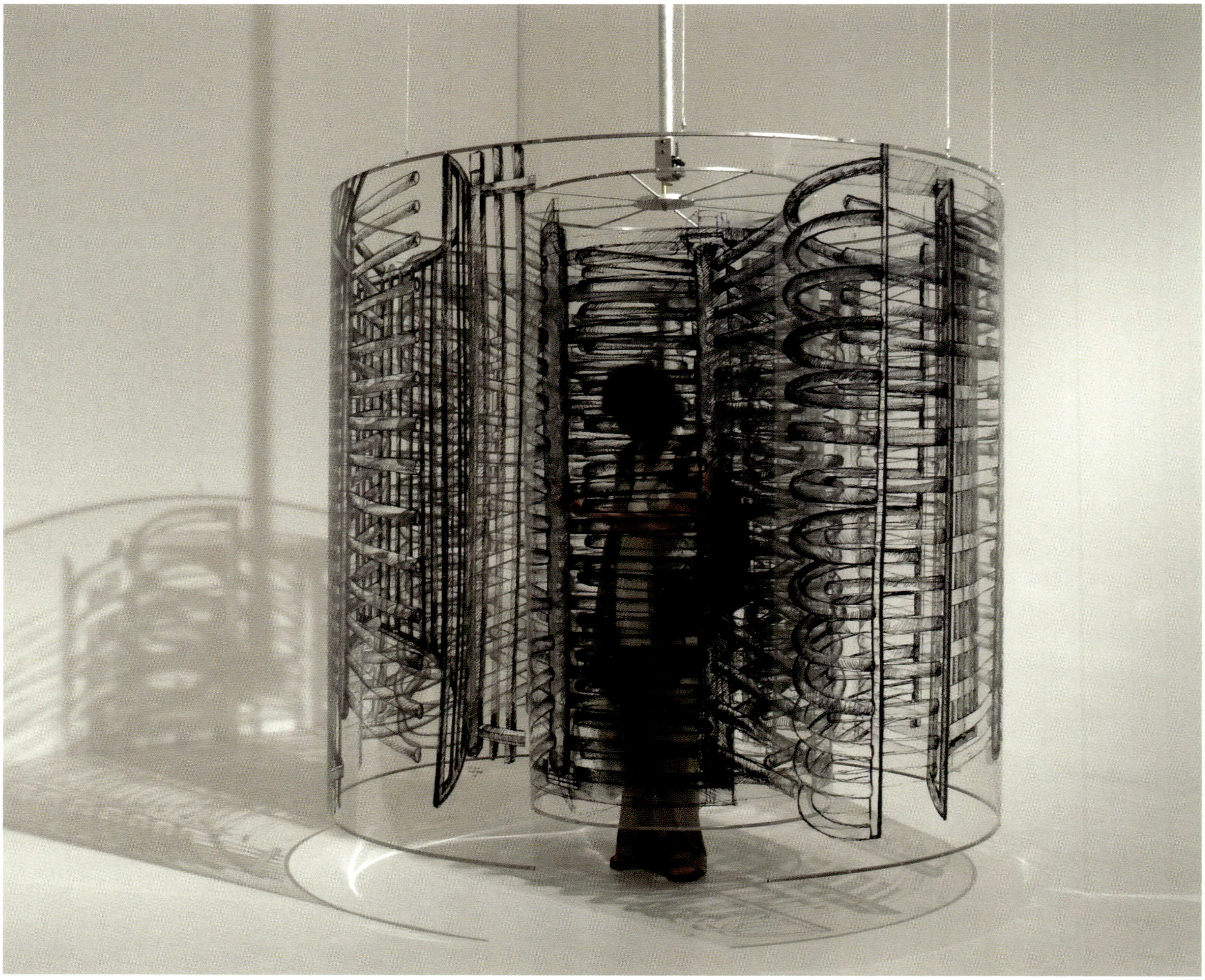

Samira Badran
Have a Pleasant Stay!
Installation. Transparent printed polyester with metallic rings, 200 x 220 cm.
Commissioned by the 9th Biennale of Sharjah, 2009.

Answers to her question varied from person to person. "Drink the water in my parents' village"; "go to Haifa and play soccer with the first Palestinian boy you see on the street"; "visit my mother, hug and kiss her and tell her that these are from her son"; "go to Bayt Lahia and bring me a photo of my family, especially of my brother's kids." Her art project thus comprised of her answers, appearing in Arabic with English translations, displayed next to photographs showing the artist carrying out the participants' requests.

TJ Demos commenting on Jacir's work writes, "when we view the piece, we become displaced, owing to the ambiguity of representation, to the divisions between text and image, and to the multiple stories and fragmented structures of identification". He then mentions the anecdote of a certain Munir who was born in Jerusalem and who lives and works in Bethlehem, a ten-minute car-ride south of Jerusalem. Though he carried a valid passport issued by the Palestinian Authority along with a West Bank Identity Card issued by the Israeli military authorities, Munir was denied an entry permit to Jerusalem on his mother's birthday. He now asked Jacir to go to his "mother's grave in Jerusalem on her birthday and put flowers and pray". The photograph of Jacir, who flew all the way from New York, shows her own shadow cast over the grave. Demos notes that the artist's "shadow also becomes ours as we gaze at the picture". Thus, he concluded through Jacir's work "we share a proximity with the excluded".[11]

Checkpoint

In a 2009 installation by Samira Badran (Tripoli 1954), the viewer does not merely "share a proximity with the excluded" but gets trapped within the claustrophobic space of a turnstile every Palestinian living under Israeli military occupation is squeezed through in the process of crossing from one sealed area to another. The daughter of refugee parents from Haifa who went to work in Libya soon after 1948, Badran who grew up in Ramallah and who has been living for the last three decades in Barcelona is a *homo viator* artist who, similarly to Jacir, is only permitted to visit her home country for the limited period granted to a tourist. Initiated by her intermittent trips, her art never ceases to be charged with an "aesthetic of expedition".

To reach Ramallah from Ben Gurion Airport Badran always has to go through the Qalandia checkpoint, which had become one of the West

Bank's largest checkpoints and is equipped with the most sophisticated surveillance systems in the occupied territories. By making the grounds of her work the daily experience of Palestinians attempting to cross the Qalandia checkpoint, she capsulates the microcosm of her people's dispossession as it unfolds in the oldest site of flying in Palestine.

Located between Jerusalem and Ramallah, the village of Qalandia was the site of the first airport in the country. It was built in the 1930s by the British Mandate authorities to serve as a military airport. After the 1948 debacle, when the salvaged Palestinian territories fell under the jurisdiction of Jordan and henceforth were identified as the West Bank in reference to the Jordan River, the village expanded into the site of the Qalandia refugee camp and the airfield was turned into a civilian airport. Throughout the two decades following Palestine's fall, as Jerusalem was a city divided between Jordan and Israel—in accordance with the 1948 ceasefire agreement—the Jerusalem Airport served as the Palestinian gateway to Arab capitals during a period that was characterised by the secular nationalist movement's call for Arab unity against all imperialist policies in the region.[12] In the meantime, three generations of boys growing up in the refugee camp adjacent to the airport have been recorded as having "had dreams of becoming airline pilots".[13]

With the fall of the rest of Palestine in 1967, the Israeli closure of the Jerusalem Airport announced the onset of the Palestinian ghetto. The annexed airfield was transformed into an Israeli domestic airport that eventually had to close down following the outbreak of the 2000 Uprising when kids from the refugee camp started hurling rocks at passing aircrafts. The original road block at Qalandia was converted into an Israeli army base with a watchtower, barricades and razor-barbed wires. In time, it evolved into the abominable monstrosity of a checkpoint called "terminal" by the Israelis with its labyrinthine iron-barred passageways looking more like cages for quarantined human beings. The few square kilometres of terrain on which the checkpoint was constructed are partly covered with a corrugated zincked roof ribbed by concrete walls. The 'terminal' is furnished with Israel's national pride in security fencing technology including high-tech surveillance cameras, magnetic spindle gates, iron pens and barriers, biometric devices, high-speed x-ray machines and multiple turnstiles automatically operated by remote control.

The single most outstanding characteristic of the Qalandia checkpoint however is how its hangar-like construction right next to the Apartheid Wall harbours the illusion of a mere border crossing between two sovereign states when everybody herded through its plethoric congestion of commuters knows that both sides of the checkpoint fall under Israel's control. The 'facade of legitimacy' it purports includes benches, waiting zones, iron queuing barriers, empty parking lots where no Palestinian car could reach. It also includes 'friendly welcome signs' in large Hebrew lettering followed by an Arabic translation with hollow slogans such as "Our Hope Together".[14]

After going through the first turnstile, the person facing a surveillance camera stands in a waiting zone for a signal from the Israeli soldier to proceed through another set of turnstiles. Topped with cheerful wishes the automatic set of turnstiles with their iron bars protruding in all directions recall attractive carnivorous plants like the Venus Flytrap whose leaves covered with spines snap shut its 'jaws' once its prey steps in. "Entry is one by one–Please await your turn patiently", warns one sign in three languages. Another became the title of Badran's installation.

Titled *Have a Pleasant Stay!*, Badran's installation represents the grinding machine by which Israel's brutal colonial policies of land confiscation and the destruction of living space are expressed in what a Palestinian sociologist calls a "*spacio-cide*".[15] "The system of spatial control", adds a Palestinian anthropologist, "is not simply about controlling and containing resistance but is primarily a mechanism of disinheritance".[16]

To fully apprehend Badran's installation whose height reaches that of the Qalandia turnstiles, there is no way for the observer to remain a passive outsider. The two attractive and transparent cylindrical structures enclosing the turnstiles are erected one inside the other. Operated by a small motor, every turnstile's rotation automatically switches on the recorded sounds of clanging metal. As each turnstile is composed of a chain of transparent polyester bars that look unthreatening, the wholly transparent installation invites the viewer to venture into it. Once inside the first cylinder, the asphyxiating space accompanied by the rattling and slamming sounds of the iron spindle gates forces one to seek the way out, only possible by going through the second cylinder with its protruding bars. One by one observers reenact passing through a checkpoint which a Palestinian media and communications expert describes as a space "in which solitude is experienced as an emptying of individuality as a temporal experience concerned only with the present task of passing through."[17]

The observer passing through Badran's installation may experience for a brief moment the suffocation of being trapped that every Palestinian commuter experiences at an Israeli checkpoint. It is only upon emerging from the transparent installation that the relieved observer may realise that Palestinian commuters of all ages who continue to line up daily to go to work, to school or to whatever takes them to the other side of a checkpoint are an obstinate breed of people who remain unhindered by Israel's latest inventions of brutality. Conquered but undefeated, they go on with their lives, and every daily crossing only reinforces each individual's determination to resist.

Flying Boy and Gaza Kites

Badran's form of dialogism contributed to cementing in Demos' words the "fragmented structures of identification" as much as works by Sansour, Suleiman and Jacir before her did. As for how dialogism manifests itself in Hani Zurob's *Flying Lesson* painting series, there are two key anecdotes involving flying that need to be briefly recounted. Separated by 22 years, the feat of imagination each incident radiates in the daily lives of Palestinians living under Israeli military occupation cannot be underestimated. The artist lived through both incidents that will be remembered for generations to come. The first flying incident expounded a lesson of mythical dimensions that eventually steered the course of the national struggle; the second represented a symbolic sign that boosted the popular call for freedom.

Hani was 11 years old when he, like all other children in the Rafah refugee camp, first heard grown-ups speaking with wonder and admiration about a heroic "flying boy". Details of the incident were scarce and unclear. The Israeli military censor had banned printing any details in the Palestinian-owned Arabic newspapers published in Jerusalem that usually reached Gaza late. Only banner headlines appearing in red announced a guerilla operation carried out by a Palestinian "flying boy". Thanks to radio reports from neighbouring Arab countries and for confirmations ascertained by an alarmed Israeli press, within days all details of what was to be referred to as the "Night of the Flying Boy" spread like wild fire throughout the refugee camps.

The guerilla operation took place during the moonless night of Wednesday 25 November 1987. A Palestinian youth born and raised in a refugee camp in Lebanon flew a homemade hang glider less than three metres long. Powered by a lawn mower-sized engine and a simple propeller, he buckled himself into position and set out on a night journey towards the land where all his forebears were born and from where he knew he would never return. He was carrying no food, neither torch, nor compass. He strapped himself with a light machine gun, a pistol with a silencer, and a few grenades. With both hands free he clung to a single tubular bar connected to the wings and occasionally shifted his body's weight to meet the favourable waft of wind.

The region he had to cross had been under the Israeli military occupation since Israel's 1982 invasion of Lebanon. There, Israel had built a 40 kilometre security zone that was honeycombed by heavily fortified bases buffered by security shields with a series of patrols and electronic fences equipped with the most sophisticated detection systems. For the "flying boy" to avoid detection, he had to buoyantly float at tree-top level. In the dead of night, he could have only heard the purring of his engine and the gentle beating of the cold wind against his nylon wings.

As soon as he was assured that he safely crossed the Israeli security zone, he landed in a field of thistles just north of the Israeli settlement of Qiryat Shemona, built in 1950 on the ruins of al-Khalisa, a Palestinian village whose original inhabitants were expelled in 1948. Many of the dispossessed villagers ended up living with their offspring in Nabatiyyeh refugee camp in southern Lebanon.

Leaving his glider behind resting on its tricycle wheels, he headed towards the nearby Gibor army encampment. On his way there, he spotted an army truck outside the base. With his pistol, he took out the driver and seriously wounded his companion. Hardly a sound was heard in the winter night save for the two muffled thuds. Upon crossing the road, he found himself standing before the entrance of the military camp. He hurled a hand grenade at the sentry and followed it by a spray of automatic gunfire. The guard panicked and ran away inside the army base. The Palestinian youth followed him there with more grenades and automatic fire killing five soldiers and wounding six others before one of the wounded soldiers managed to shoot him down.

The following morning, the Popular Front for the Liberation of Palestine-General Command announced its responsibility for the operation.
A photograph of the anonymous freedom fighter with his glider that

was taken just before his nocturnal journey was distributed to the international press. The smiling face in the photograph showed a youth only a few years older than Hani was at the time.

By the time the full story reached people throughout the Gaza Strip and the West Bank, the anonymous kid who managed to penetrate the heavily guarded security zone on what children understood to be a homemade 'gigantic kite' and who single-handedly stormed an Israeli army base killing six soldiers, was overnight turned into a mythic hero. In Gaza, Israeli patrol troops were taunted by Palestinian kids crying out "six to one". On the walls of the refugee camps "6:1" was the freshest graffiti to sum up the birth of a legend.

Offended Israeli soldiers started shooting live ammunition in the direction of kids who undauntedly faced them with a hail of stones. Within days, street confrontations between kids and units of the Israeli army spread out from one refugee camp to the other. Propelled by an imagination only schoolchildren revelled in, an uprising against 21 years of military occupation was soon to encompass the entire population of the Gaza Strip and the West Bank. Spearheaded by children, the popular uprising referred to as the "Intifada" evolved into a primarily non-violent movement, calling for civil disobedience, general strikes, boycotts of Israeli products and refusal to pay taxes. Though the ultimate price the children, their parents and their relatives had paid has been painfully high, the hope that the movement inspired was eventually to turn a new page in the history of the Palestinian people's struggle for freedom.[18]

The other incident involving flying took place more recently. It was not as much of a political catalyst as the "flying boy" incident was, but it was not any less significant as it took place in an equally calamitous period for the Palestinians. Only five months after Israel's massive military assault on the besieged people of the Gaza Strip in which some 1,400 Palestinians were killed including more than 300 children, the United Nations Works and Relief Agency (UNRWA) included in its summer camp for children a competition day for flying kites.

The day was set for Thursday 30 July 2009. This was a dream of a competition for the children who were known to have never ceased to fly their homemade kites in their separate neighbourhoods whenever the skies were clear and free from Israeli warplanes. Organised on the beach near Bayt Lahia in the North, boys and girls from all the Gaza Strip travelled there that day with their homemade kites.

Apparently, the dream of flying had not been confined to children who survived Israel's wars and who continued to live under a never-ending blockade imposed by Israel in compliance with the Egyptian government. Two months before that day, an American writer travelling to Gaza with a delegation of journalists noted "everywhere we go we see these kites". During her visit she wrote that she met a number of grown-ups in Gaza who confided to her that at night, "when they close their eyes they float up from their beds, through their windows, beyond the lights of the patrolling Israeli ships and armed trucks, and out into the night sky, free to roam the world".[19]

According to *The Guinness Book of World Records*, the number of kites flying simultaneously and in the same place had been set the previous year at 967. That day, Gaza's children smashed the official record reaching 3,710 kites flying simultaneously. For that one day, it was the boys and girls of Gaza who ruled the skies way above the Israeli army vehicles stationed across the barbed wire fence in the distance.

The Artist's Child

After putting the final touches on *Untitled*, the one painting in which his own features have been clearly defined for the first time, Hani Zurob seemed to conclude a whole cycle of works through which he had been wrestling with a leitmotif that preoccupied him for years, namely his self-representation within his compositions. Having moved on from suggesting his own face in his expressionistic paintings created in Ramallah, which attempted to speak of the self as a hermeneutic vehicle of the other, to the crowning figure contorting his own likeness in the earliest experimental series he completed following his arrival in Paris; and from the suggested features he superimposed over his gestural abstractions in his attempt to capture the memory of his Gaza childhood to the concealed faces interchanged between the self and the Palestinian other which ended up engrafted in a succession of portraits reduced to black blobs of tar that he finished painting just before leaving for his residency in Essoyes, the underlying process that evolved over the preceding six years in regards to the subject fixation he upheld may be summed up in the way the artist spurred his imagination, ultimately leading him to replace the mirror with the photograph. Zurob's *Flying Lesson* series is mainly comprised of large paintings whose compositions proceed from a photographic image. This time, the photograph is not of himself but of his son Qudsi.

At first glance, the general viewer may wonder: how come the father is so obsessed with exclusively picturing his son in his new series of paintings? Does his identification with Qudsi go as far as to nullify his old self from the picture? Could the artist see his child's biological resemblance to him as being commensurate with his own appearance so that the child as the subject of his painting substitutes the artist's earlier interpretations of his own features? In such a case, would any painting in the *Flying Lesson* series relate to the Gaza artist's memory of the "flying boy" incident he lived through as a child? Or, to what extent was the 2009 series prickled by the thrill of his homeland's children who during the same year gained a world record in flying kites, weaving the Gaza skies with colour?

Most importantly, how does the metaphor of flying in Zurob's painting allegorise the relationship between the father and the son as each goes on his own journey in a different direction: the child obliged to fly away from his father every six months to be in Jerusalem with his mother, while the artist pursues an inward journey to find expression to his own *longing* for the child during his absence; an expression which is inseparably associated with the sense of *be-longing* the parents wish to instil in him?[20]

Hani Zurob is not the only Palestinian artist whose child had inspired his art. Steve Sabella (Jerusalem 1975) who happened to be a close friend of his had preceded him in creating a series of works that were triggered by photographs of his firstborn. As a prelude to the discussion on Zurob's last series of paintings, examining his friend Sabella's work reveals how two artists differ in giving expression to a vital concern of Palestinians whose children are growing up in exile.

Sabella had never heard Cecile, his three year old daughter, utter a single word in Arabic, a fact which baffled him. Though she was born in his city of birth, the only words she babbled had been in the German of her Swiss mother, a language he does not understand. In 2007, however, after leaving Jerusalem to pursue his graduate studies in London, one day within three months of the family's arrival there he could not believe his ears when he heard Cecile address him with a sentence he could fully understand.

Flying Lesson no. 5, 2010.
Acrylic and pigments on canvas, 200 x 160 cm.

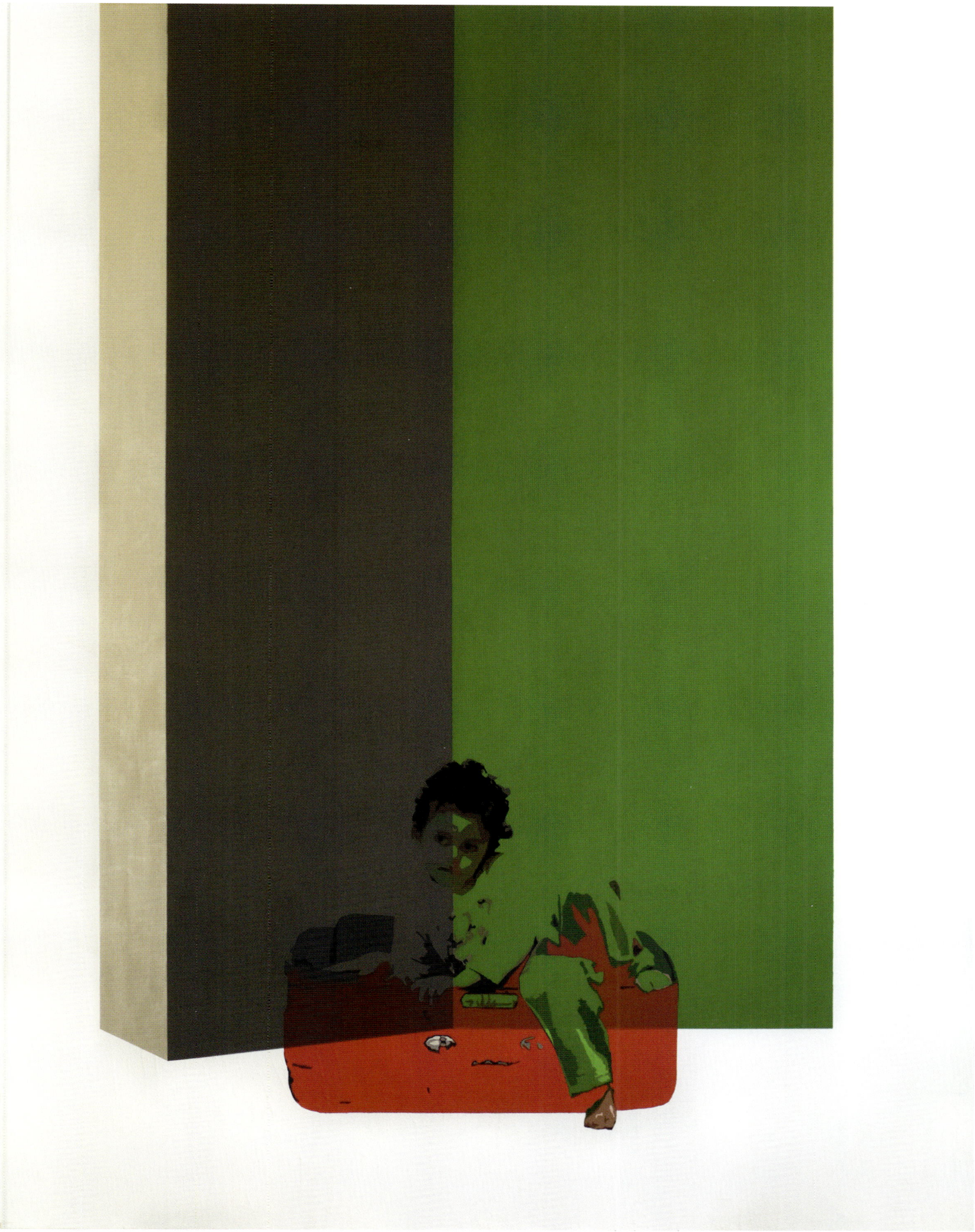

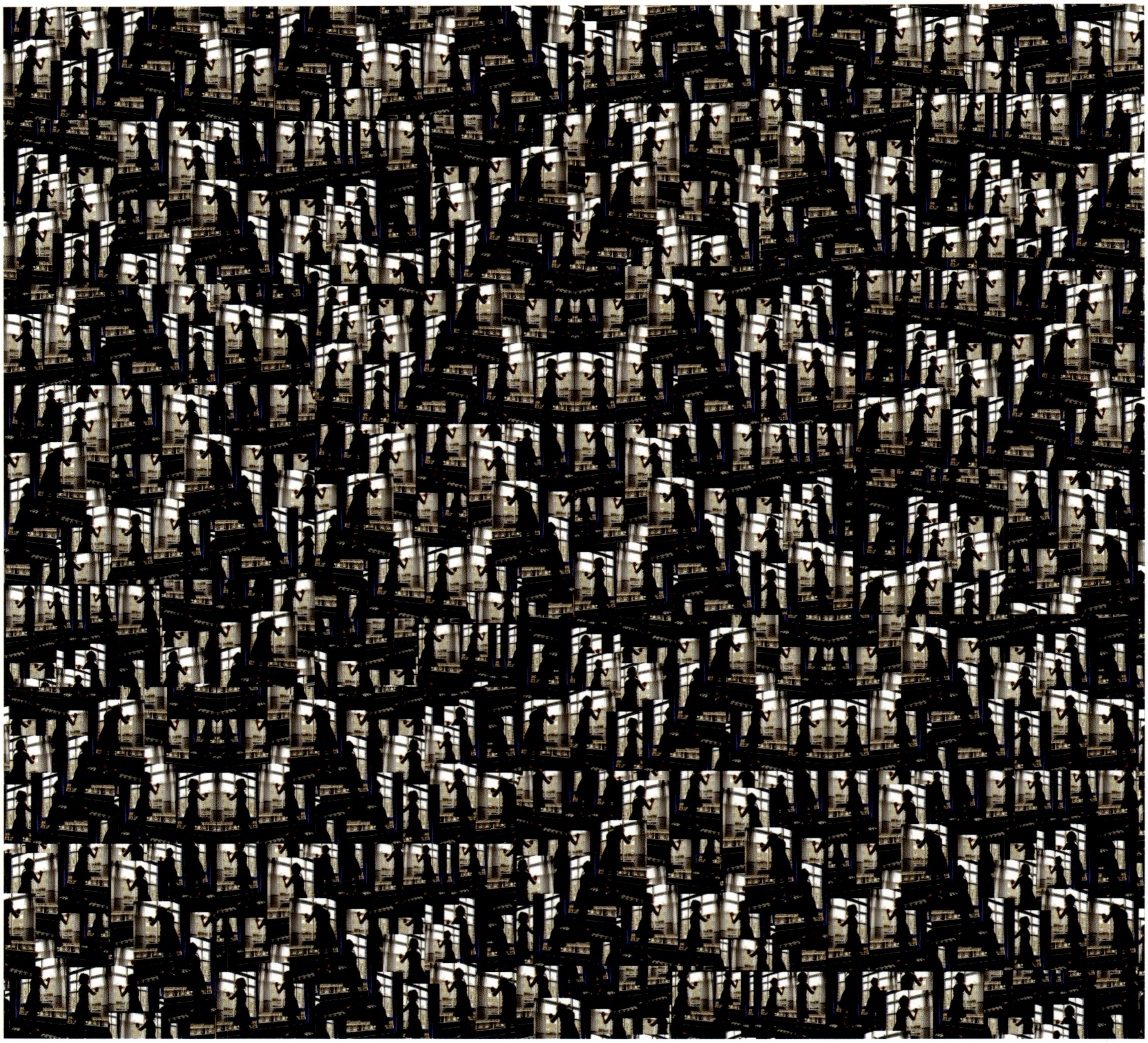

Steve Sabella
In Exile, 2008.
Lambda print mounted
on aluminium 125 x 136 cm.

It was expressed in English, her parent's common language. During that revelatory instant, he happened to be snapping photographs of her as she sat on the window ledge of their apartment looking out to a wintry sky. She broodingly said to him, "I want to go back home to Jerusalem!"

For the first time the father realised that his daughter shared with him the same sense of belonging and that she felt as disoriented and estranged as he was since their arrival in London. By 2008, photographs of her against the window panes shot from inside their apartment in addition to photographs taken of the windows from outside their building were the kernel with which Sabella created a series of five photomontages that he entitled *In Exile.* The reconstruction of photographic fragmentations depicting Cecile and the windows viewed from the inside and the outside, present us with a metaphor alluding in its structure to the experience of deracination the father and daughter shared.

Gaston Bachelard wrote that "outside and inside form a dialectic of division, the obvious geometry of which blinds us as soon as we bring it into play in metaphorical domains".[21] Sabella's reconstructed fragmentations of the two sides of the same windows represents his metaphor's embodiment of 'home' and 'exile'. By allegorising what Bachelard went on to call "the dialectics of here and there", Sabella gave a visual body to the "awareness of simultaneous dimensions" that Edward Said wrote in his description of the experience of the exiled.[22]

Using a computer program, each work in the series is composed of a multitude of digitalised miniature photographs of the windows shot from both sides. Each photograph taken from a slightly different angle acts as a unit in an overall abstract image. The combination of variable units and their alternating repetition weave together an infinite field of fragmentations denoting intricate patterns, symmetries and geometric traceries that recall prevalent characteristics in Islamic art.

During the same year, in an attempt to get a more intimate expression of the bond cemented with his daughter through their shared experience of exile, Sabella sought to carry further the metaphor of his "dialectic of division" from one between the architectonic inside and outside of their common abode to the centrifugal dialectic between the internal and external sides of Cecile's shell. To do so, he took close-up photographs of the two sides of textiles appertaining to clothes she wears. Composed of 14 photographs, the ultimate work included a video and an artist's book containing cut-outs of textiles. The project was simply titled *Cecile Elise Sabella*.

Whereas the series *In Exile* was all composed in the sombre primacy of black and white, all images in its sequel were gently toned with pastel colours. Texture which has only been inferred in his geometric reconstructions is in his photographs and cut-outs, which mostly trace floral patterns, the main subject of observation. Sabella invites us in his artist's book to turn page after page and contemplate the countless nuances of texture between both sides of the same material. The tactile aesthetics he proposed allow us to recall the Japanese saying which likens a poem in its original language to silk embroidery and its translation to the back side of the embroidered textile.

Two artists and fellow travellers with children growing up away from home may find their inspiration in their offspring, but each goes his own way when it comes to interpreting his relationship with the child. The anecdote inducing the work of one takes mythical dimensions in the work of the other. As much as Sabella's art has been motivated by an instinctive drive, where his metaphoric language could only be expressed through the interpolations of abstraction, Zurob's work has remained reflexive; his art abounding with metaphors is rooted in figuration. Consequently, after completing his two sequels of work inspired by his daughter, Sabella moved on to explore themes beyond the sphere of his paternal life. In contrast, Zurob appears to have never ceased to rediscover themes in which his son takes centre stage in his painting.

Flying Lesson

Hani Zurob launched his *Flying Lesson* series with a diptych. It was the first diptych he ever painted. Unknowingly, the artist adopted a painting format whose history, going back to the Byzantine tradition, had always been associated with travelling. It was first used as a portable icon composed of two equal panels that were joined together with hinges to allow them to be folded for protection during the journey and be unfolded for prayers upon reaching one's destination.

Flying Lesson no. 9, 2011.
Acrylic and pigments on canvas, 81 x 65 cm.

Zurob's diptych, however, whose horizontal dimensions exceed two metres long, is the largest he has explored thus far in his career. And as the tradition of portable diptych brought together emblematic images

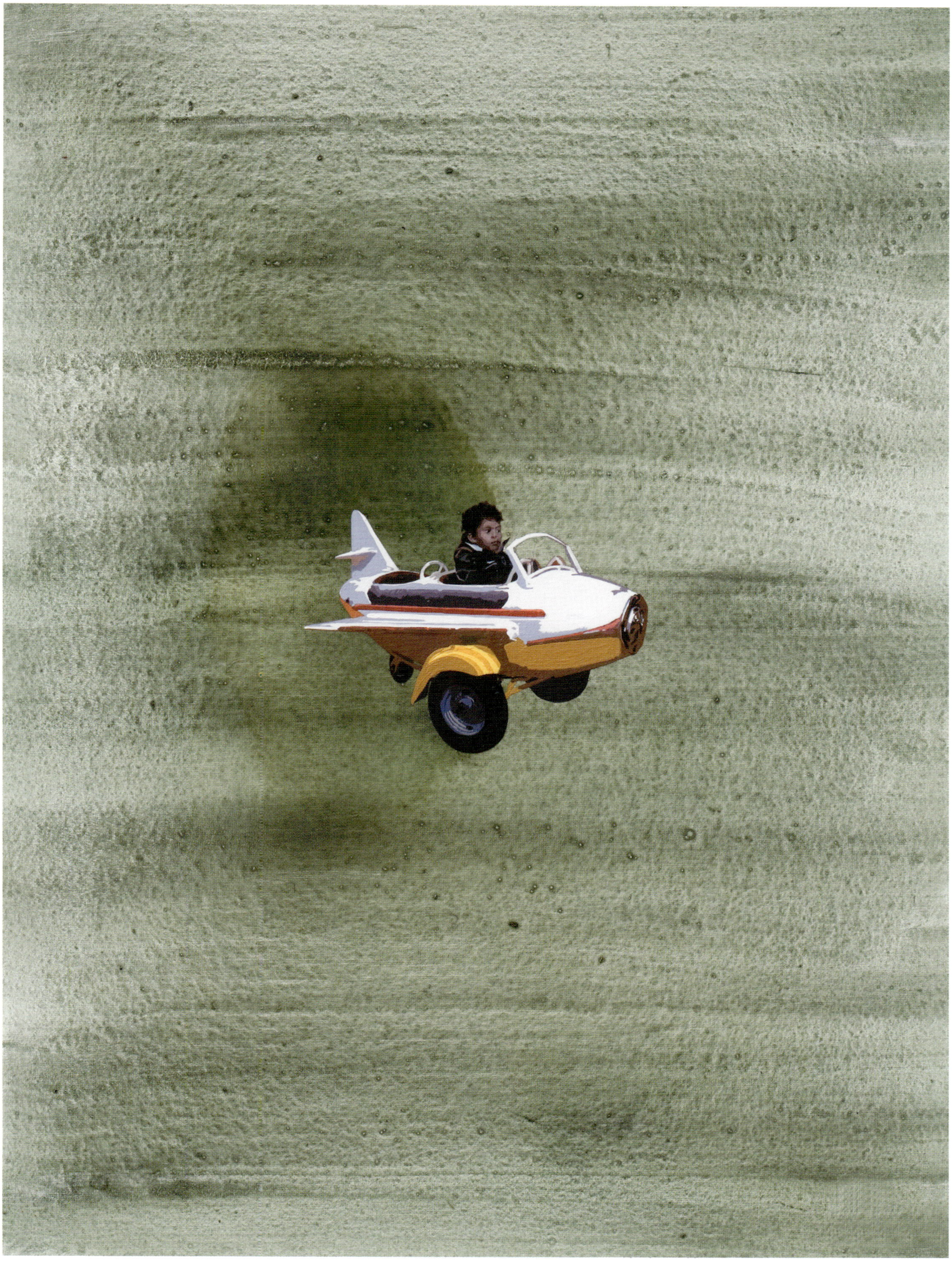

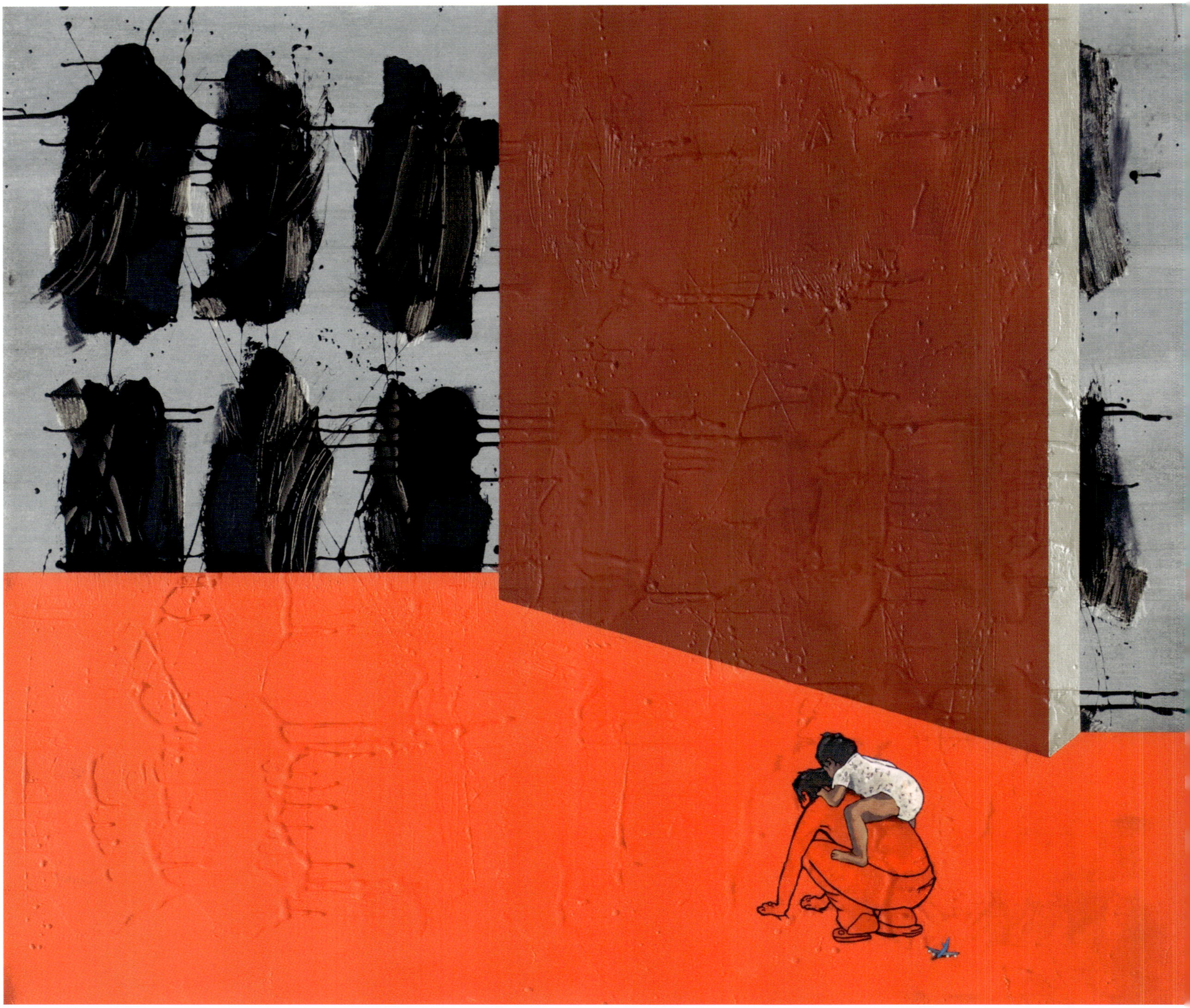

Flying Lesson no. 1, 2009.
Acrylic, oil, tar, pigments
on canvas, 100 x 240 cm.

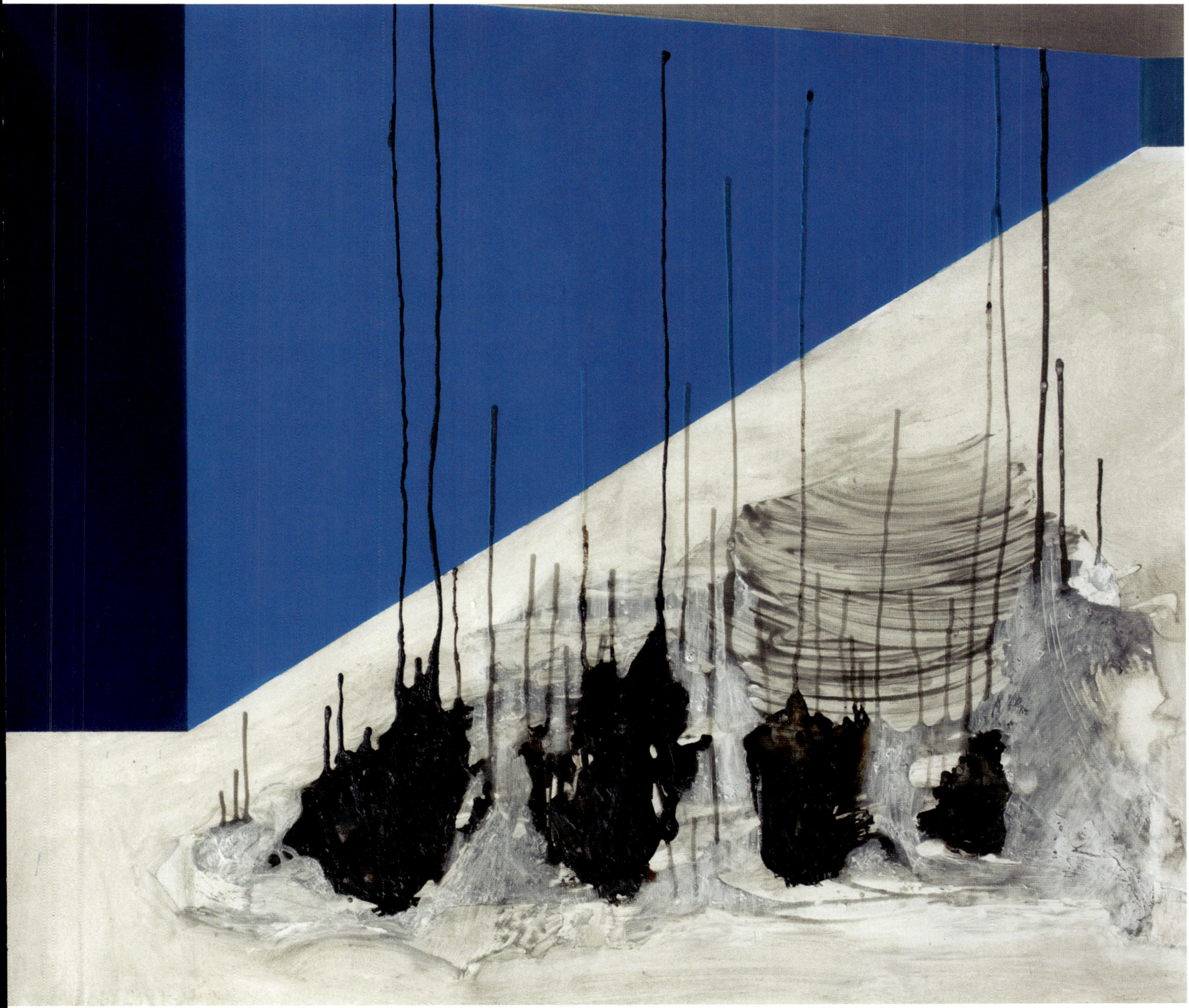

representing two worlds, the physical on one panel and the metaphysical on the other, Zurob's two canvases bring together emblematic images from his own two worlds, that of the present in which he is living and the one of the future that he is dreaming for his child.

In the extended timeframe he braces together to embody his two worlds, the artist's own figure appears diminished within the diptych's composition. In all the series subsequent paintings, it is totally absent. But the most radical components marking his departure from earlier work is not that the artist's child occupies a central stage in every painting of the series but in the precision Zurob displays in reproducing his son's photographic image and more importantly in how he has turned away from the allover free-flowing gestural expression to arrive at the hard-edged definition of flat colour fields. *Flying Lesson no. 1*, whose title epitomises the whole series, is the only painting that retains traces of gestural expression amidst the razor-edged definition of its solid colour planes.

The two canvases of the diptych, whose composition is structurally linked, stretch out like an open book. The composition's reading leads the eye to move from right to left in the same direction as reading Arabic script. For a more comprehensive apprehension of the opposite sides of the painting, however, one's eye has to exercise what I call "a stereoscopic reading" whereby only by simultaneously relating images from both canvases, each of which represents different moments in time, the painting's full dimensions may be appreciated.

In a right to left reading, the first component of the painting upon which the eye falls on is the dominant block of space in white sharply sliding across the right canvas. The space traces the silhouette of the now familiar image of the Apartheid Wall Israel built in the West Bank. Viewed in perspective, The Wall's glaring whiteness amidst the solidity of adjacent opaque colours evokes the sensation of an after-image. Just as an after-image is a temporary visual sensation which ceases once its external cause fades, the void assuming The Wall's massive shape seems to suggest its eventual disappearance. In the meantime, whirls and dripping blobs of tar smearing The Wall's absence do not gravitate downwards as the whole space imagined by the artist appears lopsided. The drippings of tar thus appear to sprout upwards as wild shrubs in a wasteland.

In such a warped and disorienting world, a stereoscopic reading allows us to adjust our eyes to see how the illusion of space assumes opposite angles of vision. In the right canvas, which represents the exterior appearance of the artist's prediction, one's eye is led to look from the ground up on The Wall against the weight of a steel blue sky. In contrast, in the left canvas, which displays an interior space, the eye is led to look from the perspective of a low-flying helicopter down to the ground which is carpeted with the colour of dried blood. Going back and forth between the colours of blue and blood, as between the two angles of vision, allows one to see, as in a theatrical setting, how each side of the spectacle placidly flows into the other the way a present moment slips into the past and an experience in the present leads into an anticipated moment in the future.

To avoid past traumas for the child who could not understand why his father could not travel with him and his mother, a toy passenger aircraft with tiny rolling wheels had been bought for Qudsi to prepare him for his upcoming trip. The photograph showing the two year old mounted on his father's back and trailed by the toy captures the crouching artist on the brink of demonstrating the first lesson in flying. It was snapped by Sabreen's cell-phone days before the boy was to take his first flight to his mother's city of birth.

The figure of the barefoot child mounted on the back of his father, who assumes the position of his child in the *Heritage* painting, is the first element the eye notes in the boxed space of the left canvas. Casting no

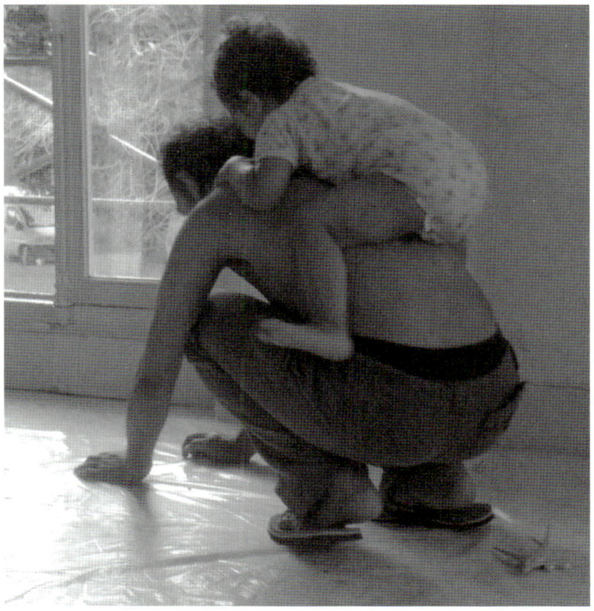

The artist and his son at home, Paris, 2009

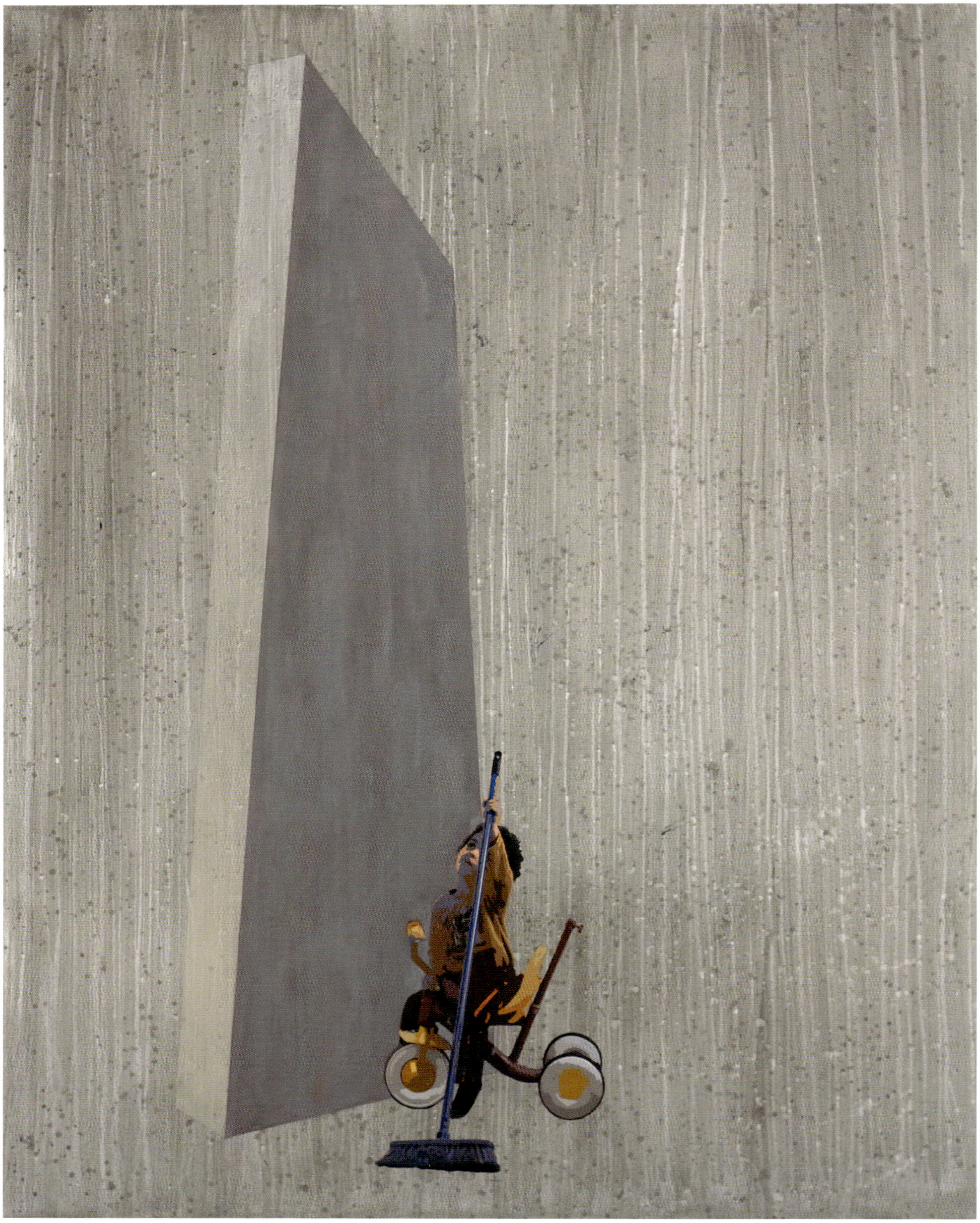

Flying Lesson no. 6, 2010.
Acrylic and pigments on canvas,
200 x 160 cm.
Private collection, Dubai.

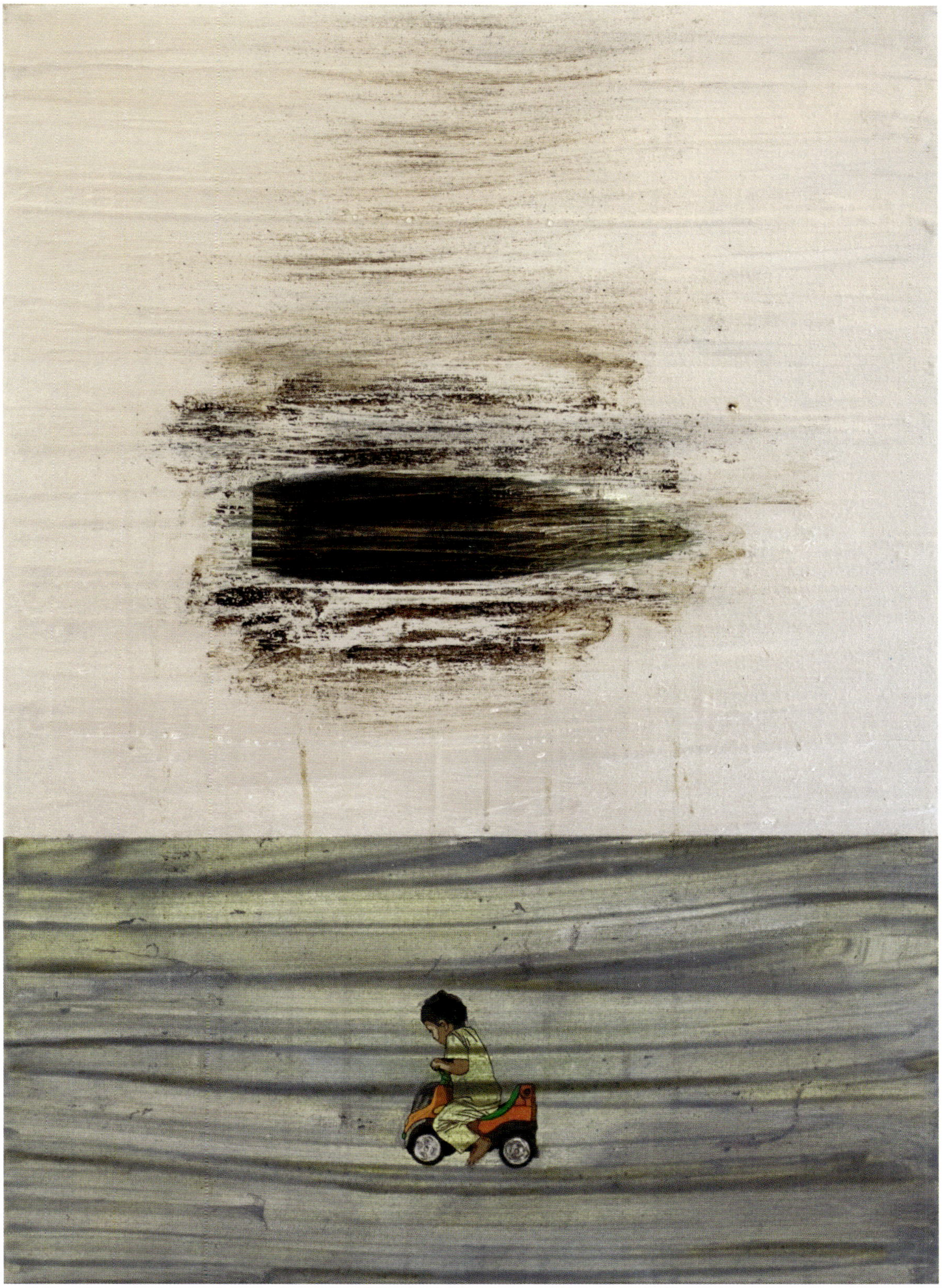

Flying Lesson no. 2, 2009.
Acrylic, oil, tar on canvas,
73 x 54 cm.
Private Collection, Manama

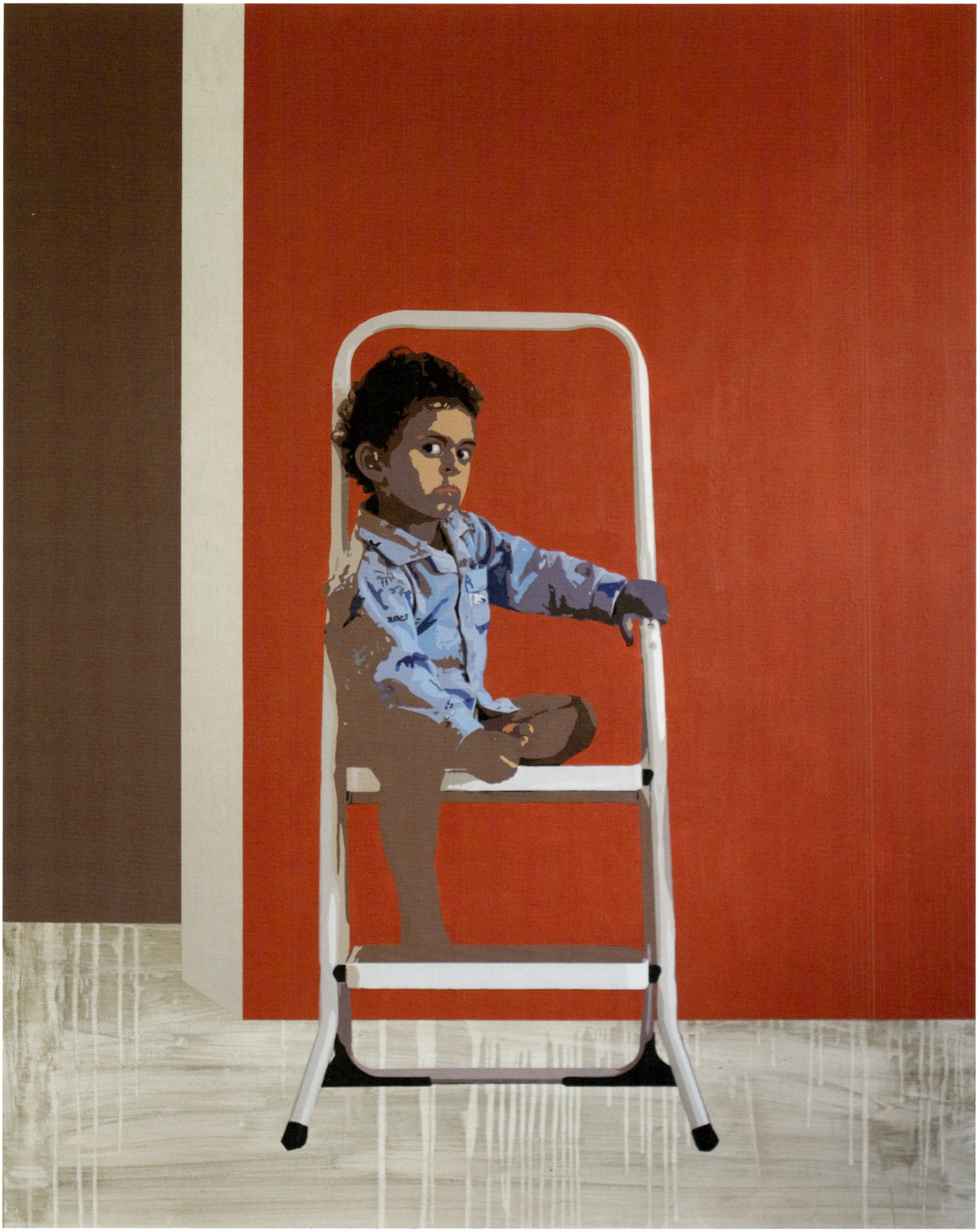

shadow, the figures, trailed by the toy aeroplane, appear diminutive in contrast to the towering walls of the interior space. Turning their backs to The Wall, they appear to be heading towards an equally massive wall set up in metallic grey. Against its sombre hardness, heavy brush strokes loaded with tar suggest phantoms of human figures hanging off a string. Boxed in from all sides with no exit in sight, the first lesson a child could learn from a position that looks more like a frog's readiness to leap could only proceed by standing up on one's own feet. From there on, flying could only take on a vertical direction.

•

In all subsequent paintings in the *Flying Lesson* series, the composition assumes a vertical shape. In each of them, the photographic image of Qudsi occupies a pivotal position. Like all parents who wished to keep in John Berger's words "a memento from a life being lived" photographs of Qudsi mostly snapped off-guard were originally taken to be shared via email with family and friends in Gaza and Jerusalem. By extracting the photographic image of the child from its physical environment and incorporating it in his imaginative painting, the private intent of the photograph acquired the status of a public image.

When John Berger first wrote on the distinction between the private and the public photographic image, he called for "an alternative use of photographs" through which a context of the photograph would be recreated so that "narrated time becomes historic time". Comparing the conventional "unilinear way" of photographs with how "memory works radially", he proposed having "a radial system… to be constructed around the photograph so that it may be seen in terms which are simultaneously personal, political, economic, dramatic, everyday and historic".[23]

Some 30 years later, Zurob appears to be intuitively wrestling with ideas about the making of his paintings, in this series in the context of his child's photograph. Through it, he seeks to transcend the limitations of the private image of his son in the manner that he had transcended the conventions of his own self-portrait—originally copied from a photograph—which he chose to name *Untitled*. Each of his paintings through incorporating moments of "narrated time" of the personal and the everyday aspire to converge these, through metaphoric insinuations, with the mythical, political and the historic. By borrowing Berger's term "radial system", each painting in the *Flying Lesson* series may thus be described as a ray in

Waiting no. 1, 2010.
Acrylic and pigments on canvas,
200 x 160 cm.

this "system". Together they operate like memory, "that is to say with an enormous number of associations all leading to the same event" as was originally captured in the photograph. All such associations bind in the painting's reading.

In most of the series' paintings, each composition vertically conceived is intuitively structured within the approximate ratio of proportions adhering to the construction of the Golden Section whereby the rectangle subdivides into a square and another rectangle. In Zurob's painting, the square is usually perceived in its upper part and the horizontally rectangular shape is defined right below it. The horizontal line between the two quadrangles determines the composition's weight *vis-à-vis* the placement of the boy's photographic image. At times the line is visibly delineated; at other times it remains invisible. With the solidity of the underlying structure, the hard-edged painting method of the background oscillates between transparent layers of colour applied with highly visible brushstrokes and opaque coatings of solid colour. Each time, different metaphoric associations are alluded to by means of the painting method which concurs with the minimal components in each composition. Through such components, Zurob relays the changing codes embedded in the child's posture, positioning, and dimensions of his figure in relation and in proportion to the surrounding abstract components in which his photographic image is incorporated.

In all the series' paintings, movement is implied not only through the photographic image that shows the boy driving his red push-car or his yellow tricycle but also through the overall rendering of the background. In one painting, the image of the boy driving his car is superimposed over a background horizontally composed of wavy brushstrokes of a translucent greenish blue with a sharply defined horizon that evokes the image of a surging sea. The boy's movement thus takes on the appearance of seafaring under a menacing cloud loaded with tar. In other paintings the background maintains an airy transparency of overlapping and often crisscrossing brushstrokes resembling the woven patterns of a textile that looks light enough to fly away at the slightest waft of wind. Such mythical evocations underlie the orientation in which the boy—seen in profile driving his vehicle—appears heading in the same right-to-left direction in which Arabic script is written.

In contrast, in the two paintings where the background is composed of solidly opaque colours both photographic images capture a frontal image of the boy as he is anchored in a seated position before what appears to be a massive wall akin to the diptych's walls. Despite appearing to be grounded however, all codes infer associations with travel.

The superimposed photograph of Qudsi viewed lounging on a suitcase and submerged in the subdued colours of the Palestinian flag of the background appears as a literal illustration of the Palestinian verse which has turned into a refrain that Palestinians living in Israel and under Israeli military occupation repeat at every occasion to declare their rootedness: "my homeland is not a suitcase/ and I am not leaving". Such a rhetorical declaration of belonging associated with the photographic image of the child who travels every six months to his parent's homeland is a further reinforcement of an earlier painting in which we see the photographic image of Qudsi sitting on the stepladder usually used by his father to reach the highest parts of a large painting. Through its structure which recalls the movable stairway that rolls up to the plane's entrance, the physical act of painting and the association with flying converge. The seated boy holding onto the rail stares defiantly back at us as if to dare us to think that his make-believe set of stairs would indeed lead him up into the sky.

•

Each vertical painting following the diptych appears to be characterised by the simplicity of its rendering and by a literality of its metaphoric associations. The one other painting in the series which stands out for its complexity is *Flying Lesson no. 4*. By employing a sort of stereoscopic reading of his earlier diptych, it is possible to see how Zurob brings together in his work two distant moments in time to express prediction and apprehension. In the case of this painting, the employment of what may be called a "prismatic configuration" reveals how the naturalistic depiction of two distant places brought together in light of a third component—in what otherwise looks as an absurd representation of space—allows us to comprehend how the very embodiment of 'flying' is elucidated beyond what is being seen by the naked eye.

The quality that sets this painting apart is that it no longer serves as a context for Qudsi's photograph. To its last detail, the painting itself replaces the photograph. Its uniform painting method employs a superfine modelling and shading technique that captures the tonality and sharpness of photographic exactitude. With almost invisible brushstrokes, the painting's surface appears flawlessly flat and its photorealist rendering is as poised as a *trompe-l'œil*. Upon examining the compelling impact of its life-like components, however, one is baffled by its enigmatic sense of space. As the eye roams over the painting, one realises that the image is viewed from three different angles of vision that converge in the painting from three imaginary distances. From each angle, the one component of the image appears to be independent from the other two and yet each of them forms part of the whole as if each part is reflected on a different plane of a prism. One cannot help but recall what John Berger called "a radial system" and how the camera's own reflexes preserve the image of reality through a prism.

Within the compositional construct of the Golden Section, the upper square space is reserved for the boundless sky. Its foreground is dominated by an image of the jetway, that is, the retractable passenger ramp that usually extends between the airport terminal and the aircraft's door. In contrast, the painting's lower rectangular space is occupied by the image of the airport's runway and its environs. What throws off the observer is how the jetway and the runway are brought together from two distant angles of vision. The jetway may be viewed this way from the passengers' lounge whereas the runway and its environs just below it could only have been viewed in this manner from within the aeroplane soon after takeoff. The lateral and the aerial view produce two vanishing points of perspective that face two opposite directions. And yet, each is seen within the space of the other.

In such a space that lacks visual 'logic', where the illusion of depth is disorienting, what looks far and what looks near all appear on the same flat plane. The *here* and the *there* appears to be interchangeable as the case is often noted in Arabic colloquial expression.[24] In between the sky and the ground where the nebulous horizon fades we see at its far edge a distant silhouette of Qudsi in his car heading leftwards out of the painting's frame. The clarity of the figure's details which make it look much closer fools the eye and augments the spatial ambiguity as its silhouette appears to be neither in the sky nor on the ground. Writing on "the logic of images", Gottfried Boehm's words may be borrowed to describe the spatial ambiguity Zurob expressed. He wrote, "midway between pure tangibility and ethereal dream: it is the paradox of a real unreality".[25]

While the convergence of the near and the far in *Flying Lesson no. 4* advanced an interpretation of the artist's experience of separation from his son, his *Flying Lesson no. 7* with an equally ambiguous sense of

Flying Lesson no. 4, 2010.
Acrylic, oil and pigments on canvas, 200 x 160 cm.
Private collection, Abu Dhabi.

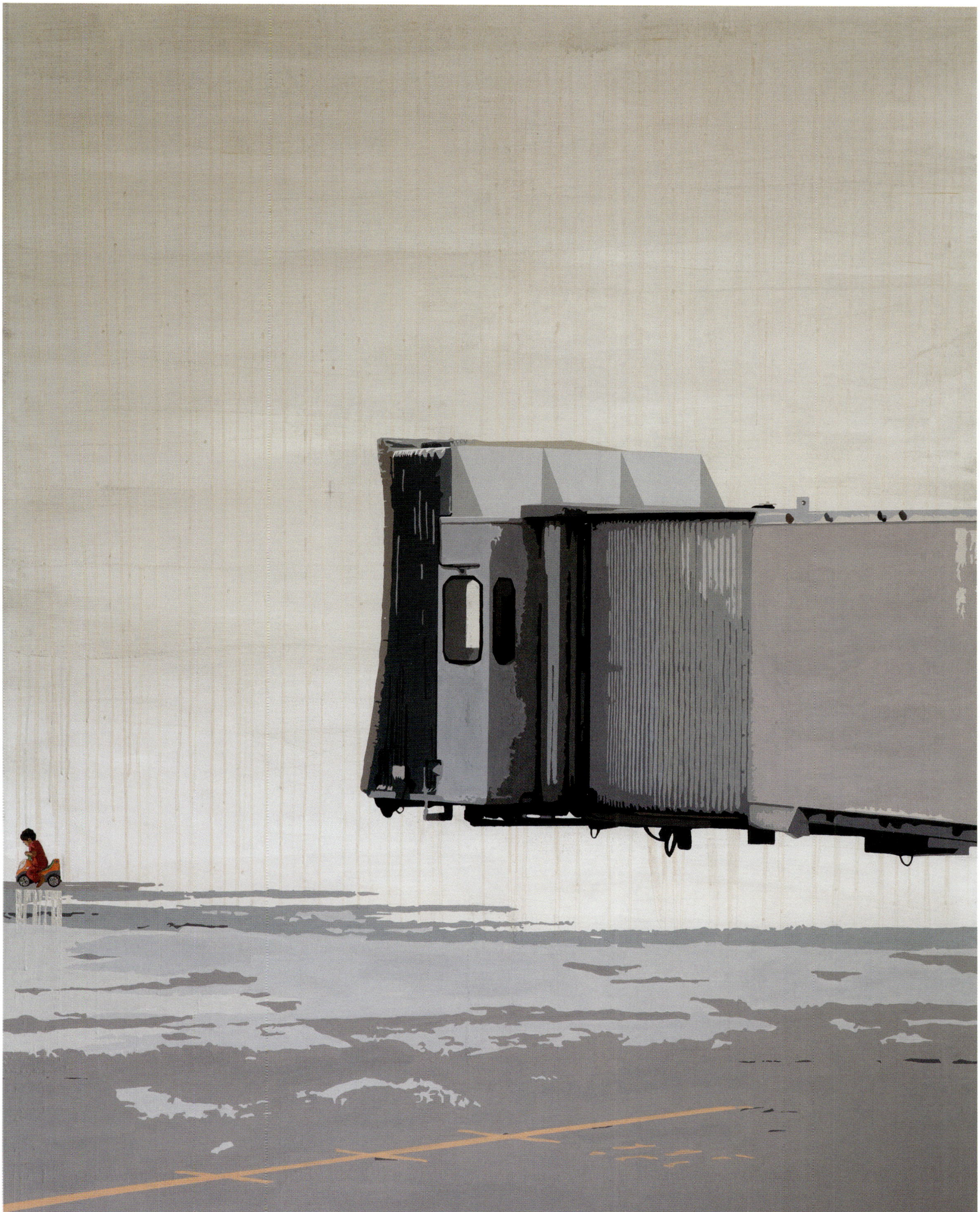

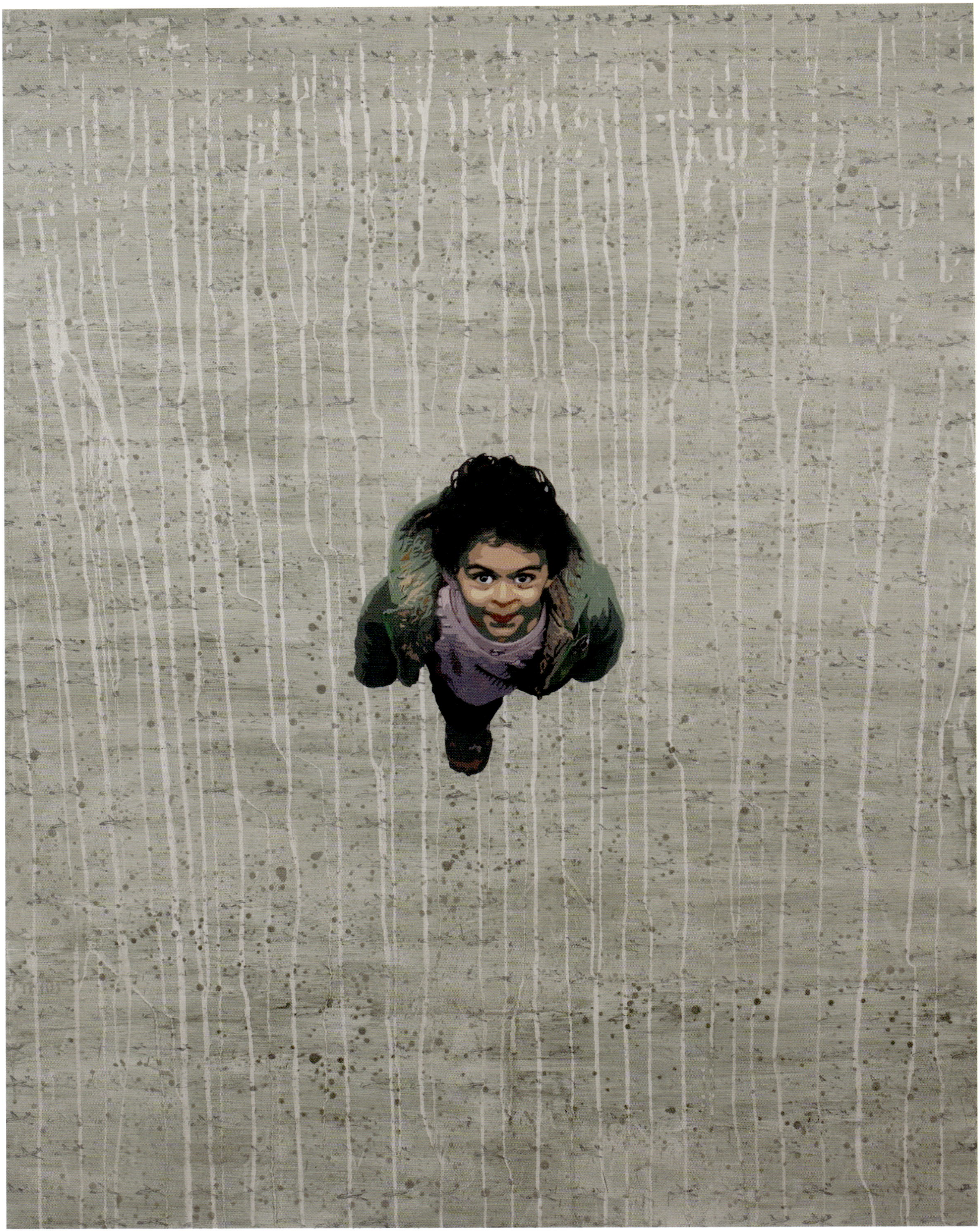

space invites us to dwell in the realm of metaphor. Again, working from another photograph the viewer crosses over to an "ethereal dream" to enter into "the paradox of a real unreality".

At first glance, the painting's foreground and background appear to share the same flat plane. The photorealistic rendering of the boy's image occupying the middle of the canvas was extracted from a photograph the father had taken from his studio's balcony as the son was walking and looking upwards at him. The boy's foreshortened figure, which is the only form highlighted with colour tints, seems to be affixed to an inane grey background assuming the shades of asphalt. Vertically streaked with an uneven dribbling of fluid stripes, the flat background turns upon a closer look into a sky crammed with a multitude of distant aeroplanes. Repeatedly stamped on canvas and veiled with the translucent shades of grey, their density appears like a long-faded page of Arabic script. By turning our eyes back on the painting's central figure and taking our distance from the painting, the boy appears to float above a wintry sky. His protruding foot makes him look as if he were floating on air as he leaves behind a grey world above the clouds.

In *Flying Lesson no. 4*, the bridge of steel the father saw his son crossing at the airport is left suspended in midair. In *Flying Lesson no. 7*, the son's flight to Jerusalem in real life takes on the unreal stance of a legend linking earth to heaven.

It was back in Essoyes after his partner together with their son flew to Jerusalem that Hani Zurob was left to face himself as if it were for the first time. In his seclusion, his self-reflection as the other of his observer was finally bound not only to compel him to reveal his full features for the first time but, more importantly, to proceed by affiliating his awareness of the self with flying. While other Palestinian *homo viator* artists of his generation like Emily Jacir and Samira Badran—to paraphrase Merleau-Ponty—lent their own bodies to confer presence to the absent others, the Gaza artist intuitively sensed that his "very essence", in the words of Avicenna, "is something beyond his body". For him, Qudsi, flesh of his flesh and bone of his bone, whose rare name in Arabic literally means "Jerusalemite" or "my Jerusalem" as well as "my holy one", is the archer's arrow aimed at the homeland that it may grant presence to his absent father and affirm continuity to his grandparents. In the meantime, it is through painting that the exiled artist experiences his own ascent to the country of his birth.

Flying Lesson no. 7, 2011.
Acrylic and pigments on canvas,
200 x 160 cm.

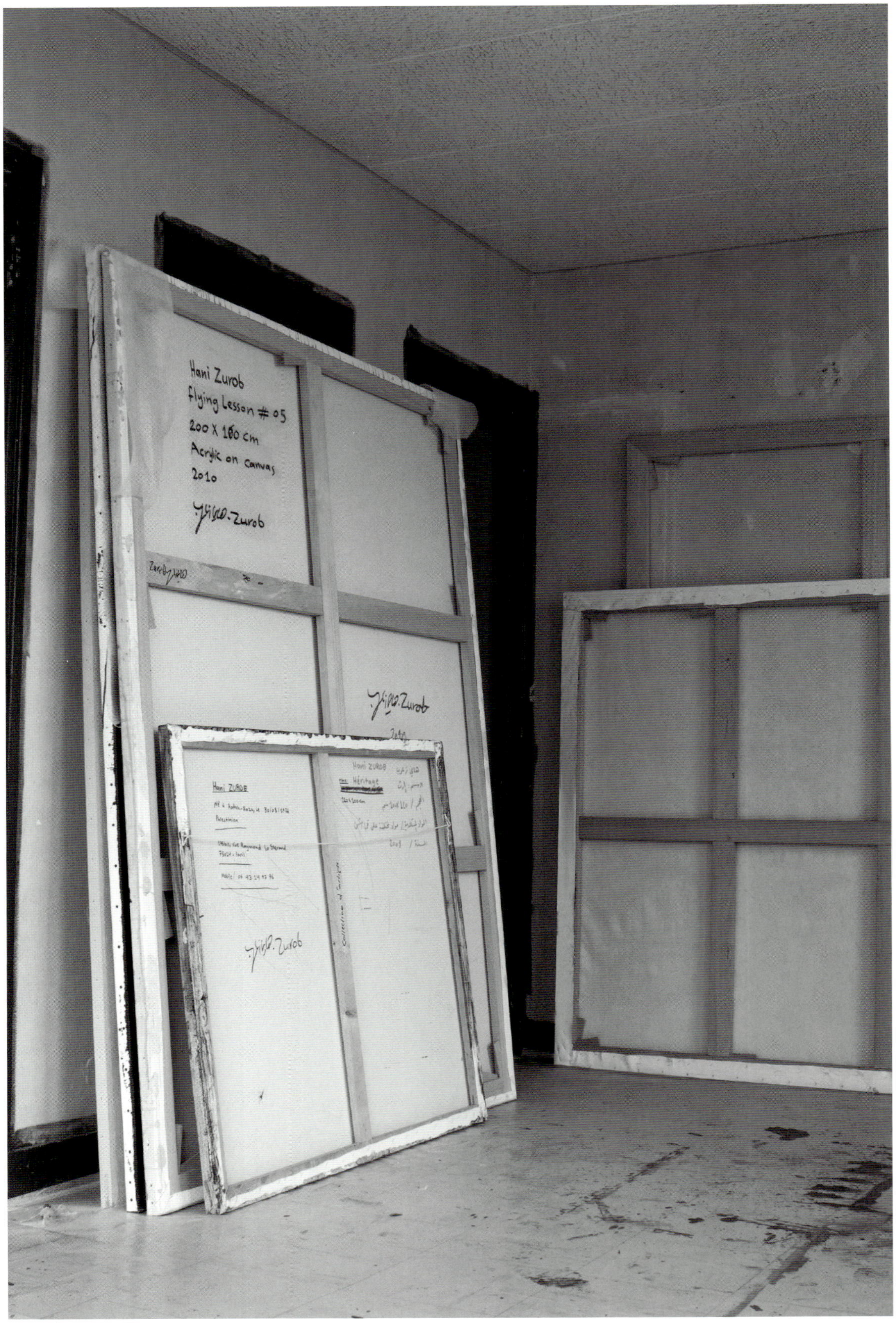

The artist's studio, Bobigny, 2012.

6.

Sky

We live in memory and by memory, and our spiritual life is at bottom simply the effort of our memory to persist, to transform itself into hope, the effort of our past to transform itself into our future.

Miguel de Unamuno
Tragic Sense of Life, New York: Cosimo Classics, 2005, p. 9.

One lives after one is through painting what one is painting.

Ad Reinhardt
Art as Art, Berkeley, Los Angeles: University of California Press, 1975, p. 128.

"The old will die and the young will forget", that is how Israel's architect and first prime minister, David Ben-Gurion, explained away the ethnic cleansing of Palestinians he ordered in 1948.[1] At the time, one of the military commanders who executed a decisive part of Ben-Gurion's master plan was no other than Yitzhak Rabin who led the expulsion of the civilian population of Lydda and Ramle that included Hani Zurob's grandparents.[2] Over four decades later, shortly before he signed the ill-fated Oslo Peace accords, Rabin, then Israel's fifth prime minister fostered similar wishful thinking. Speaking of the Gaza Strip, the region in historic Palestine that is most populated with refugee camps, he said "if only it would sink into the sea".[3]

Since 1948, the old did indeed die but their children have not forgotten. No wonder that in today's Israeli public discourse they are considered "a demographic time bomb".[4] Believers in an exclusively Jewish state see in Palestinian children—whether born to Christian or Muslim families—a threat that represents the implicit call for a democratic state in which all its citizens are entitled to equal rights, regardless of their religious origins. That is what the artist from the Gaza Strip instinctively recognised as he was turning away from the mirror of his self-portraits to see himself in the photograph of his own son.

In the meantime, the Gaza Strip did not sink into the sea. But Israel's intensive bombardments, particularly during the wars it waged in 2006 and 2009, left its soil contaminated with a high concentration of toxic metals that cause fertility problems that exert serious effects on new born babies, including deformities and genetic pathologies.[5] Bereaved and pauperised by Israel's wars and pitiless years' long blockade, the people of the Gaza Strip continue to hold out to the last. Across its sea, with the same verve and faith in life, Hani Zurob doggedly goes on painting, irrespective of how many artists of his generation claim the death of painting.

Since 1839, when French history painter Paul Delaroche, seeing the earliest photographic image, declared "from today, painting is dead", and the declaration has been proclaimed on different occasions throughout the turbulent history of the twentieth century. By century's end and through the first decade of the twenty-first, media arts and computer-generated imagery have mushroomed on a global scale. Overnight, young art practitioners were wallowing in notoriety. Their novel forms of self-expression, which turned their creations into spectacles, were believed by some to represent the last nail in the coffin of easel painting.

In the meantime, what seems to have been overlooked is that the history of Modern art in the Western world which knew dissenting movements throughout the last century has been predominantly a history of painting. Despite Alexander Rodchenko's 1920s call to abandon easel painting altogether for an "art into life", and the 1950s and early 1960s black paintings of Ad Reinhardt calling for "art as art"; and since the readymade appropriation of Marcel Duchamp's urinal in 1917 to Andy Warhol's incorporation of the Brillo Box in his work in 1964, followed by decades overflowing with conceptual art, painting has never ceased to be reinvented. Just as cinema did not nullify theatre nor did television nullify cinema, painting has continued to thrive independently from whatever newly invented form of media has been employed as a tool of self-expression.

Discussing Postmodern and contemporary art, Arthur C Danto explains that "artists liberated from the burden of history were free to make art in whatever way they wished, for any purposes they wished, or for no purpose at all".[6] His writing on the subject of "art after the end of art" rings true in response to questions raised by the debate revolving around the 'death of painting'. He points out that "what had come to an end was that narrative but not the subject of the narrative".[7] In this way, any further discussion of today's painting must rethink the way of seeing that overleaps all bounds of a master narrative. This is particularly pertinent in non-European cultures, where such a narrative had been long claiming universality in recounting the history of Modern art. It allows the opening of a whole new vista on Modern art created by non-Western artists whose language, as hybrid as it may come these days, springs from different cultural sources that freely flow in and out of the Western tradition.

Though the death of painting has been declared upon the birth of photography in France, Hani Zurob, whose paintings evolve out of the photograph, may be called, in Danto's definition, a "photographist" painter.[8] Born during the decade when the distinction between Modern and contemporary art began to emerge in the art history of the West, he came of age as a painter when art from the margins of the world in which he found himself had already succeeded in making inroads into what used to be referred to as the mainstream.

Having become aware of international artists around him whose conceptual art abrogates the language of his choice of expression and having left back home painters whose work is steeped in nationalist rhetoric imagery, Hani Zurob kept his distance from what Achille Bonito Oliva called "the internal tension between globalisation and tribalisation" dominating the period.[9] In Paris, the exiled Palestinian painter went on looking inwards for his own path.

One wonders, what it is that makes one artist look inwards in search of a personal language of expression and another to be propelled outwards to join the chorus of voices that are giving shape to what is being appraised as cutting-edge art? In the case of Hani Zurob it may all go back to answering the why and wherefore that motivated him in the first place to launch his art career by taking the mirror as an indispensable tool in his self realisation as a painter.

Having grown up in a cultural ghetto that was bred on post-1967 pictorial production which was saturated with didactic and nationalist iconography, could the mere sight of the self-portraits of Egon Schiele that he admired in a friend's book have been enough to inspire the young talent to find in the mirror the means by which to exercise his own originality? If so, why do none of his earliest paintings in which his own features are depicted manifest any trace of influence stemming from the Austrian artist's style?

Cut off from all art history and particularly that of his own culture, in which self-portraits are actually the rarest genre of painting, one can only find the explanation in the Arab literary tradition in which Zurob was grounded. Within the traditions of a tightly-knit society, Zurob dared to face the accusations of narcissism at the earliest stage of establishing his career. To have experienced being estranged in Ramallah must have been a key factor that invited the young talent to find in his reflection in the mirror not only a sort of solace but also the most inimitable venue by which to foster an originality springing out of a truth he was sure of possessing, namely his own face and body.

Thus, his earliest attempts at self-portraits recall the image of *mir-at al-gharibah* which translates to "mirror of the estranged woman" conjured up by the eighth century Bedouin poet Dhu-al-Rummah. Over the centuries, commentators have widely written on the significance of this image alluding to how a woman estranged from her own community and obliged to live among another may risk losing touch with her own identity. To insure her difference, she continues to polish the mirror she carries to see herself clearly. That way, as the legend goes, the estranged woman is not only reassured of her identity but she keeps refreshing the memory of her origins and thus revaluing her own uniqueness.

Another example illustrating Zurob's cultural affiliation with the Arabic literary tradition may be traced through the manner in which he employed the mirror and at times two mirrors to paint himself in profile. In the process of giving shape to his trying experiences as an alien living in Ramallah, the mirror was his primary window through which he reflected his emotional state in his paintings. The decisive role the mirror played in his art recalls how Taha Husayn earlier in the twentieth century resorted to the metaphor of the mirror in many of his critical essays on literary and cultural matters of his times. Hani Zurob's employment of the mirror in his earliest self-portraits echoed the blind scholar's search for a perceptual frame to concretise his thoughts.[10]

In each one of the paintings he produced between the years 2002 and 2012, a representative selection of which has been discussed in this book, it was meaning to the personal experiences he was undergoing that he sought to embody in his art. Just as meaning had always been sought since humans first invented tools with which to paint the walls of their cave dwellings, meaning has been what iconographers and artists aspired to transmit throughout the history of art. Though Hani Zurob's painting has yet to pass the test of time, it has incessantly clamoured for a narrative that would elucidate how meaning may be read in context of the artist's life. Maurice Merleau-Ponty sums it up this way, "because we are in the world, we are *condemned to meaning*, and we cannot do or say anything without its acquiring a name in history."[11]

In Hani Zurob's art, meaning unfolds in variable ways, like the act of recounting a memory at different junctures in one's life. Each time, the recounting takes a turn to meet the moment being lived. Likewise, in every one of his canvases, the meaning's embodiment shifts from one work to another in correlation with the process of creating a new series of paintings. For example, in his *Standby* series that he started working on by replacing the mirror with the photograph he shot of himself, what started with a self-portrait ended up implying a new meaning whereby the naked body of the artist in a seated position turned into the obscured figure of a man whose disposition denotes a state of waiting. By displaying each painting of the unsettled figure right next to the other belonging to the same series, Zurob managed to reflect the arrest and unfolding of body movements through which he crystallised a Palestinian collective experience.

Subsequently, when his own photograph was replaced by that of his son, as in the *Flying Lesson* series, in each of the paintings depicting the boy, the viewer is invited again and again to reflect upon a new significance that transcends the mere representation of a likeness cherished by the artist. Each painting in the series acts as a link in a chain that elaborates on meaning. As it turns out, the painting which depicts the photographic image of the boy reclining on the red suitcase his mother carries on the flight that yearly takes him with her to Jerusalem (*no. 5*) provides such a link. In a succeeding painting (*no. 7*) in the same series, the foreshortened body of the boy looking up at us appears to float in mid-air. In the context of the boy's yearly journeying to Jerusalem, his weightlessness amidst an ethereal space embroidered with the pattern of distant aeroplanes cannot but offer the viewer a personalised interpretation of the legend of the Arab Prophet's night journey to Jerusalem. Similarly, in another painting titled *Waiting* the boy viewed standing all alone on top of a pillar calls to mind the legend of St Simeon Stylites, the fifth century ascetic saint who spent his life on top of a pillar northwest of Aleppo.

In each painting the implied meaning affiliates with associations that insinuate cultural associations, fostering memories of home. For example, the painting series *Marbles' War* evoked by his boyhood memory of playing marbles in the alleyways of the refugee camp was conceived during the same period his child began to play with his fairy toys in their small apartment. Similarly, the subject of *Heritage* interwove the contrast between the joyful memory of summer days he had spent on the beach in Rafah with the sight of his child crawling away from the sea in Normandy. That is how meaning in his paintings continues to be read through memory, whereby memory always courts the legacy of the past like that cherished by Zurob of the grandfather Hajj Thabet who had bequeathed the key of the house he left behind in Wadi Hunayn to the painter's father. Just as the key of the ancestral home was an object that never ceased to revive memory, paintings of the child have repeatedly sought to perpetuate the legacy that transforms memory into hope.

By bringing two distant worlds close together—that of memory and the other of exile where his son was born—Zurob's paintings unravel a peculiar representation of space that is shrouded in enigma. Since he settled in Paris, his representation of space has either been totally obscured with tar as in his *Standby* series and his *Untitled* painting, or compressed as in *Heritage*. As for his last series of paintings, *Flying Lesson*, all reference to space appears to continue shifting from one angle of vision to another. In a number of paintings, space appears flat and unreal as in the image of the boy peddling his push-car beneath what looks like an ocean (*no. 2*) or where the boy is viewed standing all alone on top of a pillar (*Waiting no. 6*) or when he is pictured riding his tricycle and facing a massive wall with a sweeper in hand (*no. 6*) or where the boy in his pedal aeroplane is imagined flying through a haunted sky (*no. 9*).

The shifting quality of space Hani Zurob portrays finds perhaps its most intriguing expression in paintings maintaining simultaneous perspectives with no fixed point of view as in *nos. 1*, *4* and *7* in the *Flying Lesson* series. The angle of vision on the right side of the diptych (*no. 1*) points from the ground level up whereas on the left side of it the angle of vision is more of an aerial view. Yet both sides are conceived together as a continuous composition within the same frame. Similarly, in the painting (*no. 4*) the jetway and the runway are viewed from two distant angles of vision that converge on the same plane and they are equally viewed together in an unbroken continuity. In his painting of the boy looking up at us (*no. 7*) his foreshortened body, which is the central theme of the painting, thrusts forward in the direction of the surface of the canvas whereas all the aeroplanes in the background are viewed flying sideways

Waiting no. 6, 2011.
Acrylic and pigments on canvas, 81 x 60 cm.
Private Collection, Manama.

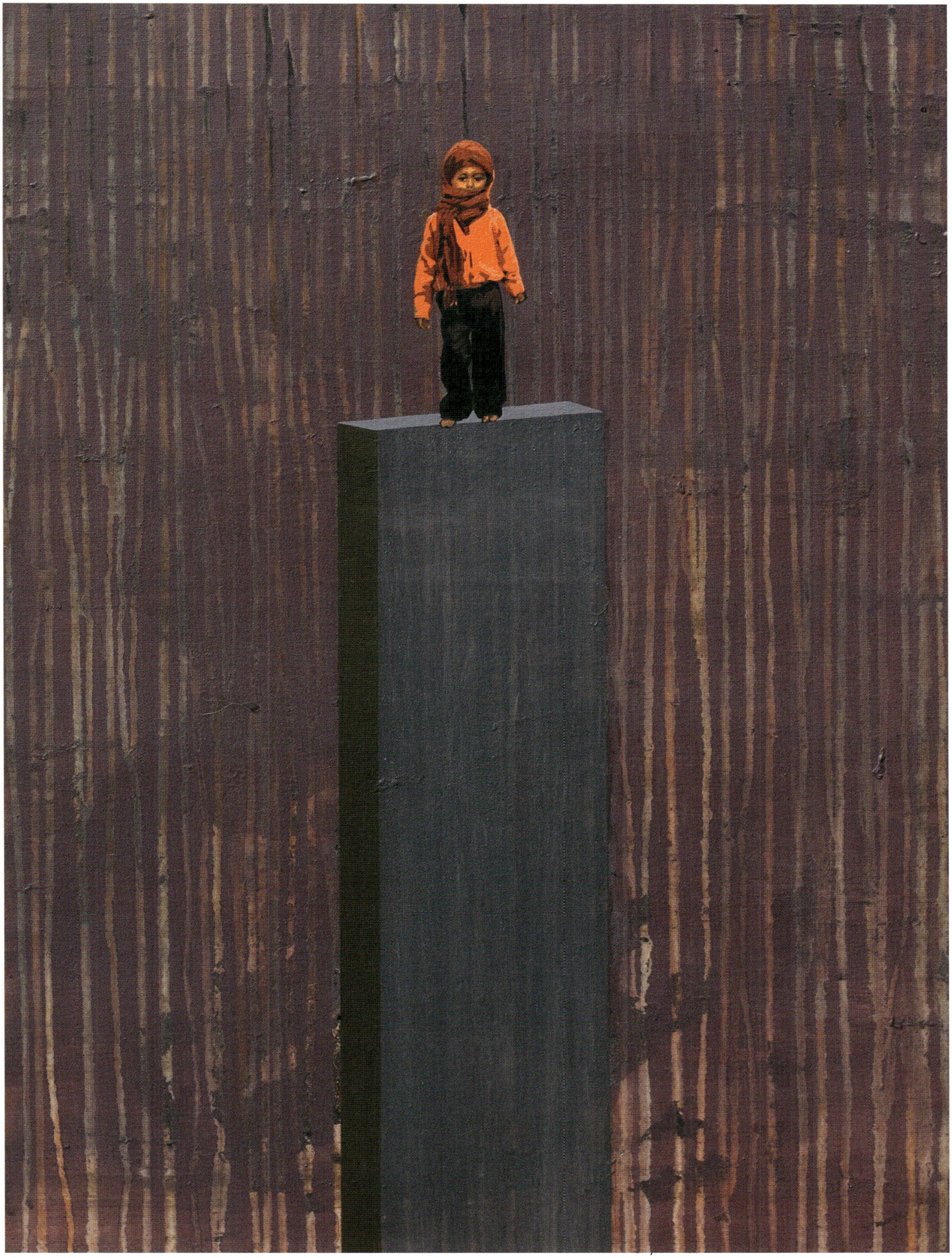

in the same direction from right to left as threads of what looks like rain falling vertically from top to bottom completes the weaving pattern. Were we to look for an expression that may best sum up how space with a multiplicity of perspectives is represented on the same plane, the German word *blickwechsel* coined by Hans Belting meaning "shifting focus/ exchanging glances" seems to sum it up. Though Belting applies the term to speak of studying Arab and Western culture placed "side by side and on the same level, so that neither would be overvalued or undervalued", the German scholar's "shifting focus/exchanging glances" between the two cultures finds a resonance in paintings created by an Arab artist who upon finding himself in the West continued "shifting focus" within the same space of a figurative painting, and "exchanging glances" between the literary tradition of his home culture and the visual tradition immortalised in the country of his residence.[12]

•

Today, Hani Zurob's flow of paintings continues to undergo transitions and transformations. Their creator realises that the journey he embarked on has only begun even though its trajectory seems measureless. From the confines of the choking space he was brought up in over 30 years ago and the underground life he was obliged to carve for himself in the open prison of the West Bank, he is now on the threshold of a new beginning. The sky is stretching before him since he took wing to the city that has been sheltering generations of artists surviving other fascisms and other wars.

Since his arrival in Paris, when he portrayed the experience of the self and the Palestinian other in a fluid and interchanging manner which was his own way of reflecting Rimbaud's declaration "je est un autre" (I is an other), the grounds have been paved for a day to come when the other embraced shall belong to an identity beyond his own. In the meantime, like all exiles before him, he is getting used to living simultaneously in two distant worlds, as distant from each other as the mirror he used for the self-portrait is from the photograph he used of his son. In the act of painting, the painter seems to have constantly sought to recover the distance he sensed between being *here* before the mirror, to being *there* inside the painting. His years of shuttling between figuration and abstraction in his art mirrors his perpetual state of being between 'here' and 'there'.

I Was Born There, I Was Born Here was the title of Mourid Barghouti's book documenting his first return visit home together with his son from years of exile where the son was born.[13] During all the years the father spent away from his native village of Deir Ghassanah, which lies north of Ramallah, it was the "I was born there" which the son had been hearing. In the course of the brief visit, the son could at long last see for himself the ancient hills and olive trees he had been told about, walk through the village square, meet relatives for the first time and most importantly behold with his own eyes Dar Ra'd, the ancient family stone-house. There, he could stand right under the dome shielding the large white room in which his father was born.

At present, "I was born there" is all that the father painter can say to his son. As for the rest of us, who see his paintings, perhaps only verses by Palestine's national poet Mahmoud Darwish may more readily sum up the determined pursuit of Hani Zurob:

> I am from there. My 'here' leaps
> From my footsteps to my imagination…
>
> I am he, who I was or will be,
> Made and struck down
> By the endless expansive space.
>
> One day I shall become what I want.[14]

Notes

Preface

- **1.** Barghouti, Mourid, *I Was Born There, I Was Born Here*, Humphrey Davies, trans., London: Bloomsbury, p. 79–80.
- **2.** "Facing the Forest: Israeli and Palestinian Artists", *Third Text*, no. 7, summer 1989, pp. 77–95.

Introduction

- **1.** *Bound, Blindfolded and Convicted* (April 2012) is the culmination of four years of investigation by the Defence for Children International-Palestine Section (DCI-Palestine), supported by the United Nations. *The Impact of Child Detention: Occupied Palestinian Territory*, 2012, is a report by Save the Children in collaboration with the East Jerusalem YMCA Rehabilitation Programme, which strives to repair the psychological damage, which often includes sexual abuse. *Children in Military Custody* (June 2012), is by a delegation in September 2011 of a group of nine British lawyers funded by the United Kingdom Foreign and Commonwealth Office, which aimed to determine whether Israel is complying with the standards of international law and children's rights.
- **2.** Articles 2 (discrimination); 3 (child's best interests); 37(a) (solitary confinement as a form of torture); 37(b) (premature resort to detention); 37(c) (non-separation from adults); 37(d) (prompt access to lawyers); and 40 (use of shackles).
- **3.** Nader Abu Amsha, quoted in "Healing Traumatised Children", *Palestine News: Reports*, *PSC*, spring 2012, p. 7.
- **4.** See also Harriet Sherwood, "The Palestinian Children—alone and bewildered—in Israel's Al Jamale jail", http://www.guardian.co.uk/world/2012/jan22/palestinian-children. The spokesperson, Mark Regev, is also notorious for making the sordid claim on BBC's Newsnight to its incredulous presenter Gavin Esler that Hamas used Palestinian children as human shields: http://youtuberepeater.com/watch?v=yJxXnm51-RQ&name=Israeli+Spokesman
- **5.** Kamal Boullata, born Jerusalem in 1942, displaced in 1948 and exiled in 1967, relates his experience of living in a 'no man's land' between the place of beginning and the shifting places of exile, and the influence of

cultural memory on his paintings in the chapters "The View from No-Man's-Land" and "To Measure Jerusalem: Explorations of the Square", in *Palestinian Art from 1850 to the Present*, London: Saqi, 2009, pp. 309–337.

• **6.** Said, Edward, *The Question of Palestine*, [1979], New York: Vintage Books, 1992, p. 5.

• **7.** Boullata, Kamal, "Notes on Verbal Dominance and Visual Expression in Arab Culture", in *Neighbours in Dialogue*, Beral Madra and Ayse Orhun Gultekin eds., Istanbul: Norgunk Publishing House, 2005, p. 11.

• **8.** Khoury, Elias, "In Defence of Metaphor", in *Belonging and Globalisation: Critical Essays in Contemporary Art and Culture*, Kamal Boullata ed., London: Saqi, 2008, p. 75.

• **9.** Barghouti, Mourid, *Midnight and Other Poems*, Radwa Ashour trans., Todmorden, Lancs: Arc Publications, 2008, p. 160.

• **10.** Bacon, Francis in David Sylvester, *Interviews with Francis Bacon*, London: Thames and Hudson, 1993, p. 12.

• **11.** Matthew Gale and Chris Stephens suggest that Bacon's approach to painting may be illuminated more by poetry than among the works of fellow painters. In *Francis Bacon*, London: Tate Publishing, 2008, p. 26.

• **12.** The word 'troubadour' is the Anglicisation of the Spanish *trovador*, which almost certainly derives from the Arabic *tarab-u-dur*, *tarab* meaning, "the delight in music when one is transported by it", and *dur* meaning "to go around" or a "refrain" in a song. (Kamal Boullata, personal note.)

• **13.** Boullata, Kamal, "Notes on Verbal Dominance and Visual Expression in Arab Culture", *Neighbours in Dialogue*, p. 19; Said, Edward, "Identity, Authority, and Freedom: The Potentate and the Traveller", *Reflections on Exile and Other Literary and Cultural Essays*, London: Granta, 2000, pp. 403–404.

• **14.** Serres, Michel, *The Troubadour of Knowledge*, Sheila Faria Glaser with William Paulson trans., Ann Arbor: University of Michigan Press, 1997, p. 93.

• **15.** Ricoeur, Paul, "Memory and Forgetting", in *Questioning Ethics: Contemporary Debates in Philosophy*, Richard Kearney and Mark Dooley eds., London and New York: Routledge, 1999, p. 7.

• **16.** Ricoeur, Paul, *Memory, History, Forgetting*, Kathleen Blamey and David Pellauer, Chicago and London: University of Chicago Press, 2006, p. 89.

• **17.** Ricoeur, Paul, "Memory and Forgetting", in *Questioning Ethics: Contemporary Debates in Philosophy,* 2006, p. 9.

1. Grounds

- **1.** Shammout, Isma'il, *al-Fan al-Tashkili fi Filastin*, (Art in Palestine), Kuwait, 1989, p. 59–60.
- **2.** For a more global view see my entry on "art" in Philip Mattar (ed.) *Encyclopedia of the Palestinians*, New York: Facts on File, Inc, revised edition, 2005, pp. 81–90.
- **3.** See 'Anani, Nabil and 'Isam Badr, *al-Fan al-Filastini fi al-Ard al-Muhtallah*, Ramallah: Gallery 79, 1984, pp. 33–38.
- **4.** Alberti, Leon Batista, *On Painting*, Cecil Grayson trans., London: Penguin Classics, p. 61.
- **5.** The scarce examples of self-portraits in profile in European art include Alberti, *Self-Portrait* c. 1436, bronze medallion, (National Gallery, Washington, DC); Caravaggio, *The Taking of Christ*, 1602 (National Gallery of Ireland, Dublin); Goya, *Self-Portrait*,1799 from his etching series *Los Capprichos* , (British Museum, London); Courbet, *The Meeting*, 1854, (Musée Fabre, Montpellier) and *L'Atelier* 1855, (Musée d'Orsay, Paris) de Chirico, *Self-Portrait*, 1911, (Metropolitan Museum of Art, New York) and Duchamp *Self-Portrait in Profile*,1957 (Metropolitan Museum of Art, New York).
- **6.** Apart from those artists who copied their own features from studio photographs, Arab artists who painted self-portraits from a mirror belonging to the first generation of the twentieth century may be counted on one hand. Mahmud Said (1897–1964) was foremost among Egypt's pioneering artists. In Lebanon where the tradition was more widespread, they included George Corm (1896–1971), Mustafa Farrukh (1901–1957) and Omar Onsi (1901–1961). Throughout the history of modern Arab art, however, no Arab painter surpassed the Syrian-born and Berlin resident Marwan (1934) in making his self-portrait a pivotal theme in his art. See my study, "Qira'at al-jasad fi lawhat Marwan" (The Reading of the Body in Marwan's Paintings), *al-Akhar*, no. 2, autumn 2011, pp. 158–177.
- **7.** The subject of the 14 pronouns in Arabic in which the 'he' leads the list of pronouns and the 'I' occupies the position before the last deserves an independent study. See my text and drawings around the subject in "Manshur Jinsiyasi" (Sex-pol Manifesto) *Mawaqif*, no. 28, summer 1974, pp. 46–59.
- **8.** For a discussion covering the thousand year old tradition of autobiographic writing in Arabic which includes the use of the third person, see Dwight F Reynolds ed., *Interpreting the Self: Autobiography in the Arabic Literary Tradition*, Berkeley: University of California Press, 2001.

- **9.** For a thorough discussion of this masterpiece in modern Arabic literature see Fedwa Malti-Douglas, *Blindness and Autobiography: 'al-Ayyam' of Taha Husayn*, Princeton, NJ: Princeton University Press, 1988.
- **10.** The term *'dédoublement'* has been devised by Phillippe Lejeune in his *Le pacte autobiographique*, Paris: Editions du Seuil, 1975, see Malti-Douglas, p. 95–96.

2. Between Exits

- **1.** My translation of "There" by Najwan Darwish appeared in its entirety in *The Virginia Quarterly Review*, vol. 84, no. 3, Summer 2008, p. 214.
- **2.** Bachelard, Gaston, *The Poetics of Space*, Maria Jolas trans., Boston: Beacon Press, 1969, pp. 5–6.
- **3.** Berger, John, *Hold Everything Dear: Dispatches on Survival and Resistance*, London & New York: Verso, 2007, pp. 10–11.

3. Standby

- **1.** *Song of Myself: And Other Poems* by Walt Whitman, Robert Hass and Paul Ebenkamp eds., Berkley, CA: Counterpoint Press, 2010.
- **2.** For more on al-'Ali's use of the bitumen substance see my two books *Istihdar al-Makan: Dirasat fi al-Fan al-Filastini al-Mu`asir* (The Recovery of Place: A Study of Contemporary Palestinian Art) Tunis: Alecso, 2000, pp. 116–119 and *Palestinian Art from 1850 to the Present*, London: Saqi 2009, pp. 137–139. During the early 1980s when Palestinian painter Munira Nusseibeh (Jerusalem 1942) was living in Abu Dhabi, she also employed the petroleum product as a medium in combination with gold leaf to comment on life in a traditional oil-rich Arab society. See *Istihdar*, pp. 236–237.
- **3.** For a history of the 'peace process' dating it back to the mid-1970s see William Quandt, *Peace Process: American Diplomacy and the Arab-Israeli Conflict Since 1967*, Washington, DC: Brookings Institution Press and Berkeley and Los Angeles, CA: University of California Press, 3rd edition, March 2005.
- **4.** "Mes faims, c'est les bouts d'air noir". From "Fêtes de la faim", J Harding and J Sturrock, *Arthur Rimbaud Selected Poems and Letters*, London: Penguin 2004, pp. 126–127.
- **5.** Genet, Jean, *Prisoner of Love*, New York: New York Review of Books, 2003, p. 5.

4. Mirrors

- **1.** Ricœur, Paul, *Freedom and Nature: The Voluntary and the Involuntary*, E Kohak trans., Evanston: Northwestern University Press, 1966. A further elaboration is found in his *Oneself As Another*, Kathleen Blamey trans., Chicago & London: The University of Chicago Press, 1992.
- **2.** Sartre, Jean-Paul, *Being and Nothingness*, HE Barnes trans., New York: Philosophical Library, 1956.
- **3.** Derrida, Jacques, *L'animal que donc je suis*, Marie-Louise Mallet ed., Paris: Galilée, 2006, pp. 15–79, "The Animal that Therefore I Am (More to Follow)" David Wills trans., *Critical Inquiry*, 28, no. 4, winter 2002, pp. 369–418.
- **4.** Derrida, Jacques, *Memoirs of the Blind: The Self-Portrait and Other Ruins*, PA Brault and M Nass trans., Chicago, Il: University of Chicago Press, 1993.
- **5.** In 2005, after viewing remarkable artworks by Dutch artist Desiree Palmen at Nova Icona Gallery in Venice, I suggested to the artist whose artistic interventions decry surveillance cameras installed in Rotterdam to consider going to Jerusalem to explore Israel's surveillance camera system installed in the Old City. Thanks to al-Ma'mal Foundation for Contemporary Art in Jerusalem, an art residency was granted to her the following year. See, http://almamal.blogspot.com/2010/09/artist-in-residence-desiree-palmen-2006_18.html. To view the video and photographs go to: http://www.desireepalmen.nl/oldcitysuitSTART.php.
- **6.** Foucault, Michel, *Discipline and Punish: The Birth of the Prison*, New York: Vintage Books, 1995.
- **7.** In his illuminating study of a landscape by the Turkish painter Seker Ahmet Pasa (1841–1907) John Berger analyses the "spatial ambiguity" a non-European artist employing the European tradition of painting created. Employing a term used by Heidegger, Berger calls it a "coming-into-the distance." Berger, "Seker Ahmet and the Forest" in *About Looking*, New York: Pantheon Books, 1980, Vintage International Edition, pp. 86–93.
- **8.** In Arabic one may use the past tense to stress the present continuous or the future tense. For example, to indicate that a promise shall indeed be fulfilled, the person to execute the promise confirms by saying, "*sar*" literally meaning "it was accomplished." Similarly, in the narration of a past event, or an imaginative narrative to enliven the unfolding of the event, the speaker often refers to an accomplished act using the equivalent of the present continuous tense.
- **9.** Said, Edward, *After the Last Sky: Palestinian Lives, photographs by Jean Mohr*, London: Faber & Faber Ltd, Vintage edition 1993, p. 38.

5. Airborne

- **1.** See Frederick S Colby, *Narrating Muhammad's Night Journey: Tracing the Development of the Ibn 'Abbas Ascension Discourse*, Albany, NY: State University of New York Press, 2008.
- **2.** Hitti, Philip, *History of the Arabs*, Hampshire & New York: Palgrave Macmillan, (10th edition), 2002, p. 598.
- **3.** McGinnis, Jon and David C Resiman, *Classical Arabic Philosophy: An Anthology of Sources*, Indianapolis/Cambridge, 2007, pp.178–79.
- **4.** See Kamal Abou-Deeb, *The Imagination Unbound: 'al-Adab al-'Aja'ibi' and the Literature of the Fantastic*, London: Saqi, Oxford: Oryx Press, 2007.
- **5.** In Arabic, all words related to "flying" from "pilot" (*tayyar*) to "aeroplane" (*ta'ira*) and "airport" (*matar*) derive from the trilateral root verb 'tar' of which words for a winged being like "bird" (*tayr, ta'ir*) and "duckling" (*tuwair*) are made. As words like "airline", "flight" and "flying" are interchangeable, so are words such as "aeroplane", "kite" and "glider". Differentiation is defined only by adding a qualifier such as "paper aeroplane" or "nylon aeroplane" to the word meaning "aircraft".
- **6.** For further discussion of Na'wash's painting see my book *Istihdar al-Makan*, pp. 137–139.
- **7.** Bourriaud, Nicolas, *The Radicant*, New York: Lukas & Sternberg, 2009, p. 113; Bourriaud, *The Radicant*, p. 108.
- **8.** Bourriaud, *The Radicant*, pp. 113–114.
- **9.** Coincidentally, three years after the release of Suleiman's film, when Banksy, the British graffiti artist, visited the West Bank, one of the nine images he stencilled on the Palestinian side of the Apartheid Wall, which attained widespread iconic popularity among Palestinians, was the silhouette of a skirted girl holding onto the threads of a bunch of balloons that are lifting her straight up in flight towards the crest of The Wall.
- **10.** Demos, TJ, "The Ends of Exile: Towards a Coming Universality?" in *Altermodern: Tate Triennal*, catalogue of exhibition curated by Nicolas Bourriaud, London: Tate Britain, 2009, p. 84.
- **11.** Demos, TJ, "The Ends of Exile: Towards a Coming Universality?", p. 85.
- **12.** Airlines connecting the Jerusalem Airport with Arab capitals included the Lebanese companies Air Liban and Middle East Airlines, the Egyptian Misr Air, the Kuwaiti Trans Arabia Airlines and the Jordanian Arab Airways and Air Jordan of the Holy Land. Documentary photographs of visiting guests including the popular Egyptian singer Farid al-Atrash and the Hollywood star Katherine Hephern illustrate the article by Nahed Awwad, "In Search of Jerusalem Airport", *Jerusalem Quarterly*, no. 35,

pp. 51–63. http://palestinearchives.org/images/ArticlesPdf/35_airport.pdf. On the rise of Arab nationalism during this period see, Adeed Dawisha, *Arab Nationalism in the Twentieth Century: From Triumph to Despair*, Princeton, NJ: Princeton University Press, 2005.

- **13.** Hammami, Rema, "Qalandia: Jerusalem's Tora Bora and the Frontiers of Global Inequality", *Jerusalem Quarterly*, no. 41, spring 2010, p. 38, pp. 29–51. http://palestinearchives.org/images/ArticlesPdf/41_Qalandia.pdf
- **14.** Kotef, Hagar and Merav Amir, "(En) gendering Checkpoints: Checkpoint Watch and the Repercussions of Intervention", *Signs: Journal of Women and Culture in Society*, vol. 32, no. 4, summer 2007, pp. 973–96.
- **15.** Hanafi, Sari, "Spacio-cide: Colonial Politics, Invisibility and Rezoning in Palestinian Territory", *Contemporary Arab Affairs*, 2(1): p. 106–121. http://www.informaworld.com/smpp/content~content=a908133156~db=all
- **16.** Hammami, "Qalandia: Jerusalem's Tora Bora and the Frontiers of Global Inequality", p. 33.
- **17.** Tawil-Souri, Helga, "Qalandia Checkpoint: The Historical Geography of a Non-Place", *Jerusalem Quarterly*, no. 42, 2010, http://www.jerusalemquarterly.org/ViewArticle.aspx?id=345.
- **18.** For a quick glance at the political period during which the "Night of the Flying Boy" reigned see *Journal of Palestine Studies*, vol. 17, no. 3, spring 1988, "Palestine Chronology: 16 November 1987–15 February 1988", p. 204–240. For a description of the incident based on the Arabic press with the photograph of the child and the glider and for reviewing art created by the children's generation of the First Intifada, see my book, *Faithful Witnesses: Palestinian Children Recreate Their World* with Preface by John Berger, New York: Olive Branch Press, 1990; Windrush Press, Gloucestershire, UK, 1990. Note the colourful drawing of a girl seated on a winged horse flying over Jerusalem by an eight year old girl, p. 119.
- **19.** Ratner, Emily, "Dreams of Flight", *Counterpunch*, 10 June 2009. http://www.counterpunch.org/ratner06102009.html.
- **20.** For a more comprehensive discussion I proposed on the relation between *be-ing*, *longing* and *be-longing*, see "Sharing a Meaning: An Introduction" in *Belonging and Globalisation: Critical Essays in Contemporary Art and Culture*, Kamal Boullata ed., London: Saqi 2008, pp. 11–21.
- **21.** Bachelard, *The Poetics of Space*, p. 211.
- **22.** Said, Edward W, *Reflections on Exile and Other Essays*, Cambridge, MA: Harvard University Press, 2002, p. 186.
- **23.** Berger, John, "Uses of Photography" (written in 1978) in *About*

Looking, pp. 52–65. The subject is further elaborated in his chapter entitled "Appearances" in his book *Another Way of Telling*, New York: Vintage International, 1995, pp. 83–129.

• **24.** In Arabic, just as the use of the past tense could be used to stress a future action (as noted in Endnote 7, Chapter 1) the words indicating "here" (*huna*) and "there" (*hunak*) are often interchanged. Perhaps the most common example may be found in long-distance phone calling. For example, Nadia in New York is calling Basima in Beirut; Dalal answers the phone. Nadia asks Dalal, "is Basima here?" instead of asking, "is Basima there?" Similarly, the interchange between "here" and "there" is evident when an Arab asks for directions to a place in an Arab city, the respondent pointing the finger in the destination's direction often answers "the place is here" when the place would actually be some ten blocks away!

• **25.** Boehm, Gottfried, "Par-delà le langage? Remarque sur la logique des images", *Trivium*, 1-2008. URL: http://trivium. Revues.org/index252.html.

6. Sky

• **1.** Bar Zohar, Michael, *Ben-Gurion: The Armed Prophet*, New Jersey: Prentice-Hall, 1967, p. 157.

• **2.** Morris, Benny, "Operation Dani and the Palestinian exodus from Lydda and Ramle in 1948", *Middle East Journal* 40, no. 1, winter 1986, pp. 82–109. See also Ilan Pappé, *The Ethnic Cleansing of Palestine*, London: Oneworld Publications, 2006.

• **3.** Hass, Amira, *Drinking the Sea at Gaza: Days and Nights in a Land Under Siege*, New York: Picador, 2000, p. 9.

• **4.** Masalha, Nur, *Imperial Israel and the Palestinians: The Politics of Expansion*, London: Pluto Press, 2000, p. 175. See also "The Koenig Report: Demographic Racism in Israel", *Middle East Research and Information Project, (Merip)*, no. 51, October 1976, pp. 11–14.

• **5.** See "The Potentially Widespread Contamination of the Soil of Gaza due to Israeli Bombing" by Drs Mario Barbieri, Maurizio Barbieri and Paola Manduca. Their press release dated 17 December 2009 followed a conference held jointly with medical practitioners from al-Shifa Hospital and representatives of the Palestinian Ministry of Health: http://www.countercurrents.org/manduca171209.htm

• **6.** Danto, Arthur C, *After the End of Art: Contemporary Art and the Pale of History*, New Jersey: Princeton University Press, 1997, p. 15.

• **7.** Danto, Arthur C, *After the End of Art: Contemporary Art and the Pale of History*, p. 4.

- **8.** Danto, Arthur C, "Photographism in Contemporary German Art" in his *Embodied Meanings: Critical Essays and Aesthetic Meditations*, New York: Farrar Straus & Giroux, 1994, pp. 304–311.
- **9.** Oliva, Achille Bonito, "The Globalisation of Art", *Belonging and Globalisation: Critical Essays in Contemporary Art and Culture*, Kamal Boullata ed., pp. 41–48.
- **10.** In his *al-Maraya al-Mutajawira: Dirasat Fi Naqd Taha Husayn* (Adjacent Mirrors: A Critical Study of Taha Husayn), Cairo: al-Hai-at al-'Amma lil-Kitab, 1983, Jabir 'Usfur discusses the different literary subjects in which Taha Husayn employed the mirror in his critical writings. For further reading on the subject see Pierre-Louis Reymond, "Les Miroirs de Taha Hussein, Romancier et essayiste Egyptien, réflexions sur la société de son temps" in Jackie Pigeaud ed., *Miroirs: XV Entretiens de la Garenne Lemot*, Rennes: Presses Universitaires de Rennes, 2011, p. 301–307.
- **11.** Merleau-Ponty, Maurice, *Phenomenology of Perception*, Colin Smith trans., London: Routledge, 2002, p. xxii. Italics are in the original quotation.
- **12.** Belting, Hans, *Florence and Baghdad: Renaissance Art and Arab Science*, Deborah Lucas Schneider trans., Cambridge, MA: Harvard University Press, 2011, p. 5.
- **13.** Barghouti, *I Was Born There, I Was Born Here*, 2012.
- **14.** Darwish, Mahmud from *Jidariyya* (Mural), Sargon Bulos trans., Beirut: Riyad Najib al-Rayyes Books, 2000, *Banipal*, no. 15/16, autumn/spring 2003, p. 23.

Bibliography

- **Abu-Deeb, Kamal,** *The Imagination Unbound: 'al-Adab al-'Aja'ibi' and the Literature of the Fantastic*, London: Saqi, Oxford: Oryx Press, 2007.
- **Alberti, Leon Batista,** *On Painting*, Cecil Grayson trans., London: Phaidon Press, 1972; reprint ed., London: Penguin Classics, 2005.
- **'Anani, Nabil, and 'Isam Badr,** *Al-Fan al-Filastini fi al-Ard al-Muhtallah* (Palestinian Art Under The Occupation), Ramallah: Gallery 79, 1984.
- **Associated Press,** "Gaza Children go for World Record for Kite Flying", 30 July 2009, http://www.msnbc.msn.com/id/32223159/.
- **Awwad, Nahed,** "In Search of Jerusalem Airport", *Jerusalem Quarterly*, no. 35, autumn 2008.
- **Bachelard, Gaston,** *The Poetics of Space*, Maria Jolas trans., Boston: Beacon Press, 1969.
- **Barbieri, Mario, Maurizio Barbieri and Paola Manduca,** "The Potentially Widespread Contamination of the Soil of Gaza due to Israeli Bombing", http://www.countercurrents.org/manduca171209.htm
- **Barghouti, Mourid,** *I Was Born There, I Was Born Here*, Humphrey Davies trans., London: Bloomsbury, 2012.
- **Baroud, Ramzy,** *The Second Palestinian Intifada: A Chronicle of a People's Struggle*, London: Pluto Press, 2006.
- **Bar Zohar, Michael,** *Ben-Gurion: The Armed Prophet*, New Jersey: Prentice-Hall, 1967.
- **Belting, Hans,** *Florence and Baghdad: Renaissance Art and Arab Science*, Deborah Lucas Schneider trans., Cambridge, MA: Harvard University Press, 2011.
- **Berger, John,** *Hold Everything Dear: Dispatches on Survival and Resistance*, London & New York: Verso, 2007.
- **Berger, John,** *Another Way of Telling*, New York: Vintage International, 1995.

• **Berger, John,** *About Looking*, New York: Pantheon Books, 1980, Vintage International Edition, 1991.
• **Boehm, Gottfried,** "Par-delà le langage? Remarque sur la logique des images", *Trivium*, 1. URL: http://trivium.revues.org/252
• **Boullata, Kamal,** *Qira'at al-jasad fi lawhat Marwan* (The Reading of the Body in Marwan's Paintings), *Al-Akhar*, no. 2, autumn 2011.
• **Boullata, Kamal,** *Palestinian Art: From 1850 to the Present*, London: Saqi Books, 2009.
• **Boullata, Kamal,** "Notes on Verbal Dominance and Visual Expression in Arab Culture", *Neighbours in Dialogue*, Beral Madra and Ayse Orhun Gultekin eds., Istanbul: Norgunk Yayincilik Publishers, 2005.
• **Boullata, Kamal,** *Istihdar al-Makan, Dirasat fi al-Fan al-Tashkili al-Filastini al-Mu'asir* (The Recovery of Place: A Study of Contemporary Palestinian Art), Tunis: al-Munazzhama al-'Arabiyyah lil-Tarbiyah wal-Thaqafa wa-l-'Ulum (ALECSO), 2000.
• **Boullata, Kamal,** *Faithful Witnesses: Palestinian Children Recreate Their World*, New York: Olive Branch Press, Interlink Imprint, 1990.
• **Boullata, Kamal,** "Manshur Jinsiyasi" (Sex-pol Manifesto), *Mawaqif*, no. 28, summer 1974.
• **Bourriaud, Nicolas,** *The Radicant*, New York: Lukas & Sternberg, 2009.
• **Chomsky, Noam, and Ilan Pappé,** *Gaza in Crisis: Reflections on Israel's War Against the Palestinians*, London: Penguin, 2011.
• **Colby, Frederick S,** *Narrating Muhammad's Night Journey: Tracing the Development of the Ibn 'Abbas Ascension Discourse*, Albany, NY: State University of New York Press, 2008.
• **Danto, Arthur C,** *After the End of Art: Contemporary Art and the Pale of History*, New Jersey: Princeton University Press, 1997.
• **Danto, Arthur,** *Embodied Meanings: Critical Essays and Aesthetic Meditations*, New York: Farrar Straus & Giroux, 1994.
• **Darwish, Mahmud,** *Jidariyya* (Mural), Beirut: Riyad Najib al-Rayyes Books, 2000, Sargon Bulos trans., *Banipal*, no. 15/16, autumn/spring 2003.
• **Darwish, Najwan,** "Hani Zu'rob Jadir bi-Alamih" (Hani Zurob Worthy of his Pain), *Al-Akhbar*, 8 December 2008.
• **Darwish, Najwan,** "Lawha Sadimah takhtazil al-Lahdha al-Mu'attalah" (A Combative Painting Sums up the Idle Moment), *Al-Akhbar*, 17 September 2008.
• **Darwish, Najwan,** "There", Kamal Boullata trans., *The Virginia Quarterly Review*, vol. 84, no. 3, summer 2008.
• **Dawisha, Adeed,** *Arab Nationalism in the Twentieth Century: From Triumph to Despair*, Princeton, NJ: Princeton University Press, 2005.
• **Demos, TJ,** "The Ends of Exile: Towards a Coming Universality?", *Altermodern: Tate Triennal*, Exhibition catalogue, London: Tate Britain, 2009.
• **Derrida, Jacques,** "The Animal that Therefore I Am (More to Follow)", David Wills trans., *Critical Inquiry*, 28, no. 4, winter 2002.

- **Derrida, Jacques,** *Memoirs of the Blind: The Self-Portrait and Other Ruins*, PA Brault and M Nass trans., Chicago, Il: University of Chicago Press, 1993.
- **Finkelstein, Norman G,** *"This Time We Went Too Far": Truth and Consequences of the Gaza Invasion*, New York: Or Books, 2010.
- **Foucault, Michel,** *Discipline and Punish: The Birth of the Prison*, Alan Sheridan trans., New York: Vintage Books, 1995.
- **Genet, Jean,** *Prisoner of Love*, Barbara Bray trans., New York: New York Review of Books, 2003.
- **Hammami, Rema,** "Qalandia: Jerusalem's Tora Bora and the Frontiers of Global Inequality", *Jerusalem Quarterly* no. 41, spring 2010.
- **Hanafi, Sari,** "Spacio-cide: Colonial Politics, Invisibility and Rezoning in Palestinian Territory", *Contemporary Arab Affairs*, vol. 2, no. 1, 2009.
- **Hass, Amira,** "Expressing the Closure of Thought", *Haaretz*, 9 January 2006.
- **Hass, Amira,** *Drinking the Sea at Gaza: Days and Nights in a Land Under Siege*, New York: Picador, 2000.
- **Hass, Robert and Paul Ebenkamp,** *Song of Myself: And Other Poems by Walt Whitman*, Berkley, CA: Counterpoint Press, 2010.
- **Hitti, Philip,** *History of the Arabs*, Hampshire, UK: Palgrave Macmillan, 2002.
- **Journal of Palestine Studies,** "Palestine Chronology: 16 November 1987–15 February 1988", *Journal of Palestine Studies*, vol. 17, no. 3, spring 1988.
- **Kotef, Hagar and Merav Amir,** "(En) gendering Checkpoints: Checkpoint Watch and the Repercussions of Intervention", *Signs: Journal of Women and Culture in Society*, vol. 32, no. 4, summer 2007.
- **Laïdi-Hanieh, Adila,** "L'Art Palestinien entre Modernité et Contemporanéité", *L'Art Même*, no. 40, autumn 2008.
- **Levy, Gideon,** *The Punishment of Gaza*, London: Verso, 2010.
- **McGinnis, Jon, and David C Reisman,** *Classical Arabic Philosophy: an Anthology of Sources*, Indianapolis: Hackett Publishing Co, 2007.
- **Malti-Douglas, Fedwa,** *Blindness and Autobiography: 'al-Ayyam' of Taha Husayn*, Princeton, NJ: Princeton University Press, 1988.
- **Masalha, Nur,** *Imperial Israel and the Palestinians: The Politics of Expansion*, London: Pluto Press, 2000.
- **Mattar, Philip,** *Encyclopedia of the Palestinians*, ed., New York: Facts on File, 2000, rev. ed. 2005.
- **Merleau-Ponty, Maurice,** *Phenomenology of Perception*, Colin Smith trans., London: Routledge, 2002.
- **Middle East Research and Information Project,** "The Koenig Report: Demographic Racism in Israel", *Merip*, no. 51, October 1976.
- **Morris, Benny,** "Operation Dani and the Palestinian exodus from Lydda and Ramle in 1948", *Middle East Journal 40*, no. 1, winter 1986.
- **Nakhleh, Khalil,** *Globalized Palestine: The National Sell-Out of a Homeland*, Trenton, NJ: The Red Sea Press, 2011.

- **Oliva, Achille, Bonito,** "The Globalisation of Art", *Belonging and Globalisation: Critical Essays in Contemporary Art and Culture*, Kamal Boullata ed., London: Saqi, 2008.
- **Pappé, Ilan,** *The Ethnic Cleansing of Palestine*, Oxford: Oneworld Publications, 2006
- **Quandt, William,** *Peace Process: American Diplomacy and the Arab-Israeli Conflict Since 1967*, 3rd ed. Washington, DC: Brookings Institution Press and Berkeley and Los Angeles, CA: University of California Press, 2005.
- **Ratner, Emily,** "Dreams of Flight", *Counterpunch*, 10 June 2009. http://www.counterpunch.org/ratner06102009.html
- **Reymond, Pierre-Louis,** "Les Miroirs de Taha Hussein, romancier et essayiste Egyptien, réflexions sur la société de son temps", *Miroirs: XVes Entretiens de la Garenne Lemot*, Jackie Pigeaud ed., Rennes : Presses Universitaires de Rennes, 2011.
- **Reynolds, Dwight F,** *Interpreting The Self: Autobiography in the Arabic Literary Tradition*, ed., Berkeley: University of California Press, 2001.
- **Ricœur, Paul,** *Oneself As Another*, Kathleen Blamey trans., Chicago and London: The University of Chicago Press, 1992.
- **Ricœur, Paul,** *Freedom and Nature: The Voluntary and the Involuntary*, E Kohak trans., Evanston: Northwestern University Press, 1966.
- **Rimbaud, Arthur,** *Selected Poems and Letters*, J Harding and J Sturrock trans., ed., London: Penguin, 2004.
- **Said, Edward W,** *Reflections on Exile and Other Essays*, Cambridge, MA: Harvard University Press, 2002.
- **Said, Edward W,** *After the Last Sky: Palestinian Lives. Photographs by Jean Mohr*, London: Faber & Faber Ltd, Vintage edition, 1993.
- **Sartre, Jean-Paul,** *Being and Nothingness*, HE Barnes trans., New York: Philosophical Library, 1956.
- **Shammout, Isma'il,** *Al-Fan al-Tashkili fi Filastin* (Art in Palestine), Kuwait: Matabi' al-Qabas, 1989.
- **Taghdisi-Rad, Sahar,** *The Political Economy of Aid in Palestine*, New York: Routledge, 2010.
- **Tawil-Souri, Helga,** "Qalandia Checkpoint: The Historical Geography of a Non-Place", *Jerusalem Quarterly*, no. 42, summer 2010.
- **'Usfur, Jabir,** *al-Maraya al-Mutajawira: Dirasat Fi Naqd Taha Husayn* (Adjacent Mirrors: A Critical Study of Taha Husayn), Cairo: al-Hai-at al-'Amma lil-Kitab, 1983.

Video

- **Habie, Jessica,** *Meet Me out of the Siege*, 14-minute video, New York: Eyes Infinite, 2006.

Index

Black Dog Publishing Limited
10A Acton Street
London
WC1X 9NG

t. +44 (0)207 713 5097
f. +44 (0)207 713 8682
e. info@blackdogonline.com

British Library Cataloguing-in-Publication Data.
A CIP record for this book is available from the British Library.

ISBN 978 1 907317 91 0

Black Dog Publishing is an environmentally responsible company. *Between Exits: Paintings by Hani Zurob* is printed on sustainably sourced paper.

reuse recycle reduce

art design fashion
history photography
theory and things

black dog publishing
london uk

www.blackdogonline.com